D1616724

INVEST WITHOUT STRESS

INVEST WITHOUT STRESS

WHAT SUCCESSFUL INVESTORS KNOW

Anne Farrelly

CAMDEN PRESS

WEST LOS ANGELES • CALIFORNIA

© Anne Farrelly, 1995

This publication is designed to provide accurate and authoritative information in regard to the subject matter covered. It is sold with the understanding that neither the author nor the publisher is engaged in rendering legal, accounting, or other professional service. If legal advice or other expert assistance is required, the services of a competent professional person should be used.

Publisher's Cataloging in Publication
(Prepared by Quality Books Inc.)

Farrelly, Anne.
    Invest without stress : what successful investors know / Anne Farrelly.
    p. cm.
    Includes index.
    ISBN 0-9647723-9-6

    1. Investments—Handbooks, manuals, etc. 2. Finance, Personal—Handbooks, manuals, etc. I. Title.

HG4521.F37 1996   332.024
                                    QBI95-20669

Camden Press
Post Office Box 642347
Los Angeles, CA 90064

To my mother, Betty
my daughters, Beth and Kristen-Anne
and Steven Scott

Contents

*"Nowadays we can hardly count our blessings,
one of which is surely that we don't have to
do all that counting—computers do it for us.
Information is easily had.
Education is readily available.
Opportunity knocks, it jiggles the doorknob,
it will try the window if we don't have
the alarm system on."*

All the Trouble in the World
P. J. O'Rourke

Preface

If you are like most people, just the *thought* of investing can make your blood pressure rise. The vast number and variety of investment products can be intimidating in itself. Add to this your feelings of inadequacy about your financial aptitude, and you have the ingredients for a lot of stress.

The good news is *profitable investing is something anyone can learn to do.* Although the number of investments seems overwhelming, there are only three basic ways to invest your money. Whether you have $1,000 or $1,000,000, the principles of investing are the same, and they are not difficult to grasp. All you need is the motivation to increase your wealth, a little time, and the right information.

As a broker, I often hear my clients complain that no investment book answers their questions in a way they can understand. Indeed, although there are many investment books available, they appear to be either so dense that novice investors cannot extract much practical information or they lack much of the information I believe investors need to invest safely. Thus, my primary goal in writing this book was to present all the essential information without confusing jargon or "investment-speak."

Invest Without Stress is a step-by-step encyclopedia that gives easy-to-digest answers to questions about any and all investments you may encounter—questions you may not even know to ask. Armed with this pocket adviser, you will be able to match your financial goals with investments that are suitable for you.

Although successful investing starts with knowledge, *acting* on that knowledge is key. Therefore, I have included an action plan to get you started and checklists to apply when engaging a broker. (If you already have a broker, don't be surprised if your new expertise engenders more respect and better service!)

It is my hope that *Invest Without Stress* will empower you to stop worrying about your money and start growing it. The investment arena is not stressful once you learn what all successful investors know—*Knowledge is the best prescription for your financial health.*

—Anne Farrelly

Wise investing can guarantee millionaire status if you start early enough. With the threat of inflation and taxes eroding the money you work so hard to earn, investing makes a lot of sense. All you have to do is learn how.

Chapter 1

Why Invest?

*"I can't take it with me I know.
But will it last until I go?"*

Simultaneous Departure
Martha F. Newmeyer

Ready or not, at some point society retires most people from earning a living. When that happens to you, your financial needs will be met from Social Security and whatever cash and investments you have accumulated.

Prudent saving and investing is not only insurance for a solvent and comfortable retirement, it may alleviate unforeseen cash-flow deficits brought on by unemployment and medical emergencies. Without savings, you can forget about buying a home, college for your children, and other costly necessities and indulgences.

As a nation, Americans save less of their incomes than citizens of most other industrialized countries, and only about half of what they saved in the 1970s. Our lack of savings is due partly to our desire for immediate affluence. Since World War II, we have admired the acquisition of material goods and ignored the rewards of delayed gratification.

According to a study by Arthur E. Little, a major independent consulting firm, eight out of ten Americans currently working will have less than half the savings they need to retire comfortably. Many individuals not covered by employer-sponsored retirement plans will have less than one quarter of what they will need.

The money you save and invest is increasingly important in maintaining your current standard of living during retirement. Nothing is likely to affect your material quality of life and your overall stress level as much as the money you save, how well you invest it, and how soon you get started.

INVESTMENT BASICS

A primary investment fact of life known to successful investors:

> *Earning a good living is not enough to guarantee financial stability without sound investing. Money doesn't just make money. It must be cultivated.*

For most Americans, investing is a rather haphazard, unenlightened process. Millions of people are not equipped to handle their finances because our educational institutions have ignored the study of managing and investing money. Consequently, many fail to take advantage of the better investment opportunities, leaving their savings mostly in low-yielding CDs and money market funds that fail to keep pace with inflation.

Learning to exploit the financial markets, as the rich have always done, is the best way to maximize savings growth. And, with less money to invest, you need the growth that certain investments offer even more than the rich. If that idea seems hopelessly complicated and difficult, I assure you, it's not. Regardless of how much money you have to invest, the principles of investing are democratic. With the possible exception of transaction costs, the potential risks and rewards in the financial arena are the same for you as for any multi-millionaire.

Regardless of your formal education, you do not lack the ability to invest profitably—you lack only instruction. Even the rich cannot invest more successfully than you unless they know more than you. You do not need to examine every type of investment product and actually are better off avoiding the more exotic inventions of Wall Street. As a matter of fact, it all boils down to only three basic investment categories: *debt*, *equity*, and *hard assets*.

Basic Class	Type of Investment
Debt/Loans	Corporate, Municipal, Government Bonds Certificates of Deposit Mortgages, Trust Deeds
Equity	Common Stock
Hybrid Debt/ Equity	Preferred Stock Convertible Bonds and Stock
Hard Assets	Real Estate (Partnerships, REITs) Precious Metals (Gold, Silver) Precious Stones (Diamonds, Rubies) Fine Art (Paintings, Sculpture) Collectibles (Baseball Cards, Antiques)

There are at least two dozen different varieties of investment products within these general categories, and every so often Wall Street creates a new one. Investment products range from the ultraconservative, super-safe to the extremely speculative. While no one class of investment works best all the time, the prime vehicles for achieving your financial goals are stocks, bonds, and mutual funds. If you want to reduce stress by simplifying your financial life, you can forget all the others.

START A SAVINGS PLAN

If you have an income, you should have a savings plan. Ideally, individuals in their 20s and 30s save a minimum of 10 percent of their income annually; 20 percent in their 40s; and 35 percent in their 50s. The percentage of savings increases with earning power.

An ideal savings plan, however, may seem impossibly out of reach. Young wage earners, for example, may have student loan obligations. Some people may suddenly be faced with meeting all family financial needs when a spouse loses a job. There will always be reasons not to save, and some of them are compelling. Nevertheless, while you may not meet the ideal all the time, it is important to save *something* on a regular basis. Like any other healthful habit, saving money requires discipline. If you have the discipline, it gets easier with time.

Whatever lifestyle accommodation it requires, the younger you are when you start to save, the less pressure you will face in later years. To adhere to a savings plan that secures your retirement years may mean buying a less expensive house than you would like or that lending institutions determine you can afford. It may mean squeezing a few more years of service out of your car before buying a new one. Or eating out less often.

The process of saving money can be inherently gratifying—what could be a better motivator than seeing your money grow? The point is, if you cannot support your preferred lifestyle *and* save money in a well-designed investment plan, then you must reorder your priorities to avoid a financial shortfall in your later years. But even if you're over 50 and have never saved a dime, don't despair. Saving and investing are like exercise—it's never too late to start, and some benefits will always accrue.

HOW MUCH IS ENOUGH?

Most financial consultants claim that people require less income when they retire. This, I believe, is debatable. Consider the realities of inflation and potentially higher medical costs. Also, once retired, you may want more money for travel and other indulgences that reward a long working life.

Retirement is likely to be a significantly longer period for you than for your parents. Although the average American's life span today is about 75 years, if you make it to 65, odds are that you'll live to 84 if you are male, 88 if you are female. With biomedical advances, it's no wonder the fastest growing segment of our population is composed of people over 85! If you retire at 65 in relatively good health, prepare to support yourself for at least another 25 years.

Throughout the nation, Americans are well behind in funding their retirements. We not only underestimate how long we will live, we tend to overestimate how much our employers and the government will contribute to our retirement. To become leaner, meaner, and more profitable, U.S. companies have cut back on employee pension and health benefits. And, according to the Employee Benefits Research Institute, more than 40 percent of workers spend rather than continue to save their company pension distributions when they leave their jobs.

Add to this the potential bankruptcy of Social Security. At the end of World War II, the ratio of workers paying into the system for each person receiving benefits was 42 to 1. According to the *Social Security Administration Trust Fund Report of 1993*, that ratio today is a mere 3 to 1! (When Social Security was enacted in 1935, average life expectancy was 61 years, even lower than the average retirement age today!) At some point, Social Security benefits may be frozen, so don't count on them to cover more than 20 percent of your needs.

Determining how much you need to accumulate by the time you retire is not an exact science. Financial consultants, brokers, and planners have the tools to calculate estimates of future retirement income based on your current savings, age, and lifestyle, factoring in a reasonable return on investment as well as an estimated inflation rate. This service is very helpful because it projects the income you can expect to receive in today's dollars when you retire, enabling you to address any shortfall as early as possible by saving more.

THE LONG-TERM PAYOFF ON SAVINGS			
	30 Years	*20 Years*	*10 Years*
Common Stocks*	9.95%	14.58%	14.40%
20-Yr Treasury Bond	6.96%	9.42%	11.86%
20-Yr Corporate Bond	7.31%	10.00%	11.57%
30-Day T-Bills	5.36%	5.44%	3.58%

* S&P 500 Compounded Annualized Return (period ending 12-31-94)
Ibbotson Research

RETIRE A MILLIONAIRE

A little extra saved and invested over a long period of time can make an enormous difference in the size of your nest egg. Instead of squandering $50 every month on frivolous expenditures, invest it. If, at age 18, you invested $50 each month, and it grew 12 percent annually, you would have $755,538 by age 60 and $1,377,000 by age 65!

If you start young enough, you might achieve millionaire status simply by contributing $2,000 to an IRA every year. If you manage to commit $2,000 each year and the account's investments grow 10 percent each year, you will have $35,062 in 10 years. If you contribute $2,000 each year for 20 years, the figure jumps to $86,005, to $301,886 after 30 years, and to $973,702 after 40 years. If your IRA contributions average 12 percent annually, you would have $1.7 million in 40 years!

Monthly Investment	$100	$250	$500	$1,000
Average Annual Profit	Years to $1 Million			
4%	90.2	67.9	51.9	37.4
6%	67.5	52.2	41.2	30.7
8%	54.8	43.1	34.6	26.5
10%	46.5	37.1	30.1	23.4
12%	40.7	32.8	26.9	21.1
15%	34.6	28.1	23.3	18.6

Turn to page 385 for a step-by-step action plan to help you get started on the road to financial security.

Summary

Most people are intimidated by the seemingly elite world of finance. Yet the journey to financial security is open to everyone regardless of income. Moreover, learning to invest need not be an overwhelming task. Many investors who became millionaires began with little cash and followed a few simple ground rules. The payoff is within easy reach if you make the time to acquire some investment basics.

O ptimal investing involves making informed choices because your profits depend on the investments you select. Before learning how to participate in the premiere investment opportunities—stocks and bonds—it is helpful to see how Americans invested for the last two centuries.

Chapter 2

Wall Street: A Brief History

"Just as war is waged with the blood of others, fortunes are made with other people's money."

Voici l'Homme
Andre Suares

Centuries ago, economic structure was very simple. Most businesses were owned and operated by one individual whose family members often shared the responsibilities. When capital was needed to expand a business, the owner used his own savings or borrowed money using his property as collateral.

With the dawning of the industrial revolution, however, factory construction and the purchase of sophisticated equipment required a far greater outlay of funds. At times, capital requirements were so great that no single lender could handle the financing.

A legal entity called a *corporation*, based on the 17th-century English prototype, evolved to become the most practical form of doing business for companies seeking to raise large amounts of capital. By issuing bonds, a corporation borrows from investors, pledges its assets to guarantee repayment of the loan, and contracts to pay interest to the bondholders. A corporation may also raise money by selling all or part of its stock to transfer ownership to investors who share in the company's profits.

Stocks and bonds attract trillions of dollars from investors because (1) the financial responsibility, and therefore the risk to investors, is limited solely to money invested and (2) they can be readily liquidated (sold for cash).

The U.S. securities market, the arena in which capital is raised and stocks and bonds are traded, plays a crucial role in expanding the total pool of capital available to finance productive enterprises, develop new technologies, and create jobs. A nation's affluence depends on the profitability of companies owned by its citizens, so it is no accident that countries enjoying the highest living standards are those with the most active and developed capital markets.

As citizens, we enjoy the benefits of our free-enterprise system, based on the concept of capitalism, which promotes private ownership of businesses and the freedom to conduct commerce without excessive government intervention. Despite its flaws, it is without question the most successful economic system ever embraced by any nation in history.

As investors, we benefit from evolved market systems that encourage savings and investment, offering opportunities to enrich ourselves by participating in the growth of the finest companies in America and abroad. Our financial markets today are highly regulated by the federal government for our protection . . . but that was not always the case.

EARLY AMERICAN MARKETS

The first financial marketplace in America began as a small settlement in 1609 when Dutch traders landed on the southern tip of Manhattan Island. To protect themselves from Indian attacks, the settlers built a high wall alongside a path connecting the East River's busy harbor with the docks on the Hudson River. They named the path *Wall Street*, and it became the logical place for traders and merchants to conduct commerce.

When the British took over in 1664, they renamed the community New York. By the early 1700s, trading in the district was brisk and organized. Commodities such as grain, tobacco, and even slaves were traded at outdoor auctions.

As long as trade with England was vibrant, there was no great shortage of capital to expand commerce in the American colonies. But when the colonists revolted against British rule and were cut off from their largest trading partner, they were denied much of the capital on which they had become dependent. By the time independence was achieved, the new government was heavily in debt to its citizens who had financed the war.

Fortunately for the fledgling republic, the first Secretary of the Treasury was a brilliant young man named Alexander Hamilton. He proposed a plan to refinance the war debt by issuing $80 million in government bonds, the first securities ever sold to Americans. The new government paid the interest on the bonds out of tax revenues.

A year later, Hamilton established the first national bank financed by a public offering of stock. (In those days, there was less distinction between stocks and bonds. Government bonds, for example, were called "public stock.") To raise capital, other banks and a few insurance companies also issued stock, and the shares were either traded among investors privately or auctioned publicly along with government securities and commodities.

Although only a handful of securities traded on any regular basis, auctioneers and brokers agreed to formal rules that addressed how trading was conducted, and mandated sanctions to punish parties who defaulted. Several merchants bought and sold securities as they did their other merchandise, *over the counter*. Today's over-the-counter market got its name from this early form of trading.

The first major attempt at stock manipulation took place in 1792 when William Duer borrowed heavily from many sources to purchase sufficient shares to take control of one of the banks. Unfortunately, the stock's price fell and Duer was unable to repay his debts. A wave of insolvencies resulted, and the consequent stock market crash was felt throughout the country. The New York state legislature reacted by ruling all public auctions of stocks illegal. The law, however, did not forbid private stock auctions, so after a few weeks, traders moved their operations from the street into a local coffee house.

On May 17, 1792, to minimize unhealthy speculation, 24 brokers and merchants drew up a set of rules which they called the Buttonwood Agreement (named after a tree under which their auctions had been held). They established commission rates and agreed to provide preferential consideration among themselves. This group could not have foreseen the profound role their private little fraternity would ultimately play in transforming an embryonic economy into the largest and strongest in the world.

Despite relatively few securities to trade, the brokerage business grew steadily. "Time bargains" (similar to modern option contracts) were so common they often surpassed cash purchases because they were cheap, simple, and satisfied the gambling propensities of the participants. These earlier contracts were not legally enforceable—parties relied solely on each other's personal honor.

THE 19TH CENTURY

Like most wars, the War of 1812 stimulated the economy with heightened demand for manufactured goods, promoting such increased market activity that brokers were required to meet on a more regular basis. Several of the more active members formed an association patterned after the much older European securities exchanges, which they called the New York Stock and Exchange Board. This exclusive club was restricted to members trading for their own accounts or for their customers. Disputes were settled by arbitration proceedings conducted by members. Punishment for rules violations ranged from fines to expulsion from membership. No appeals were allowed.

Prices of securities had been quoted privately among members for about 25 years, but to improve business, the brokers began publishing stock prices in newspapers. New regulations were adopted to ensure that the losing party to an option contract would fulfill his obligation. The exchange attracted many new customers, and by 1834, trading averaged 5,000 shares per market day.

Throughout the 19th century, the brokerage industry helped finance many companies that built such capital-intensive projects as bridges, canals, and railroads. During the Civil War, four different exchanges operated with few interruptions, though with much corruption. Trading irregularities and fraud proliferated. Corporate executives traded heavily on *inside information*, facts known to company insiders but not yet available to the public that are likely to affect a stock's price.

Banks loaned speculators up to 90 percent on their stock purchases. This high degree of leverage enabled investors to purchase several times the number of shares they might have bought with personal cash, making it easier to manipulate share prices. There were no regulations to restrict short sellers, (those who sell borrowed stock that must be purchased at some point in the future). The lack of government oversight resulted in a volatile market dominated by speculators.

In 1863, the Exchange was renamed the *New York Stock Exchange*, and two years later it moved to its present facility at 10 Broad Street. Trading volume on the NYSE exceeded 1 million shares per month on approximately 100 listed companies. Memberships, called "seats," which then numbered 1,060, became more valuable, some selling for as much as $7,000.

Runners were employed to carry information from the exchange to brokerage offices in the financial district. Conveying stock prices outside New York City was more difficult. To reconcile prices as quickly as possible during market sessions, information was actually relayed between the NYSE and Philadelphia's exchange by a series of flags situated on hilltops. The invention of the electric stock ticker in 1867 replaced the runners and flags, transmitting prices swiftly across the nation.

In 1878, the first telephone was introduced to the NYSE, and within a few years, many phones linked brokers' offices to the exchange trading floor. Without telephones, daily share trading volume could not have reached the millions typical of the early 1900s. Still, the principal market players were mostly merchants and financiers. The number of small investors was insignificant.

In 1896, Edward Jones, a former publisher of the *Wall Street Journal*, and market analyst Charles Dow, published an index based on the price movement of 11 stocks that was used as a barometer of overall market activity. The *Dow Jones Industrial Average*, dubbed "the Dow," became the most widely quoted index among investors.

THE GILDED AGE

The late 1800s continued to experience the rampant market speculation and political corruption characteristic of the Civil War days. Enormous corporate trusts created by such titans as Andrew Carnegie, John D. Rockefeller, and J.P. Morgan monopolized entire industries. U.S. Steel's capitalization was actually three times the annual revenues of the federal government. Rockefeller's Standard Oil controlled nearly all the oil refineries in the U.S. The trust barons not only ruled the national economy, they also wielded enormous political influence.

By the turn of the century, brokerage firms were rapidly forming a major industry, and membership in the NYSE carried power and prestige. Many member firms offered "customers' rooms" that were open to the public, but only individuals who could prove they were financially responsible were accepted as customers. Stocks were still traded mostly by professional investors. Not until the population became better educated, better employed, and more familiar with the securities markets did share ownership become more widespread.

WORLD WAR I

By early 1914, the NYSE was handling more than 500 companies. But when World War I broke out in Europe later that year, the stock market became unstable under a wave of panic selling. Financial markets do not respond positively to uncertainty, and the NYSE was closed for nearly five months before order was restored. After the U.S. entered the war, the markets recovered as expanded manufacturing supplied war goods.

Average citizens had their first real exposure to securities when they were encouraged to support the war effort by buying government-issued Liberty Bonds that were listed on the NYSE. By the time the war ended in 1918, Wall Street was booming and had surpassed London as the world's most prominent and active financial center.

THE ROARING TWENTIES

For a period following the war, stock prices suffered but eventually the markets turned around and prospered for nearly a decade. The Roaring Twenties was an era stimulated by foreign trade and many new technologies that gave birth to several new industries—automobile, aviation, radio, motion picture, banking, and chemical.

Interest in new product development stimulated activity on Wall Street. The 1,800 new stock issues in 1921 expanded to 6,500 by 1929. In 1925, the market value of all shares was $27 billion, but by 1929, it had tripled to nearly $90 billion. In just four years, annual trading volume grew from 450 million to more than 1 billion shares. The number of NYSE memberships expanded to 1,375 and seats sold for up to $625,000.

With their almost unimagined improved standard of living, Americans believed nothing could dampen their growing prosperity. Millions of middle-class people, who had never invested before purchasing Liberty Bonds, were trading like professionals. It was considered chic to call your broker several times a day.

THE CRASH OF 1929

The widespread practice of purchasing stocks on credit had contributed greatly to soaring prices and high trading volume. Hundreds of thousands of Americans put up as little as 10 percent of a stock's price and borrowed the rest from their banks and brokers. Mesmerized by the potential for quick profits, they rarely bothered to address company fundamentals.

On Thursday, October 24, 1929, stock prices began a steep decline. The following Tuesday, October 29, was a day forever after known as Black Tuesday. Prices plunged as stocks were sold to cover losses when customers could not meet their brokers' demands for repayment of borrowed funds. In only five trading hours, the flood of selling set a volume record that stood for 40 years. Entire fortunes were wiped out in a matter of hours; several investors were driven to suicide. Although only a small percentage of Americans were stock investors, waves of despondency engulfed the country.

THE GREAT DEPRESSION

As stocks continued their decline for three more years, a few respected analysts insisted the crash was a "slight adjustment." But it was more than a decade before stock prices recovered, and only after the U.S. had suffered its worst depression ever. One in four banks failed, and unemployment soared. By the time stock prices bottomed in 1932, more than 83 percent of all market value had been lost.

Many believed that the speculatively high credit purchases, stock manipulation, and other unethical but legal practices of Wall Street were at least partially to blame for the crash, the subsequent bank failures, and the depression. Indeed, the harsh times that followed appeared to be retribution for speculator excess.

THE REFORMING OF WALL STREET

One of the investors who had gained wealth in the 1920s through activities now illegal was Joseph P. Kennedy, father of John F. Kennedy, U.S. president from 1961 to 1963. Joe Kennedy was a financial wizard who reputedly said of the stock market, "We'd better get in before they pass a law against it." Kennedy astutely anticipated the 1929 crash and sold his stock holdings in time to avoid losses. He continued to sell many stocks short with full knowledge that such trading might further erode economic conditions and public confidence.

By 1933, unethical practices prompted the Senate to investigate irregularities in the banking and securities industries. When faced with federal regulation, industry leaders promised to curtail certain activities such as trading on inside information, but government officials believed the time for self-regulation had passed.

In 1934, President Franklin D. Roosevelt signed the Securities Exchange Act, which declared many practices of that time illegal. The *Securities and Exchange Commission* was established to administer and interpret the many new securities laws and to protect the public by ensuring fair and honest markets.

Roosevelt, who was politically indebted to Kennedy for assisting in his election, appointed him chairman of the SEC. Officially, Kennedy was chosen for his "executive ability, knowledge of habits and customs of the business to be regulated." Or, as Roosevelt more informally put it, "Set a thief to catch a thief." Most politicians objected to his appointment, but Kennedy was able to speak to the Wall Street financiers in their own language, and the brokerage community accepted reforms more readily than it might have from a more politically palatable reformer.

THE POST-WAR BOOM

The economy remained sluggish until the advent of World War II stimulated production. As the U.S. entered the war, Wall Street played a significant role by brokering government bonds and raising capital for companies that manufactured armaments.

Trading volume rose sharply when World War II ended with Japan's surrender. Corporate America enlisted Wall Street to prepare for peacetime industrial expansion in financing many new "war baby" companies. The late 1940s was a period of relative political calm and a thriving business environment. To meet global demand for autos, clothing, and other products, the U.S. produced more than half the world's manufactured goods. In only five years, private investment in the U.S. advanced more than 500 percent.

The burgeoning prosperity was both cause and effect of an enormous increase in stock trading, and Wall Street began recruiting brokers to handle the flood of new business. Before World War I, brokerage had been a "gentleman's" profession that served mostly the conservative upper class. During the 1920s, a different type of broker had emerged, one who touted racy stocks promising fast profits. The 1929 crash so tarnished Wall Street's image that brokers were not well-respected.

Charles Merrill, whose firm had survived the bad times, recognized the broker as the key to industry respectability. Merrill initiated training programs to refashion brokers to attract investors on a grand scale. In the anti-Communist fervor after World War II, the purchase of stocks was a vote for capitalism and democracy. Wall Street took advantage of the robust market to court the average citizen like never before. New investment plans were offered that allowed customers to purchase stocks with small monthly payments.

Most investors in the 1940s had bought stocks for income; however, in the 1950s they were joined by individuals who were mostly speculators. Stocks were championed on the airwaves by Walter Winchell, the most influential radio personality at the time. In 1954, the Dow climbed above 300 for the first time since the 1929 crash. During the Eisenhower years, it exceeded 637! Annual returns from stock investments averaged nearly 20 percent during the 1950s.

THE GO-GO YEARS

A new group of stocks had became popular as brokers and their clients showed little interest in a company's past performance but focused on its future prospects. A whole new vocabulary evolved—"silicon," for instance, and "transistor." Electronic stocks were hot, and company names were chosen for their technological appeal. Prices of many new stocks quadrupled in a matter of weeks. But many eventually became worthless, prompting SEC investigations that uncovered much fraud and manipulation by corporate insiders.

The intensity of investment mania at this time was reflected in a survey conducted by the NYSE. Forty percent of the investors polled could not define the term "common stock." And 25 percent of the group believed the best reason to buy stocks was the "opportunity for quick profit." Investing in stocks had become a national pastime, causing the number of registered stockbrokers to triple since World War II. In 1952, one out of 16 Americans owned common stocks; by 1961, it was one out of six.

The number of registered brokers had doubled to handle the flood of business. A new breed of entrepreneur emerged, buying up smaller companies to form conglomerates. Participation from these investors boosted institutional trading. Annual returns from stock investments averaged 7.8 percent during the 1960s.

THE SEVENTIES

In May 1969, the prime rate (the interest rate banks charge their best corporate customers) reached a new high as the *Federal Reserve Board*, or the "Fed," tightened credit to stem inflation. The worst market decline of the decade followed as distressed customers liquidated their stock portfolios, causing many brokerage firms to fail.

Inflation raged on, and there were shortages of meat and gas. The stock market recovered for a time, but by 1974, stock prices collapsed once again in the worst decline in four decades. The gains of the post-war period were wiped out as the Dow fell below 600, where it had been 16 years earlier. Despite more disposable discretionary income than ever before, average American citizens were not inclined to buy stocks. Instead, they opted for certificates of deposit and savings accounts that paid high rates of interest. Annual returns from stocks averaged only 6 percent during the 1970s.

In 1975, the brokerage industry marked a significant break with tradition when it abolished fixed commissions. Ever since, brokers have been able to charge whatever they choose for their services.

Computers made their inevitable impact on Wall Street in 1976 when the NYSE introduced a superfast computerized system to send orders electronically from brokers' offices directly to the floor of the exchange. Since 1978, a network called the Intermarket Trading System has linked all stock exchanges, enabling traders to shop around for the best prices.

THE EIGHTIES

By 1981, high inflation had pushed the yield on long-term bonds to 14 percent, and the economy responded with its deepest recession since the Great Depression. But in the summer of 1982, the Fed managed the 16.5 percent prime rate down to 11.5 percent, and stocks rallied as depressed prices attracted investors in a buying frenzy. In 1983, the Dow hit a new high of 1297, up from 777 the previous August.

Huge corporate takeovers were commonplace, and dramatic declines in inflation, interest rates, and oil prices fueled the economy and propelled stocks higher. In the first week of 1987, the Dow soared through the 2000 level for the first time. Despite the specter of insider-trading arrests, mounting domestic and international debt, and a spike in interest rates, it sailed to a high of 2722 on August 25, 1987. The Dow had more than tripled in five years.

THE CRASH OF 1987

On Monday, October 19, 1987, stock prices dropped in the heaviest trading volume ever. Wave after wave of panic selling created the steepest single-session fall in history. Stunned brokers across the country gazed at their quote monitors in disbelief. By the close of market, the Dow had plummeted 508 points to 1738, off 22 percent. Perhaps as much as $1 trillion in stock value vanished in the short financial blood bath. Although the market managed to end in positive territory for the year, an estimated 25 million shareholders had sold all their stocks.

Some analysts blamed the crash on *program trading*, computerized buying or selling of at least 15 stocks valued at $1 million or more. Computers enable huge quantities of stocks to be traded rapidly, sometimes creating an avalanche effect.

Many worried that the 1987 crash augured another economic depression, but the economy remained healthy as inflation and interest rates continued to fall, creating the optimal environment for stocks, and prices quickly recovered. Stock investors were rewarded with annual returns averaging 17 percent during the 1980s.

THE NINETIES

After Iraq invaded Kuwait in 1990, stock markets around the world plummeted, but even before the first shot of the Gulf War was fired, markets began to recover.

Although brokerage industry earnings suffered and the number of brokers declined dramatically because of the 1987 crash, a major turnaround in 1991 brought record profits. Interest rates declined to their lowest level in 20 years, and billions of dollars flowed to brokerage firms seeking higher returns. Despite global recession, Wall Street firms hired more brokers to handle their many new customers.

In 1993, Wall Street raised more capital than ever before. As the U.S. economy strengthened, the Dow broke through 3900 in January 1994, but the fear of rising inflation prompted preemptive action by the Fed to slow the economy. The Fed began raising interest rates, which caused the worst bond market in several decades. Stocks could not overcome the higher rates and investors lost money in nearly all types of investments. Inflation, however, remained under control and corporate profits continued to rise, pushing the Dow over 4800 in the third quarter of 1995. So far, the 1990s have managed to produce healthy returns for millions of Americans who own common stocks.

Summary

It is important to recognize that the principal role of financial markets is the allocation of capital—money flows to industries and technologies that are expected to deliver the greatest returns. Wall Street has created various instruments to facilitate investor participation in these opportunities.

Your challenge is to create an investment portfolio by selecting investment vehicles that will help you attain your personal financial goals. The optimal way to become familiar with your choices is one security at a time, starting with stocks and bonds, and to acquaint yourself with the investment brokers who sell them.

*N*o matter how financially savvy you become, you may still need the services of a licensed broker to conduct your investment transactions. It is vital that you learn how to engage the right broker because these professionals are positioned to either enhance or inhibit your investment returns.

Chapter **3**

The Investment Broker

"The buyer needs a hundred eyes.
The seller not one."

Jacula Prudentum
George Herbert

The brokerage industry is unique—staggering quantities of money are routinely transferred without written contracts, handshakes, or face-to-face meetings. Phone lines and computer systems transmit bids and offers on a great variety of financial assets as well as wagers on their price fluctuations.

Understandably, the uninitiated might question the sanity

of participating in this financial fray. But despite the ostensible confusion, our market systems work surprisingly well and those who administer them are highly scrutinized and regulated for investor protection. Moreover, the optimal investment opportunities are available *only* through these licensed professionals.

Job Description

An investment broker can be anyone who earns commissions or fees for executing investment transactions that transfer ownership from one party to another. Nearly all brokers are associated with brokerage firms, banks, savings and loans, or insurance companies. They call themselves agents, stockbrokers, representatives, planners, consultants, account executives, or investment executives. But despite the range of designations, most perform similar functions, so it is not incorrect (and it is certainly simpler) to label them all "brokers."

Ideally, your broker assesses your financial goals and the degree of risk you can comfortably tolerate. He can then provide insight and advice on the array of investment choices. Although you are ultimately responsible for your investment decisions, a broker's input may help you

- set and prioritize your financial goals,
- plan for a secure retirement,
- minimize your taxes,
- determine your portfolio's asset allocation,
- increase your net worth by keeping pace with or beating inflation,
- monitor your portfolio's performance, and
- gain emotional objectivity and discipline in all types of markets.

Qualifications and Training

First and foremost brokers are salespeople, and few sales jobs pay better than brokering. The Securities Industry Association reports that the average annual production of U.S. stockbrokers was $328,710 in 1993, or $1,250 per market day. A broker's share of the revenues he generates is from 25 to 45 percent, depending on the products involved and his overall production. Note that I said overall "production."

Brokers are not paid for giving advice. They get paid solely for executing investment transactions.

Salesmanship and high production are the prime qualifications brokerage firms look for when recruiting brokers. (My story below is only one such example.) After a broker trainee

The Broker Candidate

In 1981, the California real estate market suffered a severe downturn. At that time I was employed as a real estate broker, or should I say unemployed—the market put many realtors out of work. A successful stockbroker friend, who sympathized with my career circumstances, suggested that I look into becoming a stockbroker. Although I did not fit the typical "male-and-under-30" trainee profile (less than 10 percent of brokers are women), I needed a job, so I called several brokerage offices around town.

Thanks to my strong real estate sales background and the booming stock and bond markets, several firms expressed interest in hiring me. After a number of interviews, I selected one

is hired, he prepares for the rigorous (six-hour!) securities exam, which he must pass before he is licensed to market securities. Most trainees attend sales and product training seminars to prepare for long hours of cold calling (phoning strangers from lists of "prospects") to open accounts. As a result, many develop very thick skins as well as skill in the art of telephone persuasion.

Productivity is drummed into brokers early on—low revenue production is grounds for dismissal. I remember my first days on the job. My manager provided a graph for plotting my weekly production of commission revenues. The top line on the graph was my target objective; the bottom line tracked the minimum production acceptable. Producing sufficient revenue to stay above the lower line had me working 60-hour weeks, including weekends.

of the larger firms reputed to offer the best training. This firm conducted a unique test for gauging their applicants' aptitude for the job: For three hours, each candidate impersonated a stockbroker during a mock work-day session that was held after hours at the firm's branch office.

We were given different color ribbons to wear so that the examiners could tell us apart. We were seated at individual desks with phones, and handed several pages of material explaining the drill. The goal was to earn points for certain accomplishments—one point for opening an account, two points for selling 500 shares of stock, and so on.

Before I could read through half the material, my phone started ringing. Unhappy investors complained to me of price declines in their portfolios. Millionaire clients asked for investment advice. As "Mr. Blue" (the color of my ribbon and, yes,

THE BROKERAGE FIRM

Licensed investment brokers are employed by or associated with investment firms (also called *broker-dealers*). As a brokerage firm customer, you interact with one of its *retail* brokers, who may have been hired as a trainee or from another firm. Most major firms recruit successful brokers from other firms by paying them large cash incentives to relocate with their clients in tow. Structured as "forgivable loans" amounting to thousands of dollars, they may induce a broker to change firms every three to five years.

When hiring brokers, a firm's management is notified of all prior disciplinary actions on their records. In the past, brokers with tarnished records had little difficulty changing firms,

I was a "mister") I ad-libbed repartee with my client callers, articulating what I imagined to be appropriate broker responses. (My friend had warned me that I would be evaluated on my ability to sell under pressure.)

When the exam concluded, some candidates appeared energized by the experience, but I was numb. This kind of selling differed considerably from real estate sales, and I believed I must have failed the test. Besides, if this was a typical day in the life of a stockbroker, I wasn't sure I wanted the job. I was very surprised when, two weeks later, the branch manager called to inquire if I could report to work the following Monday. I was to be paid a small salary while being trained. With two daughters to support, it appeared the prudent course. With trepidation, I accepted the position, a career change I have never regretted.

provided they were successful producers. Today management is less inclined to hire problem brokers because arbitration awards to abused clients have become larger, more frequent, and more public. While no brokerage firm has a monopoly on ethical, expert brokers, some firms may be committed to higher standards of ethics and service than others. Your choice of firm is not as critical as your choice of individual broker, but you should have an understanding of how a brokerage firm operates.

Wall Street financial firms generate revenues by (1) creating a variety of securities and investment products, including stocks, bonds, mutual funds, unit trusts, and partnerships; and (2) executing buy and sell transactions, or *trades*—the transfer of ownership of a security from one party to another —as either agent or principal.

The firm acts as *agent* when it charges commissions for trades that occur between parties outside the firm. This would include sales of stocks listed on stock exchanges and purchases of mutual fund shares that are not firm-sponsored.

The firm acts as *principal* when it trades from its own account or inventory. Securities such as municipal bonds and over-the-counter stocks are marked up or down from their wholesale prices and traded with customers or other dealers for profit. Broker/dealers assume a certain degree of market risk in maintaining their inventories, and are entitled to profit just like any other retail business.

While full-service brokerage firms provide investment advice, *discount* brokers are order takers who are paid salaries and bonuses rather than strictly commissions. Discounters generally do not get involved in the creation of investment products or research but, like full-service firms, they may act as principals in over-the-counter trading of securities, charging markups or fees that are not disclosed to their customers.

CONFLICTS OF INTEREST

The brokerage community is expected to maintain high standards of business practice and to conduct customer relationships with honesty and integrity. To ensure compliance with stringent regulations, management is required to regularly review their brokers' activities.

Despite all these good intentions, the fact remains: No firm (I've heard of) has ever hired, rewarded, or even commended a broker simply for exemplary service to his customers. The rewards—higher compensation, larger offices, and better support—are reserved for brokers who outproduce their peers. Unfortunately, brokers can be tempted by conflicts of interest because the rewards are based on the number and type of investment transactions they execute.

Commissions, markups, and fees on their products and services run from a fraction of one percent to more than 10 percent of funds invested. Complex investments typically yield higher commissions to compensate brokers for their greater sales effort. Although customers expect unbiased investment advice, an unscrupulous broker may recommend an investment *only* because of the higher compensation.

An investment generating a higher commission is not necessarily one that most benefits the customer, and is often riskier than a less costly alternative. For example, individual high-quality bonds are generally more conservative and cost-efficient than shares in a bond mutual fund.

Violating Suitability

All brokers are admonished by the New York Stock Exchange rule to "know the customer." Not only must a broker be aware of each client's financial profile and goals, she must also determine his investing experience, knowledge of securities, and capacity for risk. A broker violates the "suitability rule" if she recommends any investment that would expose a client to potential losses that could cause financial hardship—even though the client may be willing to take the risk.

Churning

When his client has no available cash to purchase an investment, a broker might recommend the sale of a security to free up the cash, typically resulting in two transactions that generate fees. *Churning*, which is always illegal, is the excessive trading with infrequent profit that results in high commission costs relative to the size of the account.

THE REGULATORS

Although there may be no profession that is similarly riddled with conflicts of interest, the nation's brokerage industry is by far the most highly scrutinized and regulated by both federal and state authorities for the protection of investors.

Securities and Exchange Commission

The SEC, an agency of the U.S. government, was established by Congress in 1934 to write and administer federal laws to ensure that the financial markets operate in a fair and orderly manner. The SEC does not get involved in evaluating securities for risk, but it mandates which investments must be registered, as well as the scope of information the financial community is required to disclose to investors.

The SEC has recently instituted a consumer toll-free hotline, (800) SEC-0330, that provides information such as how to go about filing a complaint with the SEC and how to obtain their consumer publications, as well as current investor alerts from its enforcement division.

Self-Regulatory Organizations

The brokerage community assumes a great deal of responsibility for regulating its own behavior. The stock exchanges and the National Association of Securities Dealers maintain regulatory bodies that establish rules governing trading operations. These SROs also oversee the activities of all licensed investment brokers who are fined and/or suspended when found guilty of breaking the rules.

When a broker is disciplined, he may appeal—a process that could take years. Although most appeals are ultimately decided against them, the brokers' customers are not informed of any disciplinary action until the process concludes. In the interim, a broker might relocate to another firm, leaving his prior firm with the liability for his malpractice. Despite more severe sanctions, longer suspensions, and higher awards for damages, problem brokers may be employed in a firm near you, so you need to be cautious.

Broker Education Program

To counterbalance an environment that could produce an unhealthy percentage of unethical brokers, the SEC approved a program in 1995 to educate the nation's licensed stockbrokers in regulatory and ethical issues. Brokerage firms are now required to provide regular courses for their brokers that cover internal sales practices as well as the products sold to customers. All brokers with less than spotless records are required to travel to one of 55 national facilities for the computer-based training. This program, however, does not mean you are safe in simply handing over your investment decisions to just any broker. Here's why.

First, the chairman of the SEC has admitted that his agency is too understaffed to properly monitor all brokerage firms in the country on a regular basis. So despite many effective regulations, federal oversight of individual investment brokers may be inadequate.

Second, brokers are recruited on the basis of sales skills or production rather than investment expertise, ethics, or experience.

Third, in today's competitive environment, management demands healthy production, which might pressure brokers to resort to unethical practices and push investments that are not suitable for their customers.

Fortunately, many expert, dedicated brokers maintain their integrity throughout their careers. Finding such a broker, however, is not always easy.

> *"I had never managed money. I had never made any real money . . . Yet I was holding myself out as a great expert on matters of finance. I was telling people what to do with millions of dollars when the largest financial complication I had ever encountered was a $325 overdraft in my account at the Chase Manhattan Bank."*
>
> *Liar's Poker*
> Michael Lewis

SELECTING YOUR BROKER

There is no substitute for educating yourself when it comes to choosing a broker. At all cost, you should avoid choosing a broker who is lacking in any of what I call "the three E's"— *experience, ethics, and expertise.*

Throughout my career, it has never ceased to amaze me how little attention investors give to the selection of their brokers. Years ago, I had an experience that illustrates this point.

When I was a novice broker, a woman came into my office with $30,000 to invest. I presented several investment strategies for her consideration and told her I would be in touch the following week to allow her time to consider my recommendations.

When I called her a week later as promised, she suggested that I was not a good broker because I had not persuaded her to invest her money the day we met. Apparently, upon leaving my office, she had walked across the street to another investment firm where a broker was only too happy to take her check before the ink was dry. Bewildered by the episode, I consulted my manager who counseled that I needed to recognize that my customers depend on me to tell them how to invest. He said, "Your clients depend on you to know which investments are best for them, and they want you to relieve them of the responsibility of making investment decisions."

I soon realized that my manager was right. Indeed, most clients found the investment process tedious and wanted to get it over and done with. Although this may appear to be a reasonable mindset, it renders investors easy prey for unethical brokers. Such brokers may go out of their way to appear credible and give you the impression that your financial welfare is their top priority when, in reality, they consider you an easy mark. Inexperienced brokers may have good intentions but lack a thorough understanding of the investment products. Even seasoned brokers may lack expertise because they have failed to devote the time and energy to digest the volumes of data needed to provide informed recommendations.

The reality is that brokers are no different from any other class of professionals: they can range from brilliant to financially illiterate. Mediocrity is just as rampant here as in any other profession. It is your responsibility, although quite a challenge, to weed out the unacceptable and select a broker who is experienced, ethical, and expert.

If you know nothing about investing, you face a serious dilemma because you are in no position to determine if a broker is trustworthy or competent. In fact, unethical brokers are more likely to put their own interests first with customers who are not sufficiently informed to recognize a broker's malpractice. So what can you do?

You can learn investment basics. In fact, the more you know about investing, the less important your broker's experience, ethics, or expertise become.

> *Financially aware investors are rarely victims of any type of financial fraud.*

Fortunately, you have before you all the information you need to build a solid base of investment knowledge before you begin your search for a broker. As you begin this odyssey, I suggest that you watch financial programs such as *Wall Street Week* on PBS and the business news on CNN, PBS, or CNBC to gain a sense of the current investment environment. Subscribe to the *Wall Street Journal, Investors Business Daily*, or a financial magazine such as *Fortune, Business Week, Barron's, Smart Money* or *Forbes*.

Your lawyer, accountant, or any successful investor you know can probably make a reliable broker referral. As you conduct your search, here are some things to watch out for.

Friendly Advice. If friends recommend their brokers, question if they know enough about investing to accurately evaluate a broker's expertise or integrity. It is against human nature to share negative financial experiences, and many investors and brokers may have exaggerated their financial exploits.

Industry Assistance. Do not assume that the manager of a brokerage firm will assign you a good broker—his choice may involve an agenda that has nothing to do with your financial well-being.

Personal Interviews. Do not base your selection solely on impressions gained from simply talking to several brokers. Although interviewing is part of the selection process, it is anything but foolproof.

Credentials. Do not be swayed by titles and plush offices. The title of "vice president" (as well as all other trappings of success) reflects a broker's sales skills, not expertise or integrity.

Do not be impressed by an individual who bears the title "registered investment adviser." Anyone, regardless of expertise, may apply to the SEC for this title by completing a form and paying a fee. This title merely grants the applicant the right to charge a fee for dispensing investment advice, and your only real assurance is that he has not been convicted of a felony.

Also, anyone may call himself a "financial planner." While some financial planners charge fees for providing investment plans, most are brokers who are subject to the same conflicts of interest. A financial plan may be nothing more than a questionnaire that reflects only one individual's or institution's opinion as to how you should invest your money. Many financial planners charge little or nothing for this service because they earn substantial fees when the client invests according to the plan.

Limited Scope. Investment brokers who represent only one or two investment options cannot offer you an objective approach to investing. Gold coin brokers, for example, may represent their product as viable in all economic environments. Because all markets have cycles, the more investment options a broker is licensed to transact, the less inclined he is to recommend untimely or inappropriate investments.

Bank-Brokered Investments. You do not incur less risk or lower fees by investing at banks or S&Ls where commissioned brokers may deal in many of the same products as brokerage firms.

Interviewing a Broker Candidate

When you are ready to interview your candidates, the following checklist will help you make your selection:

- ☐ How long have you been licensed? (The longer, the better.)

- ☐ Do you specialize in any specific types of investments? Do you transact in individual stocks and bonds, or do you offer only mutual funds and insurance? (Your broker should be licensed to transact in individual stocks and bonds.)

- ☐ Can you furnish me with the names of three of your clients with similar needs whom I may contact regarding your service? (Then contact them!)

- ☐ How many brokerage firms have you worked for? (Avoid brokers who change firms every three or four years.)

- ☐ Will you agree to disclose the cost of each transaction made in my account *before* it is made?

- ☐ My immediate concern is _____ (retirement, lower taxes, higher income). What are your recommendations at this time?

(When you are ready to open an account, read Chapter 20.)

Due Diligence

Once you have identified your broker candidates, check to see if any has a record of questionable conduct. The NASD and stock exchanges keep records of all settled disciplinary actions against brokers. Call the NASD hotline at (800) 289-9999 to determine if there are any criminal indictments, convictions, civil judgments, suspensions, or unfavorable arbitration decisions recorded against any of your candidates.

You may get better information by contacting the regulatory agency in charge of securities in the broker's state. For its location and phone number, call the North American Securities Administrators Association at (202) 737-0900. The absence of a negative report is no guarantee that you are in good hands, but you can at least eliminate a known offender.

There is no proven strategy for finding an expert, ethical broker; however, a good place to start is with professionals who have served you well. Your lawyer, accountant, or any successful investor you know can probably make a reliable referral.

Querying an Investment Recommendation

Do not engage any broker who neglects to ask you about your income, investing experience, and investment goals before making recommendations. When your broker recommends a particular investment, don't act until you have read the chapter in this book that covers the investment. You should also read the prospectus (if there is one) describing the investment in detail. Armed with essential information, you can ask intelligent questions and thereby save yourself from sales tactics typically reserved for the uninformed.

To evaluate an investment recommendation, ask the following questions:

- How will your recommendation serve my financial goals?
- Why is this recommendation the optimal course of action?
- What are the risks? What can go wrong? What if I have to liquidate the investment?
- What is the cost when I invest? Are there any ongoing fees or liquidation charges?

Always insist that your broker promote your participation in the decision-making process just as you would in a good doctor-patient relationship. You would not likely be comfortable with a doctor who prescribed tests and administered medicines without seeking your opinions beforehand. The same is true of a broker. If you don't feel he is genuinely interested in helping you attain your financial goals *or* if you find you cannot trust him because he has not acted in your best interests *or* if he is intimidating or pressuring, find another broker.

Summary

You do not need to learn everything a licensed broker masters, but prudent investing requires that you learn the basics. The best broker-client relationships are akin to the best doctor-patient relationships—the consumer lacks the depth and breadth of professional training, but is sufficiently informed to ask key questions to gather critical information. Whatever the source of investment advice, do not invest before thoroughly examining the investment yourself.

Never forget that you and you alone are responsible for your investing success or failure. How well you meet the challenge, expending time and energy gathering and digesting pertinent information, will ultimately determine your financial destiny.

Of all the ways to invest money, ownership of profitable businesses has proven to be the optimal means of creating wealth. The rich do it; so can you. Indeed, investors have reaped greater profits by buying stock in corporate America than by lending out their money or by purchasing real estate and other hard assets. There is no reason to believe that stocks offer less opportunity today. In fact, you may have a tough time reaching your financial goals if you choose to avoid them.

Chapter 4

The Market of Stocks

"There is a tide in the affairs of men Which, taken at the flood, leads on to fortune."

Julius Caesar
William Shakespeare

A share of *common stock* is the basic unit of ownership representing a financial interest, or equity, in a company. When you hear someone talk about the "stock market," the reference is to the trading of common stocks. (Preferred stocks, which trade more like bonds, are described in Chapter 6.)

A privately owned company goes public by selling all or part of its ownership to investors to raise capital. By purchasing common stock you actually own a part of a company's assets and stand to participate in its profitability.

Shareholders have the right to vote for the board of directors and on corporate matters such as whether to sell the company or issue more stock. Although they are invited to annual meetings and generally vote in elections by mail, because of their minority interest, individual shareholders exercise virtually no influence on a company's day-to-day management.

Almost any type of business imaginable may be found among thousands of public companies from small, newer companies to Fortune 500 megacorporations. *Blue chips* are the long-established companies with larger capitalization (number of shares multiplied by the share price) that tend to have a history of consistently paying dividends to shareholders.

Defensive companies are those in the utility, food, beverage, drug, and health-care industries which are expected to be more resilient during recessions. *Cyclical* companies are expected to flourish in stronger economic cycles but suffer during recessions. These include the hotel, airline, automobile, and home-building industries.

WHAT DRIVES STOCK PRICES?

The rationale for stock investing is simple. Investors look for companies that will increase their profits, because growing earnings ultimately drive stock prices and dividends higher.

The major challenge of research analysts working for Wall Street's financial firms is to forecast future earnings of public companies for their clients. Analysts spend years increasing their knowledge of how industries function to more accurately predict which companies will be the most profitable.

Stock prices tend to reflect corporate earnings expectations projected six months or more into the future rather than what has already occurred. When a company reports higher earnings than Wall Street's consensus, the "surprise" generally causes an immediate rise in its stock's price. However, prices often decline when earnings fall short of analysts' estimates. On July 14, 1994, for example, a respected analyst lowered his 1995 earnings estimate for the computer company MicroAge Inc. from $1.90 to $1.38 a share. The announcement precipitated a sudden sell-off resulting in a 44 percent plunge in the stock's price from $17.75 to $10!

Asset valuations also influence stock prices. If the value of a company's assets exceeds its stock-price valuation, a corporate raider may try to buy sufficient shares to take control of the company. In the 1980s, investors like Boone Pickens and Sir James Goldsmith reaped megamillions in such takeovers.

Companies may buy or merge with other companies to increase profitability. Rumors of possible takeovers or mergers can impact stock prices dramatically. Share prices of companies being acquired are more likely to rise, while the shares of the acquiring companies generally drop temporarily.

GAUGING VALUE

The price of a stock is not by itself any indication of value. If it were, a $100 stock would always indicate greater value than a $30 stock, which is not necessarily the case. Stocks are analyzed on the basis of a multitude of criteria, including price/earnings ratios and dividends.

Price/Earnings Ratio

The price/earnings ratio, or *P/E,* is one of many evaluation tools that helps identify companies that warrant further investigation, for either purchase or sale. A company's stock price is greatly influenced by its earnings growth, and the P/E provides investors with a concise picture of that relationship.

The P/E is calculated by dividing the stock price by the company's annual earnings per share. Thus, if a company's share price is $10 and it earns $1 per share in annual profits, the P/E ratio is 10 to 1. The P/E figure, in this case 10, is commonly referred to as the *multiple,* the multiple of earnings each share represents.

Share Price ÷ Earnings per Share = P/E

If you recall that company earnings are anticipated and estimated, you can see how a stock's P/E reflects investors' feelings about the company's future prospects. The P/E rises as prospects for future growth improve and declines as future earnings become less certain. Fast-growing companies generally have higher P/E multiples than slower growing, mature companies because investors bid up their prices, seeking to harness a growth pattern with potential to deliver higher returns than the market. That is why analysts generally focus on P/Es based on a company's estimated future earnings, and why it makes no sense to compare a fast-growing high-tech company's P/E with that of a utility or bank.

P/Es are frequently misused because company earnings are calculated differently. A P/E is based on past, present, or future earnings; it may include credits and charges, and the total number of shares might vary. Unless you are comfortable with accounting and finance, you should give weight only to P/Es derived from the same source so that you can observe trends rather than focus on static numbers. Pay greater attention to a company's P/E trend in relationship to its industry and to the market in general.

Let's say you are considering the purchase of two companies in the same industry. One company, priced at $20 per share, earned 40 cents per share; the other company, priced at $90, earned $6 per share. The $20 company's P/E is 50, significantly higher than the $90 company's P/E of 15. This reflects investor expectation for much faster growth for the $20 company. If you consider yourself an aggressive investor, you would probably purchase the company with the higher P/E. If more conservative and value oriented, you might consider the company with the lower P/E, but keep in mind that *falling P/Es may indicate real problems.*

Market watchers track the average P/E ratio of the *Standard & Poors 500* index (composed of 500 of some of the largest U.S. companies) to gauge whether the market in general is overvalued. In the present market, a P/E of 10 or less is considered low, 15 is considered average, and 20 plus is considered high. When inflation and interest rates are low, however, investors make allowances for higher multiples.

Dividends

The total return of a stock investment includes dividends paid by the company in addition to share-price gains. Newer companies generally reinvest profits, but as they mature, nearly all large public companies pay cash dividends to shareholders out of their earnings. A company's board of directors decides if a dividend is to be paid and how much.

Dividends generally increase in line with company profits.

For example, had you invested $8,700 in 100 Procter and Gamble shares in 1969, you would have received more than $23,000 in dividend income over 25 years, and your shares in 1994 would be valued at more than $96,000.

The percentage of a company's retained earnings paid as dividends is the *payout ratio*. The typical payout ratio is 25 to 50 percent of company earnings. When earnings slump, a company may elect to decrease its dividend, which generally has a negative effect on its stock price. It is also not a good sign when a company maintains a dividend payout that threatens its profitability.

Dividends are paid quarterly to shareholders designated *owners of record*. To qualify, shares must have been purchased before the *ex-dividend* date, approximately three weeks before the dividend is paid.

Dividends may also be paid in shares of stock. A company may elect to pay a stock dividend instead of cash when its board of directors feels that the money can be best used to expand the business or develop new products.

As you might expect, when many corporations increase their dividends, it is considered positive for the stock market— dividend yields are an indicator of corporate growth and profitability as well as investment value. In 1993, the 2,000 plus corporations listed on the New York Stock Exchange paid out more than $120 billion in cash dividends to shareholders, representing slightly less than 3 percent of their aggregate market capitalization. Historically, when this average price-to-yield rate fell below 3 percent, the market weakened. However, when rates of inflation and interest are low, and earnings and dividends are growing, investors might make allowances for a rate lower than 3 percent.

Stock Splits

If a company determines that its stock price is too high to interest investors, it may *split* the shares to lower the price. Although a split changes the number of outstanding shares, it has no effect at all on shareholder equity, and dividends are adjusted accordingly. Sometimes the announcement of a split promotes the stock's market value, but often it has no effect at all.

A stock split may be a distribution of any whole or fractional number of shares for each share held. On a two-for-one split, the share price drops 50 percent and shareholders receive one new share for each share held. On a four-for-one split, the share price is lowered to 25 percent of the current price and the company sends shareholders three new shares for each share held.

A *reverse* split decreases the number of outstanding shares. A company may reverse-split its stock when the price is too low for its stock to be used as collateral for borrowing money or is too costly to trade. (As a percentage of money involved, the transaction cost of trading 1,000 shares at $10 per share is significantly less than the cost of trading 10,000 shares at $1.) A one-for-ten reverse split gives one new share to replace each ten shares held and the price is increased tenfold. Again, shareholders have no less equity, only fewer shares representing the same total equity.

> *Now is always the most difficult time to invest.*

Warren Buffett: Profile of a Master Investor

The most successful U.S. investor amassed an $8 billion fortune by purchasing common stocks. If you had invested $10,000 with billionaire Warren Buffett four decades ago, your returns would exceed $90 million today.

Did Buffett achieve billionaire status by implementing uniquely brilliant investment strategies? No, he simply bought a handful of very carefully chosen companies. Was Buffett a market-timer? Not in the classic sense, because he bought stocks to be held *forever*. A true contrarian, Buffett got out of the stock market in the late 1960s when stocks reached outrageous prices, but he bought heavily in the 1970s as investors sold and prices were down.

Buffett believes investors do not have to do extraordinary things to achieve extraordinary results. Financial goals are reached "by owning a diversified group of businesses that generate cash and consistently earn above-average return on capital." Buffett proves that you don't have to get in on the ground floor to invest successfully. He tripled his investment in Coca-Cola shares which he purchased after they had already quadrupled in the previous six years.

Buffett is very selective about the type of business and he likes companies that produce a simple product or service for which there should always be substantial demand. He ignores political and economic forecasts, but he is quite concerned about inflation, which he believes is inevitable, and chooses companies that would be least hurt by inflation. He avoids companies with over-leveraged balance sheets. He wants to own companies that are "sensibly priced with good underlying economics that are managed by honest and able people."

Buffett's "secrets" are nothing more than common sense and an uncommon detachment from the vagaries of the stock market. While most professional investors are obsessing over stock prices, Buffett rarely looks at them but focuses solely on his companies' ability to generate cash. Buffett crunches the numbers to determine a company's *intrinsic* value—independent of its stock price. Intrinsic value, a highly subjective figure that changes over time, is "the discounted value of the cash that can be taken out of a business during its remaining lifetime." If Buffett cannot understand a company well enough to make such an analysis, or if the company cannot be bought for less than his evaluation, it is not a Buffett candidate.

Having suffered a few failures on a grand scale for which he offers no apology, Buffett shows us that you don't have to be infallible to be a very successful investor. Nor do you have to invest in a large number of companies—only five companies represent 75 percent of Buffett's Berkshire Hathaway holdings. He suggests that owning more companies than you have time to monitor increases your risk.

Buffett has been described as disciplined, patient, flexible, confident, courageous, decisive, and *very relaxed*. Not to mention rich. Although Buffett started investing at the tender age of 11, the tools he uses are available to investors of any age.

Getting rich through stock investing is not that easy but it is possible once you learn how. If you have the courage to think independently regardless of market trends and what others think and to invest consistently in your carefully chosen handful of quality companies, they may reward you beyond your financial dreams. It is my hope that this chapter has you fantasizing about the possibilities.

If you want to learn more about Warren Buffett, read *Buffett* by Roger Lowenstein and *The Warren Buffett Way* by Robert G. Hagstrom, Jr.

MARKET TIMING: WHEN TO BUY AND SELL

The direction of the stock market depends on the supply and demand for common stocks. Whether investors are buying or selling depends on the outlook for interest rates and inflation, economic productivity, social and political factors such as elections and international conflict, as well as their own personal situations such as job security and income growth. Even changes in tax rates may impact investor stock-buying patterns.

Cynicism, fear, and uncertainty are emotions that typically dissuade would-be stock investors. When stock prices are down, it's just "too scary"; when stocks rally, prices are "too high"; when the economy is strong, it might weaken; when interest rates spike up, stocks might come "under pressure" . . . and so on.

Just prior to the bull market that began in 1982, the prime rate soared to 21 percent, mortgage rates hit 18 percent, unemployment was 13 percent, banks and businesses defaulted in record numbers, and international terrorism was rampant. In 1987, the stock market crashed. Some people would have thought you were crazy to buy stocks during such turbulence, but many who did made a bundle.

There is no question that investing in stocks involves risk, but to be precise, what most investors fear is price volatility and uncertainty. If stock prices inched forward incrementally with very little volatility, everyone would invest with no perceived risk. But in a free-flowing capitalist market, there are many short-term ups and downs and cycles during which prices peak or bottom out.

A *bull* market is a period of rising stock prices; a *bear* market is a period of falling or floundering stock prices. *Historically, bull markets have lasted longer than bear markets, rewarding the more courageous investors who participate wisely and remain invested for the long term.*

Let's say you had invested $10,000 in the Aim Weingarten Fund (a mutual fund that invests in stocks) on August 25, 1987, at the peak price of that year. By the day of the crash, October 19th, the market value of your investment would have dropped to $6,463; down 35.4 percent in less than two months! Faced with this paper loss, you may have chosen one of the following options:

1. Sell, take the loss, and buy CDs.
2. Wait until the fund breaks even, sell, and buy CDs.
3. Hold on to your shares for the long term.
4. Buy additional shares at the lower price.

1. If you sold your shares and bought CDs, your investment as of March 31, 1994, would have been worth between $9,500 and $10,900, depending on the CD yield.

2. If you waited for the fund to return your $10,000, sold the shares and bought CDs, as of March 31, 1994, your investment would have been worth between $13,260 and $14,560, depending on the CD yield.

3. If you continued to hold the shares, by March 31, 1994, your investment would have been valued at $16,399.

4. If you invested an additional $10,000 right after the

crash, by March 31, 1994, your $20,000 would have grown to $40,366.

Refer to the chart on page 82 that tracks the U.S. stock market. Observe how price dips were always followed by new highs, and bear markets rarely lasted very long. Stocks performed better during periods of low inflation and low interest rates. The only decade in the last six when stocks did not outperform bonds and other fixed-income investments was the 1970s. (Oil prices hit $57 per barrel and inflation soared from 3 percent to 12 percent, causing record-high interest rates and a uniquely arduous period for stocks.)

A Standard & Poor's study offers a more scientific approach for dispelling market-timing myths. If your stock portfolio's performance mirrored the S&P 500 index from 1975 to 1994, it gained on average 14.6 percent annually. Had you missed only 10 of the market's best performing days, your return would have dropped to 11.9 percent. If you had missed 20 of the best days, the return would have fallen to 10.1 percent; 30 days, 8.6 percent; and 40 days, 7.2 percent. Out of 5,218 trading days, if you missed only 40 of the best ones, your returns would have been reduced by 50 percent! In 1991, the market rose 30 percent, but if you missed only ten of the best days, your return would have been only 3.3 percent.

Predicting the right time to buy or sell is more than just difficult—it appears that nobody has ever done it successfully for very long. Although market-timers might make accurate calls for a time, sooner or later the market outsmarts them. A Dalbar study shows that investors' attempts at market timing tend to be disastrous. For the ten years ending June 1994, the mutual funds studied generated an average annual return of 14.5 percent. However, the shareholders on average earned only 4.7 percent because many bought when prices were high and sold their shares after prices declined.

S&P 500 Annualized Total Returns. 1975-1994
If Invested in the Following Number of Days:

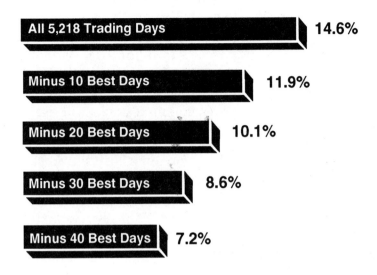

All 5,218 Trading Days	**14.6%**
Minus 10 Best Days	**11.9%**
Minus 20 Best Days	**10.1%**
Minus 30 Best Days	**8.6%**
Minus 40 Best Days	**7.2%**

A Return to Stocks

In the 1950s, a very large percentage of Americans found the stock market a good place to invest their savings because there was a fairly steady bull market and returns on bonds, real estate, and bank accounts were disappointing. By the 1960s, nearly half their savings were invested in stocks!

A shift away from stocks into other investments began in the 1970s. Inflation drove interest rates higher, and healthy returns as well as tax breaks were available in competing investments. Investors cashed out of stocks and a prolonged bear market followed.

There was no significant rebound in stock prices until the summer of 1982. As inflation and interest rates plummeted, stock prices soared. Americans returned to the market, but many backed out again when it crashed in 1987. Today U.S. households currently hold only about 20 percent of their savings in common stocks, less than half their commitment three decades ago. Perhaps they lack the knowledge or appreciation of the growth potential stocks offer; or more likely, they believe stocks are too risky. Despite these attitudes, analysts suggest that investor interest in common stocks will rise over the next decade for the following reasons:

The Spending Wave. For more than 70 years, stock market performance has been closely correlated to the number of 49-year-olds in the population. The earnings and spending of Americans typically peak at age 49, which strengthens the economy and increases the national savings rate. For the rest of this century, the number of 49-year-olds is expected to grow dramatically as the 76 million Americans born after World War II—baby-boomers—reach their peak earning/saving years. The anticipated 25 percent growth for this demographic group, combined with a 17 percent increase in the 75-plus age group, is expected to stimulate the economy and the markets.

Education. Surveys have found that the higher an individual's education, the greater the tendency to invest in stocks. Robust sales of financial newspapers, magazines, and newsletters point to increased familiarity with financial assets. As investors become better informed, they are likely to allocate more of their savings to stocks.

Growth. Stocks may be the only liquid investment capable of generating returns that outpace inflation and taxes by any significant margin.

Many analysts predict the Dow will exceed 8000 by the year 2000 based on 10 percent average annual growth. Volatility along the way should not dissuade investors with a long-term outlook.

A Case for Long-Term Stock Investing

Most of the time, nothing much happens in the stock market. The odds of making or losing money in common stocks depends less on your attempts at market timing and more on the quality of your selections and the length of time you remain invested. The only way to ensure that you participate in the major market moves is to be invested all the time. Successful investors recognize that they are not likely to find a "right" time to invest because there are always seemingly sound reasons for avoiding stocks. The key is not to hold out for the fabled "perfect" time to invest in quality stocks, but rather to *commit* to the purchase of them. Period.

According to American Funds Group, if you had consistently invested $1,000 every year since 1954 at market peaks, paying the highest prices of the year, by 1994, your invested $40,000 would have grown to a nest egg of $565,000. And that's the worst case scenario—the chances are you would have invested mostly at lower prices and profited even more.

Predictably, most investors follow the crowd, selling when most investors are pessimistic and buying when most are optimistic. A *contrarian* investor acts in opposition to the crowd. During times of uncertainty when most investors sell, contrarians buy; during periods of optimism when most investors buy, contrarians sell.

Successful investor Baron de Rothschild colorfully advised investors to buy when "blood is running in the streets." Emotionally, that is very difficult. In fact, many investors cash in during bear markets, locking in their losses, the worst possible investment mistake. Rothschild was right: *Optimal buying opportunities have always occurred during or after market declines when prices were cheaper.*

The U.S. stock market has proven to be stronger than any single event. The word "crisis" in Chinese is composed of two characters—the first, the symbol of danger; the second, the symbol for *opportunity*. The crises below caused dramatic plunges in stock prices, but within the year that followed, the market achieved record highs.

Date	Crisis	New High Reached
1950	North Korea invades South Korea	3 months later
1955	Eisenhower has a heart attack	6 weeks later
1962	Cuban missile crisis begins	7 months later
1963	Kennedy is assassinated	2 weeks later
1967	Mid-East War begins	7 weeks later
1991	U.S. enters Gulf War	11 months later

Think in terms of "time," not "timing." *Consistent, long-term exposure to quality common stocks is the key to successful investing* because as corporate profits grow, investment in them grows accordingly.

When I recommend that clients purchase stock for their retirement accounts, I often hear, "But this is my retirement money. I have to play it safe." I suggest stocks are optimal for retirement accounts because (1) over the long term, stocks have outperformed all other investment classes and (2) most people will not need to access these funds for many years.

Investing in stocks will test your fortitude and patience—some stocks and markets are roller-coaster rides while others are like watching grass grow. Stocks can suffer dramatic price swings simply because they are readily marketable assets, but over the long term, stocks offer the best opportunities for patient, disciplined investors.

*"It's like going to a beauty contest.
The idea is not to pick out the one
you think is the prettiest;
the idea is to pick out the one that
you think everyone else will think is
the prettiest."*

John Maynard Keynes

HOW STOCKS ARE TRADED

When a company first goes public, the management decides how its shares will be traded among investors, either on a stock exchange, an auction market, or over-the-counter, a negotiated market. These trading systems, which have been evolving for more than two centuries, operate very efficiently today.

The Stock Exchange

A stock exchange is a private association that provides a physical location and clerical support for its members, primarily partners and directors of brokerage firms. Trading occurs auction-style with investors exchanging bids and offers on the exchange's listed securities.

The two largest U.S. exchanges are the *New York Stock Exchange*, also known as the "Big Board," and the *American Stock Exchange*, both located in New York City. Several smaller regional exchanges are located in other U.S. cities

The Market of Stocks **61**

(Philadelphia, Boston, Chicago, Cincinnati, and the Pacific in Los Angeles). Before a company may list its shares on an exchange, it must maintain specific financial standards and publicly disclose certain information about its affairs.

Exchanges do not buy or sell securities, nor do they set prices. Trading is conducted on the exchange "floor" where each *specialist* presides over the auctioning of shares for one or more of the listed companies. Sellers willing to take the lowest prices and buyers willing to pay the highest prices are given priority trade executions. When an imbalance of customer buy and sell orders occurs, specialists may trade for their own accounts to maintain orderly trading flow. While most transactions occur electronically, specialists still accept orders on small pieces of paper just as their predecessors did 200 years ago.

The Over-the-Counter Market

Most stocks and bonds are not traded on exchanges but in the over-the-counter market. The OTC market is not a place but rather a method of *negotiated* trading which, unlike exchanges, has no central location. It is composed of numerous dealers called *market makers*. Acting as wholesalers and principals, these dealers "make a market" in the shares of one or more companies as they trade for their customers and their own accounts.

Of the more than 12,000 companies that trade in the over-the-counter market, approximately 4,900 are listed on NASDAQ, an electronic network that provides up-to-the-second price quotations. Since it was organized in 1971, NASDAQ has become the world's second-largest trading system by volume.

	Number of Companies	Market Capitalization* (in billions)
New York Stock Exchange	3,082	$5,000
NASDAQ	4,900	886
American Stock Exchange	806	119

* Total number of common, preferred, and ADR shares multiplied by share prices (4-30-95)

Price Quotations

Whether a company's stock is listed on a stock exchange or traded over-the-counter, two prices are always quoted, the *bid* and the *offer*. If you ask a broker for a stock's price, he might respond, "24 bid, 24¼ offered (or asked)."

If selling shares, you are interested in the bid, the highest price offered by a buyer. If buying shares, you want to know the offer, the lowest price at which one or more shareholders has agreed to sell.

Although the SEC is promoting change in the pricing of securities to dollars and cents, prices are still quoted in points and fractional points:

1/8 = $0.125		5/8 = $0.625	
1/4 = 0.25		3/4 = 0.75	
3/8 = 0.375		7/8 = 0.875	
1/2 = 0.50		1 = 1.00	

Sometimes shares are quoted in 16ths, 32nds, and 64ths of a point.

1/16 = $0.0625   1/32 = 0.03125   1/64 = 0.015625

A quote of 18⅝ reflects $18.625 per share. A quote of 5⁵⁄₁₆ reflects $5.3125 per share.

The Spread. The difference between the bid price and the offer is the *spread*. A quote of "24 bid, 24¼ offered" reflects a spread of ¼ or 25 cents. Actively traded NYSE-listed stocks typically have narrow spreads of ⅛ to ¼, but the spread on a small, little-known OTC company could be as high as $1.00 or more. A larger spread may indicate greater risk to market makers or low trading activity.

Stock Symbols. Every public company has a "ticker" symbol by which it is easily identified. Symbols of exchange-listed companies generally have one, two, or three letters of the alphabet; those traded over-the-counter have four or five letters. General Motor's symbol, for example, is GM; Microsoft's is MSFT.

Market Hours. During market hours, 9:30 a.m. to 4:00 p.m. EST, up-to-the-second stock quotes are readily available electronically through broker terminals and other computer networks.

Tracking the Order

When you buy or sell a security, the brokerage firm enters your order into its computer system for transmittal to its traders at the designated exchange or the firm's OTC trading desk. For an exchange-listed security, the order is sent to the brokerage firm's floor broker on the exchange or directly to the specialist to be matched with an offsetting order.

Market orders are executed immediately. Limit orders that cannot be executed are recorded by the specialist in his elec-

Stock Orders

Stocks are generally traded in 100-share increments called *round lots*. Any number of shares fewer than 100 is an *odd lot*. Investors may direct brokers to place stock orders contingent on a variety of conditions. The most common are

Market. Order executed immediately at the market price. The executed price may differ slightly from the broker's last quote, since it takes a few seconds to reach its destination. A market *sell* order is executed at the highest price acceptable to a buyer; a market *buy* order is executed at the lowest price acceptable to a seller.

Limit. Open order to buy or sell at a specified price or better. A limit order might result in an order that is filled, partially filled, or not filled at all when the limit price is "away" (too far) from the market price.

Good-til-Canceled (GTC). Limit or open order that stands indefinitely unless changed or canceled.

Day. Limit order to be held until the close of market.

Stop. Sell order that specifies a *stop price*. Once the market hits the stop price, the order immediately becomes a market order. The executed price may be higher or lower than the stop price.

Stop Limit. Stop order that becomes a limit order when the stop price is hit.

All or None (AON). Limit order to be executed completely or not at all. If you do not want to buy shares unless you can buy a certain number at a specified price, use AON to avoid partial limit-order executions.

tronic order book to be filled at a later time. When your order is executed, your broker is wired a confirmation, and the details of the trade are transmitted for public announcement.

When your order involves an over-the-counter company, it is wired to the brokerage firm's OTC trader, who looks it up in the *pink sheets* (a listing of all OTC stocks and their market makers). The trader then calls the stock's market makers to negotiate the best price on your behalf. For NASDAQ-listed companies, the trader's computer displays the market price and other pertinent data, but most orders are executed electronically without assistance of a trader, and are confirmed within seconds to your broker.

Although his own firm may be a market maker in the stock, a trader is legally bound to find the best prices for his customers among all market makers, and may have to deal with more than one to execute a large order. Unlike exchange-listed shares, OTC share prices may include dealer markups or markdowns, either in lieu of or in addition to commissions charged.

Confirmation. When your trade is executed, the brokerage firm sends you a *confirm*, a written confirmation that reports the *trade* date (date the order takes effect), the quantity, description, and price of the security traded. If the broker acted as *agent*, the confirm displays the commission charged; if he acted as *principal* (market maker or underwriter), the marked up price may be reported without specifying any commission or markup.

Settlement. When securities are purchased, payment must be made on or before the *settlement* date, regardless of whether any confirm had been received. *Settlement for stock transactions generally occurs on the third business day following the trade date.* If securities are sold, the seller must deliver the assigned stock certificates to the brokerage firm on or before the settlement date. (Before June 1995, settlement occurred the *fifth* business day following the trade date.)

Commissions and Markups. Transaction costs for buying and selling stock are based on the share price and number of shares traded during a single market session. Stock commissions are typically a fraction of 1 percent to 3 percent, although small orders for very low priced shares can cost more than 5 percent of the funds involved. The higher the stock price and the greater the number of shares traded, the lower the commission as a percentage of funds involved. (In addition to commissions, brokerage firms may charge markups that are not disclosed on OTC shares in which they make a market.)

Although their maximum commissions are generally higher than those charged by discount brokers, full-service brokers offer discounts based on a customer's trading activity. Brokers rarely offer to discount commissions—you must ask.

Short Selling

The most common form of stock investing is *buying long*. When you are "long a stock" (meaning you own it), the most you can lose is the amount of cash you invested. However, if an investor believes that the price of a company's shares will decline, she may speculate by *selling the stock short*. *Shorting* a stock involves selling borrowed shares with the expectation that the price will fall, providing the opportunity to buy them back cheaper—sell high; buy low. The short seller's profit is the difference between the buy and sell prices, less commissions.

To sell a stock short, you sell shares you do not own but arrange to borrow from the brokerage firm handling the transaction, and agree to repay the loan by repurchasing the shares in the future. A short sale cannot be protected indefinitely; it is always subject to a buy in with little notice. Short sales are very risky because the stock's price *rise* is potentially unlimited, and eventually the shares must be purchased to cover the account's short position. If you purchase the stock for a price higher than your sale price, you lose money.

After a short sale is executed, the firm charges the customer margin interest based on the sales proceeds plus commission (see margin, page 349.) Federal regulations require short sellers to maintain sufficient cash or securities on deposit to cover losses. If a shorted stock's price rises significantly, the firm must issue a *margin call* requiring the customer to deposit additional cash or equity to protect the firm from the liability of potential losses. Stock dividends are not paid to the short seller but to the owner, who is typically another customer of the same brokerage firm.

In 1992, Walt Disney Co. stock had the highest *short interest* on the NYSE. This means that more Disney shares had been sold short than any other NYSE-listed company. Despite the bearish sentiment, high short interest might ultimately be good for Disney's share price, as these shares must someday be purchased.

Stock Indexes

Dozens of indexes track and gauge the direction of security prices. An index not only gives you a market's track record, it also provides a benchmark for comparing the performance of any one stock or an entire investment portfolio.

The Dow Jones Industrial Average. When you hear that the market has gone up or down a number of points, the reference is probably to the Dow Jones Industrial Average, the oldest and most popular index with individual investors. The editors of the *Wall Street Journal* are responsible for the Dow, which includes 30 blue chip industrial companies listed on the NYSE:

Allied Signal	International Business Machines
Alcoa Corporation	International Paper Company
American Express	McDonald's Corporation
American Telephone & Telegraph	Merck & Company
Bethlehem Steel	Minnesota Mining & Mfg. Co.
Boeing Corp.	J. P. Morgan
Caterpillar	Philip Morris Cos.
Chevron	Procter & Gamble
Coca-Cola Company	Sears, Roebuck and Co.
DuPont	Texaco, Inc.
Eastman Kodak	Union Carbide Corporation
Exxon	United Technologies Corp.
General Electric	Walt Disney Company
General Motors	Westinghouse Electric Co.
Goodyear	Woolworth Company

The Dow industrials is the most widely quoted index, but being composed of only 30 stocks, it is hardly a perfect indicator of market movement. Distortions are inherent in any index, and the Dow is no exception. No electric utilities or transportation companies are included (they have their separate indexes), and the industries represented tend to be cyclical (more sensitive to economic cycles).

The Dow is weighted not by company size, but stock price—it assigns equal value to companies of vastly different sizes. For example, a 15 percent move in the price of a company trading at $100 is more significant than a 30 percent move in a company trading at $40. Stock splits create further distortion: A two-for-one split reduces by 50 percent the effect a stock has on the index relative to the same percentage move by any other component.

Standard & Poor's 500. When your mutual fund performance is being compared with overall market performance, the benchmark most widely quoted is the *S&P 500*. This index, created in 1957, includes 500 of some of the largest U.S. public corporations—400 industrial, 40 utility, 40 financial, and 20 transportation companies. Wall Street professionals favor this index because it offers a more democratic impression of stock-price momentum by representing a much larger percentage of the market's overall value.

NASDAQ Composite. In 1971, the NASDAQ (pronounced "naz-dak") Composite index was created to track the progress of more than 4,000 stocks listed on the National Association of Securities Dealers Quotation System. Although the index includes such large companies as Intel, MCI, Amgen, and Microsoft, it contains many emerging, speculative companies.

Other Indexes. There are a number of less familiar indexes that include:

Wilshire 5000. Composed of stocks listed on the NYSE and the AMEX, and the more actively traded OTC companies.

S&P Midcap 400. Medium-size companies listed on the NYSE, AMEX, and NASDAQ representing a broad sector of industrial, utility, financial, and transportation companies.

Russell 2000. Represents the smallest two thirds of the 3,000 largest U.S. companies.

S&P 600 Small Cap. Composed of 600 companies with capitalization under $1 billion, diversified by size and industry.

Wilshire Small Cap. Composed of 250 smaller U.S. companies screened by size, industry sector, and liquidity.

Newspaper Stock Quote Reporting

To help you monitor your stock portfolio, business sections of most large newspapers list individual stocks under the appropriate stock exchange or NASDAQ.

The first number on the left is the highest price traded in the last 52 weeks. The second number is the lowest price traded in the last 52 weeks. Next is the abbreviated name of the company, followed by its symbol. The next number is the annual dividend, expressed in dollars, followed by the annual dividend, expressed as a percentage of the stock's price. The next number is the P/E followed by the volume traded, expressed in hundreds. The next two numbers reflect the previous day's high and low prices, followed by the closing price. The last figure represents the price change from the prior market close.

NEW YORK STOCK EXCHANGE

52 Weeks Hi	Lo	Stock	Sym	Div	Yld %	PE	Vol 100s	Hi	Lo	Close	Net Chg
3	$2^3/_8$	MaunaLoa	NUT	.20	8.4	34	131	$2^1/_2$	$2^3/_8$	$2^3/_8$	...
$25^5/_8$	$17^1/_2$	MaxusEng pfA		2.50	10.0	...	60	$25^1/_8$	25	$25^1/_8$	...
17	$11^1/_2$	MaxximMed	MAM		...	56	61	$15^1/_4$	15	15	...
$45^3/_8$	$32^1/_4$	MayDeptStrs	MA	1.14	3.0	12	11270	$39^1/_4$	$37^1/_2$	$37^5/_8$	$-1^1/_2$
$25^3/_8$	$15^3/_8$	Maybelline	MAY	.32	1.3	20	335	$24^1/_4$	$23^7/_8$	24	$-^1/_4$
$19^3/_8$	14	Maytag	MYG	.56f	3.0	dd	5411	$18^7/_8$	$18^3/_8$	$18^3/_8$	$^1/_8$

"We are confronted with insurmountable opportunities."

Pogo

WAYS TO INVEST

You have several ways to participate in stock ownership:

- Select and manage stocks yourself.
- Act on broker recommendations.
- Purchase shares in mutual funds or unit investment trusts.
- Engage an investment adviser/manager.

On Your Own

Taking the time to study and analyze companies can be a profitable undertaking, and many individuals construct and manage their stock portfolios very successfully. You will, of course, need to engage a licensed broker to place the buy and sell transactions.

Your investment success depends on how well you select individual companies—not an easy task. The investment professional looks for a multitude of factors such as high cash flow and earnings growth, great management, low long-term debt, stable dividends, hidden assets, insider share ownership, promising chart pattern or other technical issues, and some future event that will spark investor interest.

As a service to customers, all large brokerage firms employ analysts to write research reports on hundreds of companies.

72   Invest without Stress

Financial firms also publish a recommended model portfolio consisting of several companies diversified among the spectrum of industries. *Value Line* and *Standard & Poor's* research reports are available at public libraries and brokerage firms.

Your goal should be to select six to 10 of the best companies you can find, and to continue to hold them until they no longer appear to be rewarding or until you find other companies that look better. To quote billionaire Warren Buffett, "We just try to buy businesses with good to superb underlying economics, run by honest and able people, and buy them at sensible prices." He advises investors to do their homework and limit their holdings to companies in industries they understand.

An abundance of financial newsletters, books, and periodicals will help you take the plunge. Start with Peter Lynch's *One Up on Wall Street* or *Beating the Street.* Lynch was one of the most respected and successful portfolio managers and his books have been an inspiration to many. For a different perspective on stock selection, I recommend *The Dividend Connection* by Geraldine Weiss and Gregory Weiss for insights into how stock dividends create value.

Bear in mind, however, that building and monitoring a stock portfolio requires substantially more effort than looking up stock prices in the newspaper every day. It helps to enjoy the analytical process, and you must have the time to do it properly.

Engaging a Stockbroker

Lacking the time or interest, consider working closely with a stockbroker. Be mindful that you can never know the track record of any stockbroker, and there is considerable disparity in levels of expertise. You are not likely to learn about any particular broker's competence until after you have invested. Few brokers research and analyze companies on their own, but typically base their recommendations on reports written by professional analysts. (See Chapter 3.)

Mutual Funds and Unit Investment Trusts

You can buy shares in mutual funds or unit investment trusts which offer the greatest diversification for your money. These securities are managed by professional advisers who spend most of their time researching and analyzing companies, and may even meet personally with company management. Performance figures, as well as other pertinent data, are available from investment brokers, financial periodicals, and management companies. Check with your broker or library for *Morningstar* and *Value Line* reports, which provide profiles of hundreds of funds. (Chapter 9 covers these investments in detail.)

Individually Managed Accounts

If you have more than $100,000 to commit to stocks, consider engaging a professional adviser/manager to select and manage your portfolio. Advisers charge a small fee for their services, generally one percent or less of your account value. Unlike a mutual fund, your stock positions are always held in a separate account in your name. (Chapter 9 covers managed accounts in detail.)

STOCK TIPS

One of the best ways to become proficient in stock investing is to investigate how successful professional investors operate. Although the pros may embrace different investment philosophies, strategies, and styles, they appear to agree on some things.

- *Do your homework.* Research companies as much as possible before investing.

- *Be wary of tips.* Don't buy companies that "sound" good —buy companies with sound fundamentals.

- *Be patient.* Don't be too quick to take profits on shares that have appreciated significantly. A stock's price may have much farther to climb before leveling off.

- *Expand your horizons.* Don't invest in companies simply because they performed very well in the past. Buy companies poised for future growth.

- *Beware of bargains.* Don't buy stocks just because they trade substantially lower than they once did. More often than not, these stocks are depressed for valid reasons. A depressed stock may revive with a "dead cat bounce" before declining further.

- *Take appropriate risk.* Don't allocate too large a portion of your portfolio to fixed-income investments with too little invested in common stocks. Rule of thumb: Subtract your age from 100 and allocate that percentage of your savings to stocks.

- *Sell your losers.* All too often investors suffer from "evenitis," a condition that compels them to continue holding depressed shares in the hope of getting even, or being "right" about having bought them in the first place. However, just because a stock declines after you bought it does not mean you made a bad choice. Assuming you did your homework, stick with the stock.

- *Be independent.* Unsophisticated investors typically jump into the market around the time it peaks, rarely buy when stock prices are extremely depressed, and they tend to panic and sell during market corrections—precisely the worst times for taking such action. Don't follow the crowd.

- *Beware of penny stocks.* Many investors like stocks trading under $5.00 per share because a smaller move up delivers a larger percentage profit. The opposite is true as well and appears to happen more often.

Patient, disciplined investors profit most. They invest with consistency and never panic. Nor do they mourn missed opportunities because they realize viable new ones are always developing.

The ever-changing investment climate requires a flexible attitude. If your ideas are set in stone, you will not be open to new opportunities and you risk getting caught with investments that sour.

Look for major trends politically, economically, and technologically. What are the leading-edge opportunities? Early investors in Wal-Mart were open to a new way to market to consumers; Microsoft shareholders recognized the potential for a new universal language for computers. You don't have to buy a company you don't understand. Observe your children and your community for growing trends and popular items.

Periodic market declines are inevitable, and astute investors anticipate and make the most of them. During the last century, there were at least 50 occasions when the stock market declined 10 percent or more. Create a shopping list of quality stocks you want to own that have become expensive on a price/earnings basis—you are likely to be given the opportunity to purchase them at a lower price in the next correction. If the market declines 10 percent, buy more; if it drops 20 percent, double up.

Keep in mind that there is little connection between a booming economy and stock prices. In the short run, the stock market overvalues certainty and overreacts to uncertainty. Systematically investing in quality companies, regardless of the market, has proven to be the optimal way to accumulate wealth. Set aside your fears, look for opportunity, and take a long-term perspective of the market.

Summary

If your savings program is not on track for reaching your financial goals, and you have not allocated part of your savings to common stocks, it is time to rethink and restrategize. Create a long-term investment program that includes stocks because you are not likely to find a better vehicle for growing your savings. The more you learn about them, the more you will recognize the unique opportunities common stocks offer.

If you think now is not the right time to buy U.S. stocks, you have dozens of other markets to exploit. If you don't want to bother with individual stock selection, purchase shares in mutual funds. Wall Street has made it easier than ever for individual investors to participate in the growth of profitable businesses all over the world.

VALUABLE STOCK MARKET TERMS

Book Value. Theoretical historical value (not market value) of a company's assets after all debts are paid. Many analysts believe that book value no longer accurately measures corporate values because of share buybacks and corporate restructurings.

Debt/Equity Ratio. A simplistic measure of a company's financial solvency. *Debt* is the total cash a company owes creditors; *equity* is the dollar value assigned to shareholder ownership. The relationship between the two is an indicator of a company's financial condition. A blue-chip company generally has a low debt-to-equity ratio, but it can lose this status if it takes on excessive debt.

Although acceptable debt/equity ratios differ by industry sector, the lower the ratio, the easier it is for a company to remain healthy and profitable because it is less burdened with costs to service debt. Moreover, lenders require a higher yield to compensate for the greater risk of lending to an overleveraged company, which interferes with its profitability.

Tender Offer. Offer from a company or group to purchase a certain number of a company's shares. The bidding entity sends a document to the shareholders outlining the terms of the offer. Shareholders are not obliged to tender (sell) their shares, but generally it is in their interest to do so, since the offered price might be the highest price at which the stock will trade in the near future or perhaps ever again. Brokerage firms handle the tender process for their clients at no charge.

Program Trading. The computerized buying or selling of at least 15 stocks with total market value of $1 million or more. Computers enable huge quantities of stocks to be traded instantaneously as they spot certain trends. Sometimes one program triggers other program trades, further accelerating the trend to create an avalanche effect.

Since the 1987 crash, stock exchanges have imposed trading restrictions to keep the market orderly when panic might otherwise prevail. One rule limits certain program trading when the Dow Jones Industrial Average moves either up or down 50 points within a trading session. Program trading routinely averages about 12 percent of total volume, but complaints are rare as long as prices are rising.

Insider Trading. Illegal trading in securities based on confidential information to which only insiders (such as a company's accountants, lawyers, and employees) are privy. Industry computers detect heightened trading activity in certain stocks, which allows suspicious trades to be traced and investigated for insider-trading abuse.

Warrant. The right to purchase a certain number of a company's shares at a fixed price prior to a specified future date. Warrants are issued by companies that plan to issue stock or raise cash by selling shares held in reserve. When the underlying stocks perform badly, warrants can expire worthless.

Average Annual Return. The annual average of an investment's total return for a period of years stated as a percentage. If total return over three years is 30 percent, the average annual return is 10 percent. The compounded average annual return is 9.14 percent.

Rule of 72. Quick calculation to determine how long it takes to double an investment at a given interest rate. Divide 72 by the rate of interest earned to get the number of years it takes money to double. For example, if an investment earns 8 percent annually, it will take 9 years to double on a compounded basis. (72 ÷ 8 = 9.)

Restricted Securities. Stocks or bonds issued in a private sale or other transaction that are not registered with the SEC.

Prospectus. The disclosure document required by the SEC to be furnished to purchasers of newly registered securities. It provides detailed information about the issuer and the particular offering.

Proxy. Written authorization given by a security holder to another party to cast a vote on issues involving the security and/or the issuer.

Share Repurchase. Program by which a company buys back its own shares in the open market. After a company's share price declines, it may take advantage of the opportunity to repurchase its shares at a lower price.

Rights Offering. Offering of common stock that entitles existing shareholders to buy newly issued shares with no commission, often at a discount from the price at which shares will later be offered to the public.

Fundamental Analysis. Study of a company's balance sheet, earnings history, and other issues that are analyzed in an attempt to discern its earnings prospects.

Technical Analysis. A statistical study of the price action of a stock relating to supply and demand, using charts and various technical indicators. The theory purports that stock prices move in patterns, and past behavior indicates future direction. Technicians, who are generally very short-term oriented, rarely consider a stock's fundamentals but rely heavily on its quantitive aspects.

Triple Witching Hour. Four times each year on a quarterly basis, stock options, index options, and index futures expire almost simultaneously. The stock market tends to behave with greater volatility as this hour is approached.

Leveraged Buyout. The purchase of a company with borrowed capital. Many LBOs are financed with junk bond offerings.

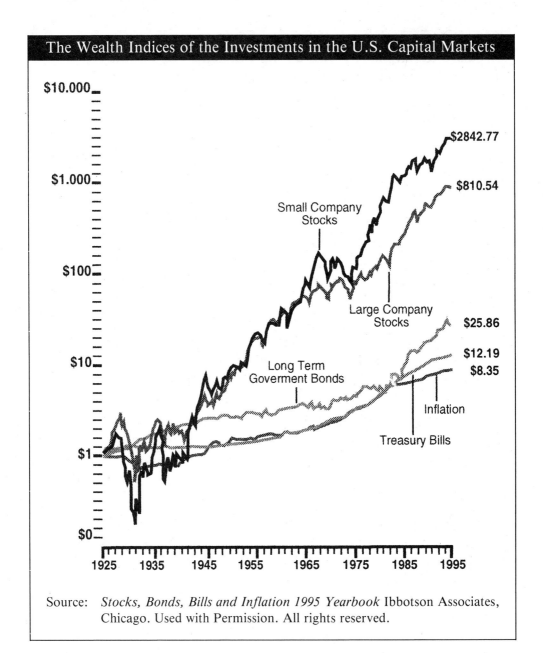

The Wealth Indices of the Investments in the U.S. Capital Markets

$10.000

$1.000

Small Company
Stocks

$2842.77

$810.54

$100

Large Company
Stocks

$25.86

$10

Long Term
Goverment Bonds

$12.19
$8.35

Inflation

$1

Treasury Bills

$0

1925   1935   1945   1955   1965   1975   1985   1995

Source: *Stocks, Bonds, Bills and Inflation 1995 Yearbook* Ibbotson Associates, Chicago. Used with Permission. All rights reserved.

*I*t may surprise you that—in spite of their rather austere "banker's gray" reputation—bonds have a rather colorful tradition. Indeed, they have been used to finance everything from Barbie dolls to World War II while serving the needs of millions of investors.

Chapter 5

The Bond Market

"It's hard to conceive of a
word more personal and emotional
than 'bond' which represents a
promise or agreement and is
used of sacred trusts."

Arthur Levitt, Jr.
Chairman,
Securities & Exchange Commission

WHAT IS A BOND?

A *bond* is a contract between a borrower and a lender guaranteeing payment of interest and repayment of a specific amount of money, or principal.

For centuries, financiers determined that the optimal way to match borrowers of money with individuals who had money to lend was with contracts called bonds. Investors lend their money when they purchase bonds to secure regular income. In fact, bonds are often referred to as *fixed-income* investments.

While the subject of bonds may seem confusing, the concept is really very simple. Let's say an old friend, who owns a small computer consulting business, has an opportunity to buy out a computer equipment service company, a business that would greatly complement his. Because the present owner insists on an all-cash deal, your friend needs to come up with $20,000 more than he has on hand. So he asks you to lend him the cash, which he promises to repay in five years with 8.5 percent annual interest. You agree, and he signs a note.

Fundamentally, you bought a *private* bond. Because of your personal knowledge of your friend's ethics and business success, you trust him to repay you in the manner agreed. But there is risk: If your friend dies before paying you back, you must make a claim to his estate to collect. If his business fails and he defaults on the note, you might lose all the money. If you need repayment earlier but your friend does not have the money, finding someone to purchase your note is unlikely.

By purchasing publicly traded bonds, you can avoid these pitfalls. First, a bond's safety is never jeopardized by the death or credit of any one person. Bond issuers must comply with strict federal regulations and disclose extensive financial information. Credit services analyze and interpret this data and assign ratings that reflect a bond issuer's financial condition so that you can know the degree of risk.

Second, bonds are *negotiable*, that is transferable, and they are publicly traded in a very active market, thereby enabling you to liquidate (cash out) quickly.

Although bonds can be very safe investments, to ensure that safety you must learn to recognize and avoid the risks involved. Bond funds are one of the most popular investments brokers sell today, but investors are often oblivious to the risks and charges involved, and not always well-informed by brokers. Do not purchase any bond or bond mutual fund until you fully understand the material in this chapter. Failure to scrutinize a bond investment can lead to financial loss, as the following true story illustrates:

In 1986, Ray Gleason (not his real name) wanted to invest his pension funds in conservative investments. A broker with a national brokerage firm recommended bonds issued by a local savings and loan yielding an attractive 13 percent. Acting solely on the broker's advice, Gleason invested $300,000 in the bonds.

About a year later, while reading his monthly statement, Gleason noticed that the bonds' interest had not been credited to his account, nor were the bonds assigned any market value. His broker explained that the S&L was shut down by bank regulators and had defaulted on the bonds' interest payments. With no buyers for the bonds, they were worthless.

When Gleason insisted the brokerage firm make good on his investment, the firm countered that it was not responsible for the S&L's problems. Attempting to recover his loss, Gleason engaged an attorney to represent him in arbitration against the brokerage firm. The panel of arbitrators ruled that the broker had done nothing wrong, and Gleason never recovered his $300,000.

The good news is that you can eliminate just about all risk once you know how to purchase bonds safely. For example, Gleason would have prevented his unfortunate loss had he properly addressed the major risk of lending money—can the borrower repay the loan? Because bonds are most likely your optimal choice if you need income, learning to purchase them safely is definitely worth the effort.

There are three major groups of bond issuers in the United States: corporations, the U.S. Government, and municipalities (state and local governments). Investors have a wide range of actively traded bonds from which to choose.

The U.S. Bond Markets *(in trillions)*	
Treasury	$3.466
Government Agency/Mortgage	1.448
Municipal	1.203
Corporate	1.252
Data from the Federal Reserve Bank as of 12-31-94	

This chapter covers corporate bonds and much of the information that pertains to bonds generally. Chapters 7 and 8 cover issues specific to government and municipal bonds, respectively.

CORPORATE BONDS

Corporate bonds, or *debentures*, represent company loans secured by their general credit. *Mortgage* bonds are collateralized by specific assets such as real estate. Bonds are the major source of financing for corporate expansion and continuing operations.

Most bonds are denominated in increments of $1,000, referred to as *par* or *face value*. The company promises to repay bondholders the bond's face value on a specified *maturity* date, and pay annual interest, ordinarily divided into two payments per year. The interest, which is stated as a percentage of the bond's face value, is called the *coupon* or *coupon rate*.

All bonds are issued for a specified term; however, most issuers retain the right to *call* (redeem or repay) their bonds prior to the scheduled maturity by including special redemption provisions in the original bond contracts.

Example of a Corporate Bond

Issuer	Coupon Rate	Maturity	Rating
American General	6.25%	5/15/03	AA −

American General guarantees to make annual interest payments of $62.50 per bond and to repay $1,000 principal on May 15, 2003.

Risks

When you purchase common stock, you become part *owner* of a company; when you buy a corporation's bonds, you become its *creditor*. A company's bonds are always a safer investment than its stock because if the company fails, bondholders have prior claim to its liquidated assets before stockholders are paid. A bond's integrity is only as good as the issuer's financial condition. Before you purchase any type of bond, you must analyze all the areas of risk.

Credit Risk. The possibility that a bond's issuer may default, that is, fail to make the interest payments or repay the loan, must be your first consideration. It is not difficult for individual investors to determine the credit risk of publicly traded bonds because most are rated by either *Moody's Investors Service* or *Standard & Poors*. These rating services analyze an issuer's creditworthiness and assign ratings that reflect its ability to repay its debts. Companies with high ratios of debt to assets are assigned lower credit ratings because their ability to repay their debts is less certain. Rating services also analyze an issuer's profitability, the quality of its management, and the economic trends affecting its industry.

Credit ratings range in descending order from AAA to D. The highest rating, AAA ("triple-A"), expresses the opinion that the issuer will not default on its debt. Conservative investors limit their purchases to *investment-grade* issues rated BBB and higher. Bonds rated BB or lower are referred to as *high-yield* or *junk* bonds. The lower a bond's rating, the greater the risk and the higher yield. Refer to page 104 for the rating scale. Rating information for individual companies is available from brokers and libraries.

Market or Interest-Rate Risk. If you sell a bond prior to its maturity, the price you get may be more or less than you paid, depending on the state of the bond market. Your broker must adjust the price of your bond to interest a buyer.

When market interest rates decline, bond prices increase because they become more appealing to investors; when market interest rates rise, bond prices decline because newly issued bonds have higher yields.

The longer a bond's life, the more sensitive its price to

interest-rate fluctuations. When interest rates rise, longer term bonds lose more market value than short-term bonds. In today's market, for example, if interest rates rise 2 percent, a two-year $10,000 bond loses $372 in market value; a five-year bond loses $829, a 10-year bond loses $1,365, and a 30-year bond loses $2,110. Market risk is not an issue when bonds are held to maturity, but it becomes an issue when you choose to sell.

Call Risk. Most bonds are issued with call provisions that allow issuers to repay bondholders prior to the stated maturity. Issuers are never obligated to call their bonds, but when interest rates decline, they are likely to exercise this right so that they can *reissue* the bonds at a lower interest rate to save borrowing costs. *Call protection* refers to the period after issuance when a bond may not be called, typically 10 years for long-term bonds. A call never works in favor of bondholders. A bond is usually called early when market interest rates have declined, causing bondholders to earn less interest when they reinvest the proceeds.

Inflation Risk. When a bond matures, the cash proceeds may have less buying power because of *inflation*. When a bond's yield is less than the inflation rate, buying power of the invested funds is sacrificed to some degree. If you purchase a two-year bond, for example, and inflation averages 4 percent annually, buying power is eroded by 8 percent during the bond's life. If your bond pays 6 percent annually, your "real" return is only 2 percent because your principal's buying power is reduced by the inflation rate.

Liquidity Risk. Liquidity refers to the readiness of the market to purchase the bonds. When lack of public awareness and low quality renders an issue less marketable, market value is reduced. Treasury securities are the most actively traded, followed by high-grade corporate and municipal bonds; unrated and low-rated bonds are generally the least marketable.

Reinvestment Risk. Market interest rates might decline by the time the bond's interest payments are received or principal repaid, allowing reinvestment of the proceeds at only lower rates.

HOW BONDS ARE TRADED

When a corporation needs capital, it generally engages a financial firm to process the initial bond offering. Before it may offer bonds for sale to the public, a corporation must file a registration statement with the Securities and Exchange Commission, and provide investors with a prospectus containing information about the company and the particular offering.

Bonds are initially offered to investors in the *primary* market; thereafter, bonds change ownership in the *secondary* market where they trade among investors. Some bonds are traded on exchanges, but most trade over-the-counter with brokers and dealers acting as principals, adding their markups to wholesale prices. Minimum purchase for corporate bonds may be $1,000 (face value), but is typically $10,000.

Yield/Price Dynamics

When you hear that the bond market is up or down, the reference is not to yields or interest rates, but to bond prices, particularly the prices of U.S. Treasury bonds. Because Treasury issues are extremely marketable, have very high credit quality, and are easily understood, they dictate the U.S. credit markets and act as benchmarks for all other fixed-income investments. In fact, investors gauge interest-rate fluctuations by tracking the yield of the Treasury's 30-year *long* bond, the bellwether for long-term interest rates.

The major factors that dictate bond prices and yields are credit quality of the issuer, market interest rates, length of the bond's maturity, and supply and demand.

Credit Quality. Credit ratings are major determinants of bond prices and yields. High-rated bonds command higher prices, resulting in lower, but theoretically safer, yields. The most creditworthy issuers pay the lowest borrowing costs; the least creditworthy issuers pay the highest.

Market Interest Rates. For a bond to sell, its price must reflect a competitive yield. Fluctuating market interest rates have the greatest impact on bond prices, so to become familiar with bond market dynamics, you must understand how bonds are repriced with *discounts* and *premiums*.

- **Discounts.** If the current market yield is 7 percent on new AA-rated 12-year corporate bonds, similar bonds with lower coupon rates are discounted to reflect a 7 percent total return to attract buyers.

  For example, a bond with a 6 percent coupon rate is discounted to $920 to reflect a 7 percent yield to maturity. When the bond matures, the holder is paid $1,000, $80 more than he paid to compensate for earning less interest.

- **Premiums.** Bonds with higher coupon rates merit premiums. A bond with an 8 percent coupon rate commands a price of $1,080 ($80 more than it pays at maturity), because it pays $80 more interest during its life, reflecting a 7 percent yield to maturity.

Analyzing Bond Yield

Yield is the return on an investment, calculated as a percentage of the amount invested. But it is really not that simple because the ultimate proceeds to be returned as principal may be more or less than your original investment. Therefore, to properly analyze a bond's total return, you must become familiar with the following terms:

Coupon Rate is the fixed-dollar amount the issuer contracts to pay bondholders until the bond matures, expressed as a percentage of the bond's face value.

Current Yield is a bond's annual *current* cash flow, expressed as a percentage of the bond's purchase price. It is calculated by dividing the total annual interest payments by the bond's purchase price.

Yield to Maturity is a bond's annualized total return if held to maturity. YTM factors in a bond's price, its future interest payments, and any projected capital gain or loss at maturity. YTM, which is calculated by brokers with special calculators, provides a reliable tool for evaluating and comparing bond yields.

Yield to Call is a bond's total annualized yield if it is called on its earliest call date. YTC factors in a bond's purchase price, call proceeds, and interest payments.

The coupon rate is generally static, but all other types of yield change as a bond's market price fluctuates and the period to maturity decreases. In the following example, the bond is trading at a discount, so its current yield, yield to call, and yield to maturity are all higher than its coupon rate.

Issuer	*Coupon Rate*	*Maturity*	*Price*
Union Pacific Corp.	6.125%	1/15/04	$93.479

Callable on 1/15/01 at 100   S&P Rating: A
Current Yield: 6.55%   Yield to Maturity: 7.068%
Yield to Call: 7.38%

Premium bonds may be preferable to discounted bonds. Because of their higher coupon rates, premium bonds yield higher current cash flows and their prices are more stable when interest rates rise.

Length of Maturity. A bond's life span influences its price because the longer the period to maturity, the greater the chance interest rates could rise, causing the bond's price to fall. The longer a bond's life, the higher the interest it generally pays to compensate for this risk.

The varying rates along the spectrum of maturities form a *yield curve*. Most of the time, short-term rates are lower than long-term rates. When long-term yields are significantly higher than short-term yields, the condition is called a *steep* yield curve. When long-term bond rates are lower than short-term rates, an *inverted* yield curve results. The curve is *flat* when rates are about the same for long and short maturities.

Supply versus Demand. The junk bond market sold off in 1989 when the supply greatly exceeded investor demand. When the stock market crashed in 1987, investors poured their stock sale proceeds into bonds, pushing up bond prices faster than ever before. Although these are extreme examples, bond prices typically move up or down during any market session because of imbalances of buy and sell orders.

Lower investor demand = lower prices and higher yields.
Higher investor demand = higher prices and lower yields.

Adjustable-Rate Bonds

When interest rates rise, the prices of bonds decline, and vice versa—*bond prices and yields move inversely to one another.*

However, when an issuer contracts to raise a bond's coupon rate when market rates rise or lower it when rates decline, the bond's price tends to remain more stable.

An *adjustable*, or *floating*, rate is usually pegged to some benchmark or index. For example, an issuer may contract to reset a bond's coupon rate each quarter to 1 percent over the 90-day Treasury bill rate.

Put Bonds

Some bonds contain a *put* provision whereby the issuer guarantees to redeem the bonds before maturity at a set price and date, at the option of the bondholder. A put provision provides a degree of protection that limits market risk.

How to Read Price Quotes

Bond prices, like stocks, are quoted in points and fractional points. The value of a point is $10 and the value of ⅛ point is $1.25. A price quote of 101⅜, for example, means the bond is priced at $1,013.75, a premium of $13.75 over its $1,000 face value. If the quote is 98⅝, the price is $986.25, a $13.75 discount from par.

1/8 =	$1.25	5/8 =	$6.25
1/4 =	2.50	3/4 =	7.50
3/8 =	3.75	7/8 =	8.75
1/2 =	5.00		

Bonds are also quoted in decimal points. If the quote is 103.85, move the decimal one digit to the right for a price of $1,038.50.

Treasury bonds are quoted in 32nds of a point. Each $\frac{1}{32}$, or *tick*, equals 31.25 cents. If the quote is 100 $\frac{5}{32}$, the price is $1,001.56 per $1,000 face value.

Basis points are used to express and compare bond yields. A basis point is $\frac{1}{100}$ of 1 percent. The difference between a yield of 8.76 percent and 8.83 percent is 7 basis points. Interest-rate fluctuations are expressed in basis points—"bond prices rose today, with the yield on the Treasury's *long* bond falling 7 basis points."

HOW TO BUY BONDS

Purchasing bonds is similar in some ways to purchasing a TV or refrigerator. Just as you would compare the features and price tags of different appliances, you ensure a satisfactory bond purchase by properly analyzing and comparing the features and prices of available bonds.

Brokers offer bonds that are listed on exchanges, inventoried at their firms, or available through other brokers and dealers. After determining your investment goals, a broker will probably make one or more specific recommendations.

Before You Buy

Bond rating guides published by S&P and Moody's are tremendously helpful in your analysis, comparison, and selection of bonds. Once you are satisfied that your broker understands your needs, ask for a copy of the page from one of these guides that describes the recommended bond.

Do not buy corporate bonds that are not listed in the S&P Bond Guide or Moody's Bond Record. A guide listing, of course, does not guarantee a safe investment, but without such assistance, you have no easy way to verify the information you are given.

If a bond is not listed in the guide or is not rated, it often signals a poor risk. Mr. Gleason's S&L bonds (in the example given earlier) were never listed in either bond guide. Had he followed this rule, he would be $300,000 richer today. Thousands of unfortunate investors in the well-reported American Continental Corp. debentures sold through Charles Keating's Lincoln S&L would not have lost their money had they also followed this rule.

Before purchasing any bond, ask the broker for the bond's issuer, credit rating, coupon rate, maturity date, price, call features, and yields. Then confirm the data in the guide.

Credit Rating. The most important step is to determine if the issuer can repay the bond. The best way to do this is to check the issuer's credit rating, which reflects the quality of its financial condition—the lower the rating, the higher the risk. The guides report the bond's previous rating and the date it was last changed.

Compare the company's total outstanding debt with its assets to determine how leveraged it is. Fiscally suspect companies with debt/equity ratios higher than 40 percent are generally assigned low credit ratings, requiring them to pay higher yields.

Price. If a broker quotes a price that differs much from the price quoted in the guide, ask for an explanation. Although a disparity might be the result of market fluctuations, the broker may be charging a high markup. Prices of exchange-listed bonds are quoted in newspapers and on computers, but prices of OTC-traded bonds may differ from broker to broker, and prices are rarely published.

Yields. Compare the yield to call, current yield, and yield to maturity of various bonds to select issues that meet your needs. If a bond's yield appears to be higher than that of all other bonds like it, you probably lack information. Sometimes a broker quotes the current yield when it is higher than its yield to maturity, the bond's total return.

Pricing aberrations that would result in higher than market yields seldom occur because fixed-income securities are market driven. If a broker recommends a bond yielding a significantly higher rate, it might be denominated in a foreign currency. If so, the bond is subject to currency risk and you have every right to be made aware of this fact. (See page 205 for an explanation of currency risk.)

Call Features. If a callable bond's coupon rate is higher than market interest rates, assume the bond will be called early. Although the rate may be attractive, you may prefer a bond that locks in a rate for a longer period.

When You Buy

When you buy a bond, there are four things to consider: transaction costs, trade confirmations, settlement, and accrued interest.

Transaction Costs. Bond commissions and markups may

differ substantially depending on factors such as credit rating, length of maturity, and number of bonds traded.

For exchange-listed bonds, brokers generally impose a set dollar commission charge per bond. Most bonds, however, are traded over-the-counter, bought and sold by brokers who resell them to the public for profit. A firm that assumes market risk by holding bonds in inventory is entitled to profit just like any other retail business, but some brokers charge higher markups than others.

Typical markups for high-grade bonds are 1 percent for bonds maturing in less than five years, 1 to 2 percent for intermediate-term (5 to 10 years), and 1.5 to 3 percent for long-term (10 years or longer). As with any product that is easier to sell, the greater the demand for an issue, the lower the markup. Treasury securities typically cost the least to trade, and high-yield (junk) bonds and long-term zero coupon bonds tend to cost the most. *It generally pays to shop around.*

Accrued Interest. Bondholders are, in effect, paid interest for each day they own a bond. When a bond is purchased, the brokerage firm calculates the interest that has accrued since the last payment was made. This *accrued* interest is then paid by the buyer to the seller to compensate the seller's ownership since receiving his last interest payment. The buyer is reimbursed the accrued interest that she has essentially *advanced* when she receives her first interest payment.

Settlement. The settlement date of a bond transaction is generally three business days after the day your order is executed, the *trade date*. This is referred to as *regular way* settlement. Some bonds, however, have a shorter settlement. For example, Treasury bills generally settle on the next day.

You must pay for purchases on or before the settlement date. When selling bonds, the assigned certificates must be deposited to the seller's account on or before the settlement date. If payment is not made, the brokerage firm must cancel ("bust") the trade. If a loss results, it is charged against the customer's account.

Trade Confirmation. After a trade is executed, the firm sends you a confirmation, or *confirm*, a document describing your transaction. For exchange-listed bonds, the confirm may show the commission, but for OTC-traded bonds, only the net price is displayed. Even if you do not receive the confirm, you must still pay on time.

After You Buy

It is important to periodically check the credit ratings of bonds you own because rating services downgrade bonds when they discover potential problems with their issuers. If the credit quality of your bond has slipped, consider selling rather than risk a further price decline, or worse, a default.

Managing Market Risk (aka Interest Rate Risk)

The most important consideration for investors purchasing investment-grade bonds is *market risk*. Properly addressing market risk requires an understanding of how the bond market operates and how to anticipate the course of interest rates.

What's good news for economic growth is generally bad news for the bond market. A brisk economy generally promotes inflation, which drives interest rates higher. But even the fear of inflation sometimes promotes a bearish scenario for bonds. Although inflation remained low in 1994, concerns that it would rise as the economy improved was the primary culprit for the worst bond market in decades. (Refer to page 221 to better understand what causes interest rates to fluctuate.)

If you determine that rates will be stable or decline, purchase long-term bonds to lock up higher rates. But if you believe rates will be rising, purchase only very short-term bonds, or create a bond ladder.

Bond Ladder. One way to manage market risk is to structure a *bond ladder*, that is, purchase bonds that mature sequentially rather than simultaneously. By purchasing bonds maturing in two years, four years, six years, and so on, you earn a "blended" yield that may be lower than purchasing all long-term bonds, but you reduce market risk. The ladder approach, which is particularly advisable when interest rates are low, is appropriate if you must have funds available for anticipated expenditures.

Bond Swaps. The strategic purchase or sale of bonds to meet defined goals is referred to as a *bond swap*. Bond swaps may be used to upgrade a portfolio for quality, to increase income, to generate tax loss, or to extend maturities to lock in rates for longer periods. For example, an investor may sell his bonds maturing in one year and invest the proceeds in issues with longer maturities and higher yields.

Ways to Invest. Wall Street offers three ways to participate in bonds:

- Select individual bonds and transact with a broker.
- Purchase shares in bond funds or unit investment trusts.
- Engage a manager/adviser to select the bonds and manage the portfolio on your behalf.

(Chapter 9 covers mutual funds, unit investment trusts, and managed accounts in detail.)

"When Milken trades junk bonds, he has inside information. Now it is quite illegal to trade stocks on inside information . . . but there is no such law regarding bonds (who, when the law was written, ever imagined that one day there would be so many bonds that behaved like stock?)"

Liar's Poker
Michael Lewis

HIGH-YIELD (JUNK) BONDS

A high-yield bond, or *junk* bond, is a bond with a credit rating of BB or lower. You might say that any bond that is not investment-grade (rated AAA through BBB) is considered high-yield.

Credit-rating services assign lower ratings to less credit-worthy issuers whose so-called junk bonds must pay higher returns to investors for assuming greater risk. Despite their attractive yields, investors have lost billions because of junk bond defaults.

Junk bonds have been around for decades. Initially, junk bond financing was typically the solution for less solvent companies unable to access the major money lenders. Beginning in the 1980s, the junk bond market virtually boomed because of their crucial role in financing numerous corporate takeovers and leveraged buyouts.

Corporate junk bonds began to receive notoriety as Wall Street bond trader Michael Milken promoted them to institutions such as insurance companies and S&Ls. Milken pitched the concept that junk bond portfolios outperform investment-grade portfolios because their higher yields more than compensate for losses resulting from defaults.

Investing in junk bonds is often compared with buying common stock because when these companies survive and thrive, their bonds rise in price often faster than their stock. Investors should analyze junk bonds as if they were equities in disguise, evaluating the same criteria.

Although historically junk bonds gave investors a rocky ride, overall they have performed very well in the last several years. The average annual default rate of corporate bonds during the 1970s was not a big concern. During the 1980s, however, the default rate picked up and finally peaked in 1990 and 1991 with rates approaching 10 percent! But in 1993, only 1.1 percent of all corporate bonds defaulted.

Today the $200 billion market is larger than ever and growing. In 1993, more than $58 billion in newly issued junk bonds were sold to investors, and analysts believe that the percentage of "junkier" junk has increased. With credit quality slipping and the prospect of rising default rates, investors should be even more vigilant regarding bonds they buy or hold.

High-yield mutual fund returns for 1993 averaged close to 19 percent, but in some other years the junk bond market was precipitously volatile with prices dropping 15 to 25 percent in days or weeks. That may appear daunting, but a corporation's bonds, even junk bonds, are always safer than its stocks. When a company is liquidated to pay its debts, bondholders, who are technically creditors, are always positioned ahead of stockholders to receive any available proceeds.

Prices of junk bonds generally fare better during strong economies when corporate defaults are less common. Conversely, during recessions, junk bonds tend to lose value as investors become more concerned about increased potential for default.

When interest rates are rising, junk bond prices are generally more stable than investment-grade bonds because of their higher yields. However, if mutual fund shareholders flood their high-yield mutual bond funds with redemption requests, forcing managers to sell all at once, the entire high-yield market could take a big hit.

Prior to 1993, brokers were not required to report prices of junk bonds as they were traded, so investors had no easy access to accurate market prices. Sharp price swings were common and brokers' quotes varied by as much as 5 percent, causing high spreads between bid and offer prices.

Despite the attractive yields of junk bonds, only investors who understand how to assess the risks should consider buying them. Sorting out better quality is not always easy. If higher yields attract you, consider one or more of the approximately 70 high-yield bond funds—diversification may be as important as expertise when you invest in junk bonds.

Summary

Besides offering liquidity and higher yields than money markets and CDs, bonds allow you to lock in your return for long periods. Before investing, learn to assess the major risks: *Will the borrower repay? Will the bond's market value erode?* If you need regular income, you will be well compensated for taking the time to learn how to purchase bonds safely.

CREDIT RATING CHART

AAA Highest quality. The issuer has exceptional ability to repay.
AA   High quality. The issuer has very strong ability to repay.
A   Good quality. The issuer has strong ability to repay.
BBB Satisfactory quality. The issuer has adequate ability to repay.
BB   Speculative. The issuer's ability to repay is questionable.
B   Highly speculative. The issuer's ability to repay is poor.
CCC Vulnerable to default.
CC   Minimally protected; default seems probable.
C   In default, or default is imminent.
D   In default, to be purchased for liquidation value only.
NR   A rating was not requested or furnished.

Investment Grade: AAA through BBB.

S&P	Moody's	Duff & Phelps	AM Best
AAA	Aaa	AAA	A + +
AA +	Aa1	AA +	A +
AA	Aa2	AA	A
AA −	Aa3	AA −	A −
A +	A1	A +	B + +
A	A2	A	B +
A −	A3	A −	B
BBB +	Baa1	BBB +	B −
BBB	Baa2	BBB	C + +
BBB −	Baa3	BBB −	C +
BB +	Ba1	BB +	C
BB	Ba2	BB	C −
BB −	Ba3	BB −	D
B +	B1	B +	E
B	B2	B	
B −	B3	B −	
CCC	Ca	CCC	
CC	C	CC	
C		C	
D		D	

*T*he investment game cannot be faulted for its lack of variety. Though the wide range of offerings may confuse you at first, it really provides an interesting assortment of merchandise. Like a big department store, there's something for every taste depending on your financial objectives. This chapter presents some of the more popular selections.

Chapter **6**

More Stocks and Bonds

"I don't know where speculation got a bad name since I know of no forward leap which was not fathered by speculation."

John Steinbeck

THE INITIAL PUBLIC OFFERING

An *initial public offering* is a company's first offering of common stock to investors. If the company itself receives proceeds from the sale of the shares, it is a *primary* offering. If the stock is previously owned, typically by company insiders, and the company itself receives no money directly, it is technically a *secondary* offering.

Owners of private companies who want to raise capital may engage an investment banking firm that specializes in corporate finance to take them public. The investment banker guides the company through a formal offering process that abides by extensive federal regulation. Generally, a group of underwriters assumes the risk of buying the new shares from the company at a discount, and then resells them to the public for profit. Occasionally, a firm represents a company as agent only, selling shares to investors on a "best-efforts" basis, in which it does its best to sell the shares at a reasonable price but assumes no risk if the shares don't sell.

During bull markets when the best prices can be obtained, there is an abundance of IPOs. In 1993, Wall Street raised a record $41.4 billion from investors to capitalize 707 private companies that went public.

To protect the investing public from irregularities, the SEC regulates the marketing of IPO shares. By law, all securities must be registered with the SEC as well as the states in which they are offered. Investors must be given prospectuses containing specific information about the companies' financial affairs. Brokers who solicit IPOs are restricted from making statements that conflict with the prospectus, which supposedly provides sufficient information for judging the worthiness of the shares.

Hot Issues

A new offering is referred to as "hot" when it is expected to be *oversubscribed* (demand surpasses supply). With healthy demand, the price of the new shares climbs quickly as they start trading in the *aftermarket* (the open or secondary market in which securities are traded among investors on an exchange or over-the-counter).

It is not that easy for retail brokers to get allotments of hot issues since the largest blocks are generally allocated to institutional investors. The few shares a broker receives are likely allocated to the broker's best customers. (Brokers are not allowed to give themselves or their relatives the opportunity to purchase new issues when there is a fairly strong demand for them.) If you are told you can get all the shares you want, the offering may be quite *cold*.

Risks

IPOs are definitely not for novice investors. It is not easy to profit in this arena, and many individual investors have sustained major losses. Because brokerage firms represent both corporate IPO clients as well as customers buying their shares, investors must consider the potential conflicts of interest.

Not long ago, after losing their money in an IPO, a group of investors brought a lawsuit against the brokerage firm that managed the offering. They alleged that certain negative information about the company had not been disclosed in the offering prospectus. They also charged that the company's subsequent financial reports were "overly optimistic."

The judge dismissed the case because the investors were not able to prove the firm had *intentionally* misled them. The court also concluded that the brokerage firm was not responsible for updating investors with information affecting the company after completion of the offering. "Buyer beware" is the lesson here.

Institutional investors typically receive the lion's share of the better offerings, leaving small investors with the more speculative deals. Institutions may also get better information about the deals offered. Quite often, institutions garner quick profits by "flipping" (selling almost immediately after purchase) their IPO shares, while small investors continue to hold as prices decline. Brokerage firms have installed special systems to penalize brokers when their customers sell their shares quickly, but institutions flip shares with relative impunity. The only profits derived in some IPOs were garnered by the institutions that sold within the first few hours of trading.

Though many fine companies go public each year, the overall track record of IPOs is dismal. A great number are badly managed, and it is often difficult to determine an IPO's prospects, even after carefully reading the prospectus. For every IPO that prospers, many more fail to realize investor expectations. Those that survive rarely generate a higher return than shares in long-established, well-capitalized companies, and only a small fraction become blue chips.

Before investing, first track several IPOs after they start trading in the aftermarket to see how they fare. Call several firms to request prospectuses of offerings on their "new issue calendars." If you are curious about an IPO, ask for and scrutinize the preliminary prospectus describing the offering (the final prospectus is printed after the shares start trading). Be sure to examine the sections that address conflicts of interest and risk. If you still want to participate, at least target the highest quality IPOs.

Note . . . The price of IPO shares includes the underwriting fees and broker commissions. Brokers are better compensated for purchases of IPOs than for shares already trading.

The fish sees the bait,
not the hook.

Chinese Proverb

PENNY STOCK

Traditionally, a *penny stock* was any stock priced under $1.00 per share, but today, all shares priced under $5.00 that are not listed on an exchange or NASDAQ are referred to as penny stock.

High-quality private companies that go public are brought to market for the first time by the larger, more prominent brokerage firms because they can be more selective. On the other end of the spectrum, some small brokerage firms specialize in underwriting low-priced stocks that typically do not have strong expectations for survival. In fact, many such stocks have been shares in companies with totally fictitious underpinnings.

The penny stock business is rife with stock-price manipulation, high-pressure sales people, and inflated brokerage commissions and markups. The spreads between buy and sell prices are generally very large, enhancing profits for market makers and severely limiting investor profits.

Brokers who specialize in penny stocks typically cold-call their prospects, sometimes operating out of "boiler room" offices. Fast-talking brokers are highly compensated for pushing penny stocks on gullible, unsuspecting investors who equate low prices with value. Unfortunately, the touted returns rarely materialize. The following case is typical.

In 1990, the National Association of Securities Dealers fined seven former employees of a small securities firm a total of $712,000 for their roles in a 1990 penny stock scheme. The NASD charged that the manager and brokers had created public demand for low-priced shares through price manipulation and high-pressure sales tactics, driving the stock's price from $1 to more than $5 within two months. Some of the brokers were fined and suspended from working for only a few days, but the firm's customers were left holding shares that eventually became worthless.

The SEC has launched a major offensive to shut down unethical penny stock operations that has already put many out of business. Brokers are now required to have customer approval in writing for purchases of non-NASDAQ, over-the-counter stocks priced under $5.00 a share. Brokers must also obtain personal information from investors about their current financial situation and investment experience. Before transacting, a broker must state in writing why the shares are a suitable investment for his client and have his client sign the statement.

Most firms now require brokers to obtain permission from their compliance departments prior to soliciting penny stocks, but abuses still occur. Be guarded when taking phone calls from brokers who tout investments, but be especially leery of those soliciting low-priced stocks.

*"Go to where the puck is going to be,
not to where it is."*

Wayne Gretsky

ELECTRIC UTILITIES

Electric utilities are public companies in the business of providing energy. Historically, utility stocks have paid dividends that average twice the yields of other public companies. As alternatives to bonds, they are generally bought by investors who seek regular income as well as some potential for growth.

The better performing utilities have delivered respectable total returns with low risk. Unfortunately, some utilities have experienced the adverse consequences of cost overruns in nuclear plant construction and a few sustained heavy losses from investing in unrelated businesses. When the utilities were forced to reduce or eliminate their dividends, the stock prices declined severely.

Utilities may no longer be the conservative, safe investments they were considered in the past. In 1993, Standard & Poor's stiffened its debt-ratings formula for the electric utility industry, declaring it a "sector in a long-term decline . . . facing slow growth in terms of demand, growing cost pressures, nuclear decommissioning cost pressures, and challenges in maintaining current earnings and operating levels."

Risks

The greatest risk to utility stocks is a significant increase in market interest rates, because investors sell their shares to purchase higher yielding bonds and CDs. High interest rates also reduce profit margins because utilities typically service substantial debt. Utilities are negatively affected by oil and gas price increases because they are heavy consumers.

The long-term Dow Jones Utility Index (page 113) illustrates how utility stock prices rose during periods of falling interest rates and oil prices, but they sustained a bear market when inflation and oil prices rose. The index peaked in September 1993 at 256.46, but corrected nearly 30 percent within the months that followed as interest rates began to rise.

Because electric utilities cannot readily raise their usage rates, the most favorable conditions for electric utilities are slow economic growth and low inflation. Fast growth could require new plant construction, which increases costs and regulatory problems.

Deregulation. The monopoly that utility companies have enjoyed as a result of government protection may be in jeopardy. Several state legislatures are taking steps to deregulate the generation and distribution of electrical power over the next several years that will allow customers to purchase power from lower bidders located hundreds of miles away. Open competition may lower prices across the board, jeopardizing utility companies' earnings and dividend payouts. Analysts are speculating on an industry shakeout with potential price wars and mergers that could shrink the nation's 170 utility companies to less than half their number in the next decade.

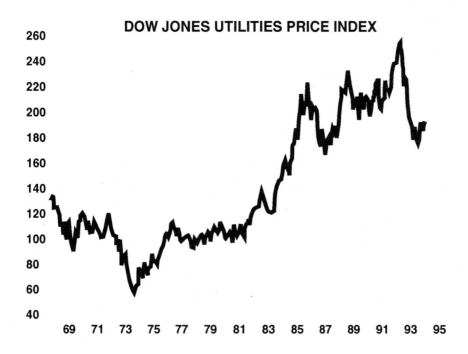

DOW JONES UTILITIES PRICE INDEX

How to Select Utilities

The challenge is to identify utility companies that will have continued earnings and dividend growth. Analysts rank public utilities according to projected performance. Dividends considered "safe" (not likely to be reduced) are generally not as high as those considered less secure. Be suspicious of utilities that pay significantly higher dividend rates because it might be an indication of major problems. Yields could be higher just because share prices have dropped. Better-performing utilities with secure dividends rarely generate the highest yields.

The following is a checklist to help you determine which utilities, if any, might be the right choice for you.

- ☐ Look for utilities with low customer usage rates and excess power.
- ☐ Because rate hikes promote higher dividends, consider utilities in states where public utility commissions are more liberal in granting rate increases.
- ☐ Purchase companies whose *only* business is running utilities.
- ☐ Select utilities with more of a residential than commercial customer base, because a weak economy has less negative impact.
- ☐ Avoid utilities planning to construct nuclear facilities. If they already operate nuclear facilities, they may be attractive because of their reduced vulnerability to oil and gas price increases.
- ☐ Avoid utilities with highly leveraged balance sheets because excess debt interferes with profitability.
- ☐ Avoid utilities with payout ratios (percentage of earnings) higher than 85 percent.

If higher inflation or interest rates appear likely in the near term, hold off buying utility stocks.

PREFERRED STOCK

A *preferred stock* is a form of equity ownership with characteristics of both common stocks and bonds that pays dividends to shareholders. "Preferred" indicates that shareholders have priority over common shareholders should the company have difficulty paying its dividends. They do not, however, have preference over bondholders because they are not technically creditors of the company.

When a company is liquidated, bondholders are paid back first along with all other creditors. Second in line are the preferred shareholders. (Only after preferred shareholders are paid do common shareholders share in the proceeds.) Preferred stocks pay higher yields than bonds to compensate for their junior position in their claim to distributed company assets in the event of bankruptcy.

Because preferred stocks do not participate in a company's growth, investors purchase them solely for their current income. Most preferreds are initially priced at $25 per share and pay a fixed-dollar or adjustable-rate dividend on the same quarterly schedule as that for dividends on common shares.

Preferred stocks are issued mostly by very large, well-capitalized corporations such as banks, utilities, and insurance companies. With nearly $75 billion in new shares issued in the last decade, chances are good that a broker will offer you one of the many preferreds on the market if you are investing for income.

A *cumulative* preferred stock is considered safer than a noncumulative issue because if the company ever fails to pay a dividend, it cannot pay dividends on its common shares until all cumulative preferred dividends in arrears have been paid.

Preferred stocks are traded on stock exchanges and over-the-counter; commissions are the same as those for common stock.

Risks

Like all debt securities, preferred stocks are subject to credit risk, market risk, and call risk.

Credit Risk. If a company defaults on paying bond interest, it may be forced into bankruptcy. If a company stops paying dividends on its common or preferred stock, however, no default is triggered because shareholders are not creditors. A company's financial strength is therefore a more critical factor when purchasing preferred stock than it is for bonds. Like corporate bonds, preferreds are rated for credit quality by S&P and Moody's.

Market Risk. Except for those with *sinking funds* (money set aside to retire the issue), preferreds are *perpetual*—they never mature. The lack of a set maturity renders preferreds more vulnerable than bonds to market risk. When interest rates rise, the prices of preferred securities may decline more than bond prices (unless their rate is adjustable).

Call Risk. Like bonds, preferreds are usually issued with call provisions allowing issuers to redeem them after a specified period of time. In the first analysis, a preferred's yield may appear very attractive, but a potential call might preclude a competitive yield. To determine the actual total return, you must amortize any price premium (the portion of purchase price higher than the call price) and deduct it from the cash-flow yield.

Corporate Tax Advantages

One of the most appealing aspects of preferreds for corporate shareholders is the *dividends received deduction*, which enables corporations to avoid double taxation of corporate dividends. (This benefit is not available to individual investors.) Current tax law exempts qualified corporations from paying taxes on as much as 70 percent of dividend income received from common and preferred shares in other corporations. A qualifying corporation in the 35 percent bracket has an effective tax rate of only 10.5 percent (.30 × 35%) on stock dividends. For example, a preferred's 8 percent yield is equivalent to a taxable yield of 11.01 percent.

ZERO COUPON BONDS

A zero coupon bond is a debt instrument that pays no interest until it matures, at which time the issuer pays the bondholder the face value (generally $1,000).

A zero coupon bond is bought at a discount from its face value, and the interest earned is the difference between the bond's price and its face value. Maturities may be as short as a few weeks or longer than 30 years. Like other bonds, zeros may be sold before they mature. Because zeros do not pay periodic interest payments, they are not appropriate for investors who need regular income.

Zero coupon bonds, created by brokerage firms in 1982, are issued by the U.S. Treasury, government agencies, municipalities, and corporations. Treasury *STRIPS* are the most liquid, but they generally yield less. *TINTS, CUBES, CUBS, TIGRS,* and *CATS* are receipts for Treasury securities that have been "stripped" of their coupons and re-packaged in the zero coupon format. The securities backing these zeros are held in trust at custodian banks. Most zeros are not issued in certificate form, but rather reported as "book entry" on brokerage firm statements.

Step-Up Bonds

Some hybrid bonds function like zero coupon bonds, but start making interest payments at a predetermined date prior to the maturity. Step-ups are issued by corporations and government agencies as a means of raising capital without the obligation to pay interest for many years. Step-up bonds may be appropriate for investors who do not need immediate income but anticipate a need at some future date.

Risks

The major risks of zero coupon bonds are the same as those for all other fixed-income investments, credit risk and market risk. Theoretically, a zero's market value increases incrementally until it matures, but its price is still subject to market risk. The lack of interest payments renders long-term zeros especially attractive when interest rates are high, but they should be avoided when rates are low.

Tax Implications

Unless a zero coupon bond is held in a tax-exempt account, the IRS requires bondholders to pay income tax each year on the *accreted* (assumed) income even though no interest was actually received. Issuers determine the amount of taxable interest that must be reported to the IRS and furnish bondholders with this information annually on the 1099-OID (original issue discount) form.

Trading and Commissions

A few zero coupon bonds are listed on exchanges, but most trade over-the-counter. Markups are included in the price.

The following is an example of a zero coupon bond maturing in 10 years offered by a brokerage firm:

Issuer	Price	Maturity	Yield to Maturity	Markup
TINT	$500.50	5/15/04	7.568%	$13/bond

This zero coupon bond's price is $500.50. The issuer guarantees payment of $1,000 to bondholders on May 15, 2004. The interest to be earned is $499.50, the difference between the bond's price and its face value, representing an annual yield of 7.568 percent. A markup of $13 is included in the bond's price.

Before purchasing, ask the broker for the price, rating, yield to maturity, and maturity date so that you can compare prices and yields.

CONVERTIBLE SECURITIES

A convertible security is a corporate bond or preferred stock that may be exchanged for a predetermined number of common shares.

Convertible securities are legitimate instruments of mainstream financing for corporate America, typically issued by smaller growth companies to save interest expense. A convertible security offers both equity and income. A company's convertible security yield is lower than its bond interest, but typically higher than its common stock dividend. When you purchase a convertible, you forfeit some interest to gain the opportunity to participate in the company's growth.

The price fluctuation of a company's common stock may affect the price of its convertible securities, causing them to be more volatile than other fixed-income issues. The convertible's higher yield, however, may provide price stability during poorly performing stock markets.

Call Features

Nearly all convertible securities are issued with call provisions that allow issuers to redeem them prior to maturity. Sometimes a company may call its convertible issue once its common shares reach a predetermined market price. Most convertible issuers expect that holders will eventually become equity owners. Many issuers call their convertible securities when they have the opportunity to convert their higher paying convertible to a lower paying common stock. In the event of a call, the holder either accepts the predetermined cash price or converts to the common shares. Assume that a company will exercise its call option when it is in its interest to do so.

Risks

The principal risks associated with convertible securities are credit risk, market risk, and call risk.

Credit Risk. Like all debt securities, convertibles are subject to downgrading in the issuer's credit rating, but they carry less credit risk than common stock because of their prior claim to company assets in the event of liquidation. Holders of convertible *bonds* have claim to corporate assets along with all other creditors, but convertible *preferred* shareholder claims are subordinate to all other debt issues of a company. Many convertible securities are rated for credit quality by S&P and Moody's.

Market Risk. Convertible security prices are exposed to fluctuating market interest rates as well as price fluctuations of the underlying common shares.

Call Risk. In the event of a call, the cash proceeds or market value of the shares exchanged may be less than the price paid for the security, resulting in a loss.

Evaluating Convertible Securities

To properly evaluate a convertible security, analyze the issuing company as if you were purchasing its common shares. After reviewing the company's credit rating and fundamentals, examine the length of time before the convertible matures or may be called. The longer this period, the greater the potential for the common stock's price to reach a level that allows for a profitable conversion. The shorter its life, the less likely it will offer any profits other than interest or dividends. A convertible security's market value is influenced by both its *investment value* and its *conversion value*.

Investment Value. A convertible's investment value is a function of its credit quality and its yield.

Conversion Value. The convertible's conversion value is determined by multiplying the number of common shares the holder is entitled to receive upon conversion or exchange by the common's market price.

Calculate the *conversion premium*, the part of a convertible's price that is higher than its conversion valuation. This tells you how much higher the common stock's price must rise before a conversion can be profitable.

Growth versus Income. Convertible securities with high conversion premiums are less sensitive to price movements of the common shares and may be more appropriate for yield-oriented investors. Conversely, issues with small premiums are typically more equity sensitive and therefore more suitable for equity-oriented investors.

Check the spread between the convertible and common yields. The greater the yield advantage of the convertible over the common's dividend yield, the more investors will value it. At some point, a convertible's greater yield over the common's compensates for the conversion premium paid. The length of time needed to hold the convertible before its yield advantage offsets the conversion premium is known as the *break-even*.

If you are more interested in income than growth, select issues with longer break-even periods, higher yields, and better credit quality. If you are more interested in growth, select issues with shorter break-even periods and lower conversion premiums, and give less weight to credit quality or yield.

Trading and Commissions. Trading costs for convertible bonds, which are listed on exchanges or traded over-the-counter, are the same as those for most other bonds. Commissions for convertible preferred stocks are the same as those for common stocks.

Convertible securities may be purchased in the mutual fund format.

PERCS

PERCS, Preferred Equity Redemption Cumulative Stocks, are higher yielding equity securities that offer the opportunity to participate in the gains of a company's common shares up to a predetermined *cap level*. PERCS prices may be less volatile than common shares because they pay larger and more secure quarterly dividends.

Unlike other convertible securities, PERCS have a *mandatory* redemption that requires the company to exchange them for its common shares. As conversion approaches (typically three years following the date of issuance), the price of the

PERCS tends to trade close to the price of the common shares or at the cap level, whichever is less.

PERCS are exposed to the same risks as the common shares with no call protection—companies may call them whenever it is in their interest to do so. Your risk is that the common stock will trade lower than the price paid for the PERCS.

Consider the PERCS' total return potential and not just its higher dividend. Because your return depends on the trading level of the underlying common shares, examine company fundamentals. Although PERCS may be sold before the mandatory redemption, buy PERCS only if you are prepared to own the common shares.

LYONs

A variation on zero coupon bonds called Liquid Yield Option Notes is one of Wall Street's latest innovations. LYONs, issued only by corporations, meld a zero coupon bond with a convertible feature that allows holders to convert their notes into a predetermined number of the company's common shares.

All LYONs have a *put* feature which requires the issuer, at the option of the holder, to purchase them from the holder on certain dates at predetermined prices. The risks of LYONs are low compared with other types of equity securities, because the put offers downside protection. In some markets, LYONs have the best combination of modest conversion premiums and price protection.

After reviewing the company's S&P and Moody's credit rating and the call provisions, determine how many shares may be exchanged for the notes and at what price the shares achieve parity (equal the cash investment). Determine if the capital gains potential compensates for market risk or the forfeiture of interest payments.

Assume the issuer will call the notes if it is in its interest to do so. By 1993, the market for LYONs declined as issuers called them rather aggressively.

Summary

While the healthy diversity of securities offered tends to confuse us, all securities are fundamentally either *equity* or *debt* or a combination of both. If you find a security so complex that you cannot understand it, don't buy it.

*B*ecause of its status as the most creditworthy borrower of money in the world today, securities issued by the U.S. government are considered to be just about the safest of all. If your personal investment motto is "safety first" when loaning your money, the U.S. government's guarantee may provide the security you seek.

Chapter 7

U.S. Government Securities

"States, like individuals, who observe their engagements are respected and trusted."

Report on Public Credit, January 1790
Alexander Hamilton

The two major categories of government securities are *Treasury* and *agency*.

TREASURY SECURITIES

Treasury securities, or *Treasuries*, are debt obligations of the U.S. government, issued and guaranteed by the U.S. Department of the Treasury to finance government expenditures and its budget deficits.

Because our government has never defaulted on any of its debts and presumably never will, the investment community considers Treasury securities to be of the very highest credit quality. Although they are not officially rated by the credit-rating agencies, government securities are assumed to be rated AAA. As a result, the government pays less to borrow your money than do the most creditworthy corporations. It is estimated that more than $3 trillion in Treasury issues are currently owned by the investing public.

Treasury securities offer investors

• **Maximum Safety**. Principal and interest are backed by the full faith and credit of the U.S. government.

• **Maximum Liquidity**. There should always be a ready market for sellers. Average trading volume of the very liquid Treasury market, the most active in the world, exceeds $100 billion a day!

Note . . . Yields of Treasury securities are not determined by the government but by the marketplace. The greater the investor demand for its bonds, the less interest the government pays to borrow.

• **Tax Exemption**. Treasury interest is exempt from state and local taxation (though subject to federal income taxes). Consequently, Treasuries may offer higher after-tax yields than high-grade corporate bonds or CDs if your state income taxes are high. To determine if your after-tax income could be higher with Treasuries, calculate the *taxable equivalent yield* you would need to earn from a taxable investment to equal a Treasury's tax-exempt yield. Ask your tax adviser for your combined state and local tax rate and compute as follows:

$$\frac{\text{Treasury Yield}}{1 - \text{state and local tax rate}} = \text{Taxable Equivalent Yield}$$

For example, if the Treasury bond yield is 6 percent and your state tax rate is 5 percent, an alternative investment must yield at least 6.3 percent to equal a 6 percent Treasury security yield.

$$\frac{.06}{(1.00 - .05) = .95} = .063, \text{ or } 6.3\%$$

Classes of Treasury Securities

The U.S. Department of the Treasury issues three types of marketable securities with varying maturities—*bills*, *notes*, and *bonds*.

Treasury Bills, the shortest maturities, are issued for three months, six months, and one year. They are available in multiples of $1,000, but the minimum investment is ten bills ($10,000 face value). T-bills resemble zero coupon bonds because they are bought at a discount from their face value, and no regular interest payments are made to holders. The interest you earn is the difference between the purchase price and the $1,000 paid out at maturity.

Treasury Notes are issued in increments of $1,000 for terms longer than one year but fewer than 10 years. Unlike T-bills, T-notes contain coupons and pay interest semiannually. The minimum purchase is $5,000 (face value) on maturities of fewer than five years, and $1,000 on maturities of five years or more.

Treasury Bonds are issued in increments of $1,000 for terms longer than 10 years, and pay interest semiannually. The minimum purchase through a brokerage firm is $1,000 (face value). The 30-year *long* bond is a widely quoted yield benchmark for long-term interest rates in the United States.

Note . . . The Treasury also issues zero coupon bonds called *STRIPS*, with maturities as long as 30 years. (See page 118.)

Risks

The U.S. government's credit is stronger than that of any other borrower, so credit risk is not a consideration. However, you do need to address *market risk*. Unlike bank CDs, Treasury securities incur no arbitrary penalty for liquidation before maturity, but sale prices depend on the supply/demand vagaries of the bond market. (See Market Risk, page 88.)

Trading

Treasury securities are initially offered through the Federal Reserve system in about 100 auctions held each year. This rather unsophisticated process involves no more than 39 authorized primary dealers, mostly large brokerage firms and commercial banks, who bid for blocks of securities to resell to their customers for profit. No single dealer is allowed to purchase more than 35 percent of any one issue.

Treasury securities may be purchased from banks and brokerage firms, or direct from the Federal Reserve Bank "at auction."

Direct Purchase. You can purchase Treasury securities direct from the Federal Reserve Bank, (800) 227-4133, commission free, but you will not know the exact yield of the securities when ordering. The Federal Reserve is not involved with resales—if you want to sell your Treasury securities, you need to engage a licensed broker.

Secondary Market. Most investors buy Treasury securities from brokers so that they can know the yield prior to purchase and can sell them at any time. Firms charge only a nominal handling fee for T-bill purchases, but T-notes and T-bonds are priced and traded like high-grade corporate bonds, with higher markups for longer maturities. (See Chapter 5, "How Bonds are Traded," page 90.)

The Real Rate of Return for U.S. Treasury Bills

Year	T-Bill Rate	Maximum Tax Rate	Inflation Rate (CPI)	Real Rate of Return
1970	6.52	50	5.6	−2.34
1971	4.39	50	3.3	−1.11
1972	3.84	50	3.4	−1.48
1973	6.93	50	8.7	−5.24
1974	8.00	62	12.3	−9.26
1975	5.80	62	6.9	−4.70
1976	5.08	62	4.9	−2.97
1977	5.12	60	6.7	−4.65
1978	7.18	60	9.0	−6.13
1979	10.38	59	13.3	−9.04
1980	11.24	59	12.5	−7.89
1981	14.71	59	8.9	−2.87
1982	10.54	50	3.8	+1.47
1983	8.80	48	3.8	+0.78
1984	9.85	45	3.9	+1.52
1985	7.72	45	3.8	+0.45
1986	6.16	45	1.1	+2.29
1987	5.47	38	4.4	−1.01
1988	6.35	33	4.4	−0.15
1989	8.37	33	4.6	+1.01
1990	7.81	31	6.1	−0.71
1991	5.60	31	3.1	+0.76
1992	3.50	31	2.9	−0.49
1993	2.90	40	2.7	−0.95
1994	3.90	40	2.7	−0.34

Courtesy Keyport Life Insurance Company

AGENCY SECURITIES

Agency securities are debt obligations of certain federally owned or sponsored government agencies. Most are repackaged mortgages on homes owned by U.S. citizens. All agency securities are assumed to be rated AAA.

Major Agency Issues

Ginnie Maes are mortgage bonds issued by the Government National Mortgage Association (GNMA), an organization that buys FHA and VA home mortgages from banks and auctions them to financial institutions. The institutions package the mortgages into "pools" to create securities to market to investors. Both principal and interest are guaranteed by the government whether or not homeowners meet their mortgage obligations. Ginnie Mae interest is paid monthly and is subject to federal, state, and local taxation.

Ginnie Maes are the most popular agency securities because they are very liquid, formally backed by the full faith and credit of the U.S. government, and pay higher yields than Treasury securities.

Fannie Maes are mortgage bonds issued by the Federal National Mortgage Association (FNMA), a federally sponsored, quasi-private corporation that provides funds to the mortgage market by purchasing conventional mortgage loans from banks and other lenders. Like Ginnie Maes, these loans are packaged into pools by financial institutions and sold to investors. They lack official government backing, but they are considered a moral obligation of the U.S. government. Interest is paid monthly, and it is subject to federal, state, and local taxation.

Freddie Macs are securities issued by the Federal Home Loan Mortgage Corporation (FHLMC), a federally sponsored corporation that loans money to member institutions so they may supply conventional mortgage loans at competitive rates. FHLMC issues both coupon bonds and mortgage securities. Interest is paid semiannually on the bonds and monthly on the mortgage securities, and it is subject to federal, state, and local taxation.

Sallie Maes are packaged student loans purchased from financial institutions. Semiannual interest is subject to federal taxation only.

Tennessee Valley Authority is a federally owned corporate agency that was established to develop the resources of the Tennessee Valley region into one of the largest electric utility systems in the country. Semiannual TVA bond interest is subject to federal taxation only.

Note . . . Ginnie Maes are the only agency issues directly backed by the U.S. government. All others are "moral" or indirect obligations of the government, so named because the government has never defaulted and is not likely to do so. The credit quality of agency securities is second only to that of Treasury securities.

Evaluating Mortgage Securities

The enormous mortgage-backed securities market is even greater in size than the corporate bond market. Ginnie Maes, Fannie Maes, and Freddie Macs refund millions of mortgages on properties located in all 50 states. (Your own home mortgage may be part of such a security.) This, in turn, encourages lower mortgage rates by providing great liquidity to the mortgage markets.

Agency mortgage securities are high quality and liquid, but they are complex fixed-income investments with a special terminology all their own.

Corporate Equivalent Yield. As *pass-through* securities, the mortgages' interest and return of principal are passed through to investors on a monthly basis, proportionate to their share of the pool. Although all individual mortgages within a pool mature on or before the stated maturity, *principal repayment may occur at any time.*

With no *fixed* maturity, mortgage bond yields cannot be calculated like conventional bonds—only projected. Out of necessity, dealers created the concept of *corporate equivalent yield* as a way to compare mortgage yields with those of other fixed-income investments. The CEY is based on a mortgage bond's *average life*, an estimated number of years before half its principal is repaid.

PSA. Over the years, the *PSA* model (developed by the Public Securities Association) evolved to help dealers estimate the timeframe of mortgage prepayment on the basis of historical prepayment, default experience, mortgage age, coupon, and geographical data. *100 PSA* denotes a normal payback; *200 PSA* indicates twice normal prepayment speed. Although it is far from perfect, the model offers investors a consistent benchmark for comparing mortgage issues.

Factor. When you purchase a mortgage security in the secondary market, the chances are that some of its principal has already been repaid. The *factor* indicates the amount of the original principal left in a mortgage investment. A new pool starts with a factor of 1.0, which declines as the principal is partially repaid. A pool with 60 percent of the principal repaid has a factor of .40, which means that 40 percent of the original principal remains.

Example of a Ginnie Mae

Security Pool	Coupon	Price	CEY	PSA	Factor
GNMA 0000520M	6.5%	92.5	7.74%	82	.890399

Average Life: 11 years   Stated Maturity: 11-20-22
Broker Markup: $25/bond

This Ginnie Mae, identified by the security number 0000520M, pays 6.5 percent annually. Because interest rates have increased since it was first issued, the price had to be discounted to $925. The dealer estimates that half the underlying mortgages in this pool will be repaid within 11 years, but all must be repaid by 2022, reflecting a corporate equivalent yield of 7.74 percent. The factor indicates that about 11 percent of the pool has already been repaid. A PSA of 82 suggests that the anticipated rate of principal prepayment will be slower than normal.

ARMs. Some mortgage securities are *adjustable-rate* rather than *fixed-rate* mortgages. Thanks to their floating rates, ARM market values are more stable as interest rates fluctuate. If you want to reduce market risk, consider agency ARMs because they may offer consistently higher returns than short-term, fixed-rate investments.

Risks of Mortgage Securities

Although credit risk is not a consideration, most mortgage securities are subject to considerable market risk because of their long maturities (20 to 30 years).

In addition to market risk, mortgage securities are subject to *prepayment risk* because there is no way to know exactly when repayment of principal will occur. This causes unique problems.

If interest rates rise, not only are mortgage bond prices sure to drop, but the prepayment of principal slows because homeowners are less likely to refinance. If interest rates decline, homeowners are more likely to pay off mortgages early, presenting return of principal to bondholders at times when it can be reinvested only at lower rates. Whether interest rates rise or decline, mortgage bonds may be adversely affected.

Note . . . It is important for investors to keep track of all principal payments and reinvest them, or risk depleting principal.

All mortgage securities are continuously subject to principal payback at face value, which is lower than the purchase price when a premium has been paid. In the last few years, prices of mortgage securities have increased as demand surpassed supply. When a flurry of refinancings to lock in lower mortgage rates occurred, many investors who had bought mortgage securities at premium prices lost money because the premiums were not recouped when the bonds were called earlier than expected. *Be careful when paying a premium for any mortgage security, as most can be repaid at any time.*

Trading

Agency securities are traded over-the-counter by brokerage firms. (See Chapter 5, "How Bonds are Traded," page 90.)

Minimum Investment. Agency security minimums are typically $10,000. Mortgage securities are available in increments of $25,000 when initially offered, but partially paid-down issues trade for less in the secondary market.

Commissions and Markups. Markups for agency securities are similar to those for other bonds traded OTC—the longer the maturity, the higher the markup.

COLLATERALIZED MORTGAGE OBLIGATIONS

In 1983, an innovative security was introduced to the credit markets, the *Collateralized Mortgage Obligation*. CMOs were developed to give institutional investors a wider range of investment timeframes and greater cash flow certainty than had been available with traditional mortgage-backed securities.

CMOs are "packaged" derivative securities that are composed of government-backed mortgages such as Ginnie Maes, Fannie Maes, and Freddie Macs. Like the underlying securities, most CMOs are assumed to be AAA-rated (although some issues are not rated AAA because they include mortgages that do not carry government backing). With more than $800 billion issued, CMOs are one of the fastest growing investments, and one of the most complicated.

Structure

Packagers of CMOs restructure the underlying securities to provide a clearer projection of prepayment timing. Each CMO is separated into *tranches* (French for "slices") or classes with different maturities and interest rates. In a "plain vanilla" CMO, all principal prepayment goes to holders of the earliest tranche until it is completely paid down; then members of the next tranche in line are paid.

The characteristics of each CMO tranche affect the functioning of other tranches in the pool. Some are as simple and safe as Ginnie Maes while others are risky and volatile because they act like shock absorbers, assuming greater market risk so that other tranches may carry less risk. Riskier CMOs generally offer higher yields initially to attract buyers.

Planned Amortization Class CMOs are designed to provide greater protection against prepayment risk, market risk, and the consequent price volatility. PAC bonds are targeted for earlier payback when interest rates rise, and later payback when rates decline. PAC bonds offer lower yields than other tranche classes because they offer greater safety.

Support Class CMOs absorb the prepayment risk transferred from PAC tranches, which renders them more vulnerable to cash flow and price volatility. SUP bonds generally offer higher yields to compensate for greater market risk.

Targeted Amortization Class CMOs are designed to provide protection from prepayment risk, but TAC bonds are not protected from interest-rate risk.

Z-Bonds are CMOs structured as zero coupon bonds that pay no current interest during the accrual phase, but they receive credit for interest that accrues to their face value. Z-bonds eventually enter the payment phase and begin to function like other mortgage-backed securities, as they pay out principal and interest on a monthly basis.

Note . . . CMO interest is fully taxable on the federal, state, and local levels, regardless of the type of mortgage securities in the portfolio.

Risks

The credit risk of CMOs composed of government agency mortgages is not a consideration, but market risk and prepayment risk may be significant. Even a relatively small rise in market interest rates can cause the average life of a CMO to stretch out dramatically, with a consequent decline in market value. A broker may advise you that the average life of a SUP tranche is five years, but if interest rates rise, the maturity extends, perhaps even doubles. Although a rise in interest rates hurts all bond prices, some CMOs are more vulnerable than others.

A recent offering of CMOs illustrates their risk. The prospectus reported that the 7.75 percent CMOs have an average life of 11.5 years under the assumed rate of prepayment on the underlying mortgages. However, the prospectus went on to say that if rates drop significantly, prepayment could occur in only 1.7 years. If rates rise, maturities could extend to 29 years! Either scenario would cause a severe drop in the CMO's market value.

Dealer inventories may have been cherry-picked by sophisticated institutional investors for the safer issues, but even these professionals have lost money in CMOs. Recognizing that problems arise when brokers and customers lack an understanding of CMOs, the National Association of Securities Dealers has released guidelines for marketing them to individual investors. Brokers may no longer imply that CMO yields or values are "government guaranteed." *Unless you understand CMOs thoroughly, it is best to avoid them.*

Trading

CMOs are traded over-the-counter by brokerage firms. (See Chapter 5, page 90.)

Minimum Investment. CMOs are available in increments of $1,000.

Commissions and Markups. Markups for CMOs are similar to those of other bonds—the lower the quality and the longer the maturities, the higher the markups charged.

Summary

Credit risk is not an issue when purchasing U.S. Treasury and agency securities, but you must consider market risk and prepayment risk. Mortgage bonds, such as Ginnie Maes and CMOs, present complications because principal may be returned prematurely to the disadvantage of bondholders. Be certain you understand these sophisticated securities before you invest.

For decades, the investment of choice for most wealthy, so-phisticated investors who want tax-free income with low risk has been municipal bonds. You don't have to be wealthy to benefit from municipal bond investment—you just have to pay taxes.

Chapter **8**

Municipal Bonds

"Anyone may so arrange his affairs so that his taxes shall be as low as possible; he is not bound to choose that pattern which will best pay the Treasury; there is not even a patriotic duty to increase one's taxes."

Judge Learned Hand, 1934
U.S. Circuit Court
Helvering v. *Gregory*

Municipal bonds, or *munis*, are debt obligations of state, county, and local governments that raise money to finance their operations, to provide many public services, and to build and maintain facilities such as schools, sewer systems, hospitals, and prisons.

Municipal bonds, a market that has grown to more than $1.2 trillion, are the major source of financing for state and local governments. They are the one investment left that continues to offer investors tax-free income.

Munis have two major advantages over most other bonds. First, the interest payments of most munis are exempt from federal taxation. Moreover, if you hold bonds from the same state with which you file a tax return, muni interest is generally *triple-tax exempt*—exempt from federal, state, and local taxation. Interest from bonds issued by the U.S. territories of Puerto Rico, Guam, and the Virgin Islands are also triple-tax exempt. This tax exemption attracts investors because munis offer higher after-tax yields than many other conservative investments.

The second advantage of munis is their solid record as very safe investments, second only to Treasury securities. Nearly all municipal bond defaults have been limited to low-rated and non-rated bonds, and only one major default has occurred in the last 50 years. In 1983, the Washington Power Supply System defaulted on $2.3 billion of revenue bonds that funded the construction of two nuclear power plants. In 1992, only $2 billion of the entire $1.2 trillion municipal bond market was in default, or .167 percent, a very small fraction indeed—and way under the corporate bond default rate.

Evaluating Municipal Bonds

The higher your income taxes, the more municipal bond investment may benefit you. When the 1993 Budget Reconciliation Act raised the top federal income tax rate, it increased the yield advantage of municipal bonds over government and corporate bonds, which are not federally tax-exempt.

To determine if your after-tax income could be higher with

municipal bonds, calculate the *taxable equivalent yield* you would need to earn from a taxable investment to equal a muni's tax-exempt yield. Ask your tax adviser for your combined state and federal tax rate and compute as follows:

$$\frac{\text{Tax-Free Yield}}{1.00 - \text{ state and federal tax rates}} = \text{Taxable Equivalent Yield}$$

For example, if a California resident's income is taxed at 34.5 percent (combined federal and state tax rate) and he purchases a municipal bond yielding 5.5 percent, the TEY is 8.4 percent:

$$\frac{.055}{(1.00 - .345) = .655} = .084, \text{ or } 8.4\%$$

If all other conservative taxable bonds and CDs are yielding less than 8.4 percent, this investor may benefit from a municipal bond investment.

Both borrower and lender benefit from tax-free municipal bonds. The federal government allows tax exemption for municipal bond interest so that state and local governments can borrow at lower interest rates. The states reciprocate by exempting Treasury bond interest. Interestingly, neither exemption is protected by the U.S. Constitution, but there is little chance of a policy change.

Tax Considerations. Although interest is tax-exempt, taxable events may occur when bonds are redeemed or sold. When sale proceeds are less than the purchase price, you may not always deduct a loss; if proceeds are more than the purchase price, the gain may be taxed as capital gain, ordinary income, or a combination of the two. For bonds originally issued at a price below par (*original issue discount*), you pay no capital gains tax on the accretion or on the proceeds paid at maturity; however, additional taxes may apply if bonds

Taxable Equivalent Yield of a 5.5% Coupon Municipal Bond

STATE	Federal Income Tax Bracket 36%	39.6%	STATE	Federal Income Tax Bracket 36%	39.6%	STATE	Federal Income Tax Bracket 36%	39.6%
Alabama	8.88	9.40	Kentucky	9.14	9.69	North Dakota	9.77	10.35
Alaska	8.59	9.11	Louisiana	8.94	9.45	Ohio	9.29	9.84
Arizona	9.24	9.79	Maine	9.40	9.96	Oklahoma	9.24	9.79
California	9.66	10.23	Maryland	9.14	9.69	Oregon	9.44	10.01
Colorado	9.05	9.59	Massachusetts	9.77	10.35	Pennsylvania	8.84	9.37
Connecticut	9.00	9.54	Michigan	9.35	9.91	Puerto Rico	8.59	9.11
Delaware	9.31	9.87	Minnesota	9.39	9.95	Rhode Island	9.58	10.24
Washington DC	9.50	10.06	Mississippi	9.05	9.59	South Carolina	9.24	9.79
Florida	8.59	9.11	Missouri	8.94	9.45	South Dakota	8.59	9.11
Georgia	9.11	9.65	Montana	9.31	9.82	Tennessee	9.14	9.69
Guam	8.59	9.11	Nebraska	9.23	9.78	Texas	8.59	9.11
Hawaii	9.45	10.02	New Hampshire	9.05	9.59	Utah	9.13	9.66
Idaho	9.36	9.92	New Jersey	9.24	9.79	Vermont	9.37	10.01
Illinois	8.86	9.39	New Mexico	9.32	9.88	Virginia	9.12	9.66
Indiana	8.90	9.39	New York	9.33	9.88	Washington	8.59	9.11
Iowa	9.20	9.72	New York City	9.80	10.39	West Virginia	9.19	9.74
Kansas	9.19	9.73	North Carolina	9.32	9.87	Wyoming	8.59	9.11

Source: Internal Revenue Service, Combined State and Federal Tax Rates—Nuveen Research

were purchased at a substantial discount to the adjusted basis (Compound Accreted Value).

Note . . . Municipal bonds are usually not appropriate investments for tax-exempt retirement accounts. All interest earned in a tax-exempt account is taxable when it is distributed from the account, so there is no reason to accept the muni's lower yield.

Call Features. Nearly all municipal bond issuers retain the right to redeem their bonds before they officially mature to better control borrowing costs. When issuers call bonds early, holders may be paid a premium of 1 or 2 percent more than the par value ($1,000).

Designation of Ownership. Most municipal bonds are either registered in the name of the holder or held in his brokerage account in the name of the firm, referred to as *street name*. Most newer bonds are *book entry*, and are assigned a computerized notation in the issuer's files with no paper certificates issued. Book entry bonds must be held at a bank or brokerage firm where issuers credit interest payments directly to bondholder accounts.

Bearer bonds, which are no longer issued, are older munis that do not identify their owners by name. Bearer certificates include coupons the owners clip and exchange at brokerage firms or banks when interest is due. Since 1983, federal law has ruled that all municipal bonds be issued in registered form.

Regulation. The Municipal Securities Rulemaking Board regulates the municipal bond industry. Unlike stocks and corporate bonds, the municipal sector is not heavily regulated and issuers are not required to register new bond offerings with the Securities and Exchange Commission. Even so, few abuses occur. The most common complaints involve unsuitable purchases of low-grade bonds and misrepresentation or omission of material facts about issues such as call features.

Risks

The major risks of municipal bonds are market risk and credit risk. Market risk is the same as for all other types of debt instruments, but credit risk is somewhat different.

Credit Risk. Although state and local governments as an aggregate had budget surpluses in the 1980s, many now run high deficits. Under severe economic conditions when tax revenues decline, some low-grade issues might default. While this would negatively affect prices of all low-rated bonds, state and federal taxes would undoubtedly rise to cover the deficits, which would create more demand and higher prices for high-quality issues.

With more than 2 million different municipal bond issues, the best way to ascertain their credit quality is to check the credit ratings granted by the independent rating services, Standard & Poor's or Moody's (see credit-rating chart, page 104).

When bonds are first issued, the issuer generally pays a credit-rating service to review the bonds and assign a credit rating. But ratings can change. The issuers of municipal bonds must provide ongoing financial reports to notify investors of any problems that might undermine their creditworthiness. Rating services evaluate these reports to enhance the integrity of the ratings they assign.

When a problem occurs that might jeopardize an issuer's ability to make interest payments or repay principal, a rating service reviews the situation and may downgrade the bonds by lowering their rating. This generally lowers the bond's market value and increases the issuer's cost to borrow in the future. Conversely, upgrades can enhance market value.

Non-Rated Bonds. Not all municipal bonds are rated by the rating services, generally for one or more of the following reasons:

- The size of a bond offering is so small that it does not require the enhanced marketing value a rating provides.

- The cost of establishing a rating history is not economically feasible, because the issuer is not prominent or issues debt infrequently.

- The bonds are not offered to the public but are placed privately with institutions.

- The assigned ratings are below investment grade and therefore offer no marketing advantage.

Non-rated bonds are not necessarily low quality, but they require considerable analysis as well as continuous monitoring. These are tasks individual investors rarely have the time or expertise to handle adequately.

Major Categories

There are approximately 85,000 issuers of municipal bonds and a great variety in the types of bonds offered.

General Obligation. To finance various public projects, state and local governments issue long-term bonds secured by the pledge of their credit and taxing power. Projects financed by *GOs* are usually approved by the electorate and serve a public purpose, such as freeways, libraries, and other public buildings. Issuers are assigned ratings on the basis of their individual credit strength, and many are rated AAA or AA.

Revenue and Certificates of Participation. *Revenue* bonds finance a wide range of municipal projects, and their safety depends on a project's ability to generate adequate revenues. Airport revenue bonds are backed by monies generated by landing and concession user fees; hospital bonds may be supported by revenues from federal and state reimbursement programs (Medicaid and Medicare) and individual patient payments.

Certificates of Participation, which finance various projects through lease-payment programs, are backed by annual appropriation rather than payments from any revenue-generating facility. Because they are budget items, their safety is contingent on an issuer's ability to manage fiscally sound budgets so that lease payments will continue.

COPs and revenue bonds must be evaluated on an individual basis. Less essential projects, such as golf courses and recreation centers, are best avoided unless the bonds are insured. The safer, more essential projects include municipal buildings, courthouses, jails, and schools. Utility revenue bonds for basic services such as water, sewerage, and electricity are generally considered safer because the population is more likely to support them, even in a very weak economy.

Housing Bonds. Municipalities issue bonds to finance the construction of low-income housing and to provide lower mortgage rates. Because property owners have the right to prepay their loans at will, most housing bonds are redeemable on any interest payment date.

AMT Bonds. Industrial development bonds, covering a range of purposes, are issued to help finance the efforts of private corporations. Credit ratings are based on the financial strength of the corporations. Interest payments are generally subject to the Alternative Minimum Tax. (A taxpayer may be subject to AMT if he takes significant deductions derived from *preference* items such as passive losses, property taxes, and accelerated depreciation.)

Federally Taxed Bonds. Some *private purpose* municipal bonds do not qualify for federal tax exemption, because their interest is treated as preference income. Although they are subject to federal taxation, they are generally exempt from state and local taxation. Always ask the broker if anything about a bond interferes with its federal tax-exempt status.

Zero Coupon Bonds. Like corporate and government zero coupon bonds, municipal zero coupon bonds pay no interest until maturity. Zeros are purchased at a discount from face value and mature at $1,000 or some other stipulated face value. Be sure to learn the call features because it may be possible for a bond to be redeemed for less than its purchase price. (See Zero Coupon Bonds, page 118.)

Short-Term Investing. For very short-term tax-free yields, you can purchase shares in a tax-free municipal money market fund or purchase *preferreds*, *floaters*, or *notes*.

- **Preferreds.** Preferreds are short-term municipal debt instruments that yield slightly more than tax-free money market funds. They are issued by mutual fund companies that leverage their portfolios to boost fund yields. Yields adjust periodically as market rates fluctuate. The minimum purchase is $25,000.

- **Floaters.** Investors with more than $100,000 may purchase 7-day demand notes called *floaters*, issued by municipalities. The interest rate is reset every seven days, and is generally higher than tax-free money market fund yields. To cash out, investors "put" the notes back to the issuer with seven days notice.

Inverse floaters, which pay the difference between long-term rates and floater rates, are very risky. They are sold mostly to aggressive managers of municipal bond funds who seek to boost fund yields. When interest rates decline, their yields increase; if rates rise significantly, inverse floaters become more difficult to sell, and market values could plummet. Avoid mutual funds that purchase inverse floaters.

- **Notes.** Revenue Anticipation Notes (RANS), Tax Anticipation Notes (TANS), and Tax and Revenue Anticipation Notes (TRANS) mature in a year or less, with interest paid only at maturity.

The Safest Bonds

If you are a very conservative investor who wants the least risk, purchase only *insured* or *prerefunded* bonds.

Insured Bonds. Approximately one third of all newly issued municipal bonds are insured for timely payment of interest and principal if the issuer defaults. Insurance coverage continues for the life of the bonds, even when the financial strength of the issuer declines. Investors typically give up only a fraction of a percent in yield for the safety of insurance.

Insurance companies insure only those bonds considered to be investment-grade (rated BBB or higher), and the coverage automatically grants bonds a AAA rating, as long as the insurance company is rated AAA by the major rating agencies.

The major insurers are MBIA (Municipal Bond Investors Assurance), AMBAC (American Municipal Bond Assurance Corporation), FGIC (Financial Guaranty Insurance Corporation), FSA (Financial Security Assurance), and Capital Guaranty. All are rated AAA by both S&P and Moody's.

If an issuer defaults, the insurance company does not pay off holders all at once, but it makes the interest and principal payments as they are due. Credit rating analysts state that the current claims-paying resources of insurers are adequate to cover payments to bondholders during severe economic conditions.

Prerefunded Bonds. When it is in their interest to call a bond issue, issuers may set aside funds in escrow accounts to redeem them on the earliest possible call date. The call date then becomes the new maturity date on which the issuer is obligated to pay the proceeds to bondholders. Prerefunded bonds that are escrowed in Treasury securities are considered safest and are given the AAA rating.

Trading

When a municipality borrows money, it publishes its intent to sell bonds along with the required documentation. Before municipal bonds can be traded among investors, they must undergo an offering process that is either *negotiated* or *competitive*.

Most larger, complex issues are sold through a negotiated underwriting in which the issuer selects a financial firm to manage a group of underwriters, called a *syndicate*, who purchase the bonds and resell them for profit. After the terms of the offering are agreed upon and announced, a short order period follows during which investors place their orders called *indications of interest*. Prices are not immediately confirmed, and bonds may be repriced to reflect demand.

Certain government obligations bonds are underwritten on a competitive basis, often because the government mandates it. Underwriters bid at auction, and bonds are generally awarded to the dealer whose bid reflects the lowest cost to the issuer. Again, your broker may not be able to confirm your purchase or your price immediately, and final confirmation may not be given for a week or more.

Once issued, municipal bonds trade among investors in an active over-the-counter market. Dealers maintain inventories ("make a market") to serve their clients' needs to buy and sell. Prices are subject to market conditions, and may vary significantly among dealers on the same issues. Although there are more than two million different issues, only a few of the most actively traded are quoted in newspapers.

Minimum Investment. Most municipal bonds are denominated in increments of $5,000 (face value), which is the smallest lot you can purchase.

Commissions and Markups. Markups on bonds range from a fraction of 1 percent to as high as 5 percent over the broker dealer's wholesale price. Generally, the longer the maturity and the lower the rating, the higher the markup. The only way to ensure fair prices is to shop and compare.

Bid Prices. Standard & Poor's has recently launched a pricing service for individual investors. By calling 800-BOND-INFO and paying a fee, S&P will provide price levels on your municipal bonds. These prices, as well as bond prices reported on brokerage firm statements, should be viewed as "reasonable approximations." Actual bid prices generally vary among

Marginal Income Tax Rates

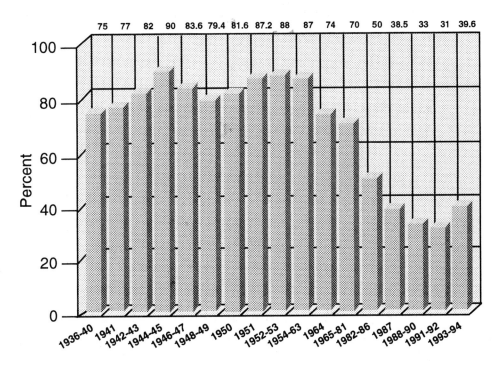

the dealers who trade bonds, a situation you will encounter when you try to sell your bonds.

Discounts versus Premiums. The purchase of a municipal bond with a price premium may be a better buy than a discount bond because a discount bond is more likely to incur a taxable gain than a premium bond. Also, relative to the prices of discount bonds, premium bond prices are more resilient to a rise in market interest rates because they pay higher current income.

Ways to Invest. You can purchase municipal bonds three ways:

- Buy individual bonds from brokerage firms.
- Buy shares in municipal bond mutual funds and unit investment trusts.
- Engage a manager/adviser to select and monitor your bond portfolio.

Before purchasing any bonds, read Chapter 5 to learn how bonds are traded and how to assess risk. For mutual funds and other managed participation, read Chapter 9.

Summary

If you need income and your combined state and federal tax bracket exceeds 28 percent, municipal bonds are probably your best choice. Insured and prerefunded bonds are safest. A carefully selected municipal bond portfolio can provide many years of solid, tax-free income.

If you would rather not be personally engaged in the tasks of selecting and monitoring your investments, you may hire professional investors to handle the job. Wall Street offers you three ways to access their services: mutual funds, unit investment trusts, and individually managed accounts.

Chapter 9

Mutual Funds and Other Managed Investments

"The future is purchased by the present."

Samuel Johnson

MUTUAL FUNDS

A mutual fund is an investment company that brings together money from many investors and invests it in a portfolio of stocks, bonds, or other securities to achieve specific investment objectives. Investors share the fund's profits (or losses), income, and expenses.

Professionally managed mutual funds have existed for more than half a century, but they are growing faster than ever. In 1950, mutual funds held $49 billion in assets, but now the nation's 8,000-plus funds hold more than $2 trillion of investors' money, more than double the total of just three years ago. In 1980, only 6 percent of households owned mutual fund shares; today 31 percent do. Counting their mutual fund holdings, Americans have more money invested in stocks and bonds than ever before.

The Benefits

Mutual funds have the potential to make money grow in three ways:

- *dividend and interest income* paid by securities in the fund;
- *capital gains* from security sales either reinvested or paid to shareholders; and
- *capital appreciation* from an increase in share price.

Mutual funds provide diversification and professional management to accommodate a full range of investment objectives. They are probably the best way for most people to invest, especially if they want to participate in the stock market. The cost of professional management is reasonable, and the mutual fund industry is highly regulated to protect shareholders.

Professional Management. Mutual fund companies prefer their managers to have extensive experience managing investment portfolios, and many hold the Chartered Financial Analyst (CFA) designation. Managers are not brokers, and they rarely communicate directly with shareholders.

A fund manager's job is to select securities that best meet his fund's investment objectives. To analyze the financial prospects of hundreds of companies, the manager gathers data from a variety of economic, financial, and statistical resources, taking into account general economic and market trends. The fund manager might oversee more than 100 different securities, deciding when to buy and sell them.

Diversification. Mutual funds offer you the opportunity to purchase an entire portfolio consisting of many different securities with only a small outlay of cash. For example, with as little as $1,000, you may participate in the growth of more than a hundred companies, spread among many different industries in both the U.S. and abroad.

Investment Objectives

Mutual fund investment objectives encompass a wide range, from higher risk portfolios seeking greater than average returns to those with more stable, conservative investments that generate regular income. Investors generally buy stock funds for their growth potential and bond funds for income. Information regarding a fund's investment objectives is found in the prospectus, which is essential for determining if a fund is suitable for your needs.

Performance

Although mutual funds offer professional expertise and diversification, they tend to rise and fall with the markets. During a bull market, most mutual funds flourish; when the market corrects, nearly all mutual funds suffer. Each fund class has different risks and rewards—those offering higher potential returns incur a greater potential for loss.

No mutual fund promises to return your original investment.

This concept is easily understood for stock funds, but for bond funds, alternative ways of purchasing bonds, such as individual bonds, do promise to return your principal at specified maturity dates.

Past performance figures of all mutual funds are available from the funds, brokers, and various financial magazines and newspapers. *Lipper, Morningstar,* and *Value Line* research reports are available on thousands of funds. Although superior past performance may be the most popular criterion for selecting a fund, it never guarantees future success.

As Table 9-1 shows, over the last 10 years of exploding mutual fund asset growth, the average U.S. stock fund

Table 9-1				
MUTUAL FUNDS				
AVERAGE ANNUAL RETURNS				
Type of Fund	*No. Funds*	*3 Years %*	*5 Years %*	*10 Years %*
Equity (Stock)	369	10.16	11.21	12.50
International	36	9.73	7.31	14.49
Taxable Bond	120	5.51	8.18	9.17
Tax-Free Bond	152	6.52	7.83	8.38
S&P 500 Index		10.54	12.62	14.78
Lehman Gov't Bond		7.15	9.57	9.77
Morningstar Research (10 years ending April 30, 1995)				

returned 12.5 percent annually, even though most under-performed the S&P 500 index's gains of 14.78 percent. The average corporate bond fund returned 9.17 percent. (Treasury bills averaged 3.58 percent.)

Net Asset Value. Each day at the close of the market, all securities in a mutual fund portfolio are priced to arrive at the price of one share, the *net asset value*. The NAV is calculated by determining the total asset value of all the fund's securities based on the day's closing prices, minus the fund's expenses, divided by the total number of shares.

$$\text{NAV} = \frac{\text{Total Assets} - \text{Fund Expenses}}{\text{Total Shares}}$$

Total Return. To calculate the total return of mutual fund shares, add together all dividends, capital gains distributions, and compounded interest on reinvested dividends, and then add or subtract any changes in the NAV.

Total Return = Dividends + Capital Gains + Interest ± Changes in NAV

Fees

All mutual funds charge their shareholders fees to cover expenses and administration costs (employee salaries, marketing expenses, legal, and transfer agent fees). All fees are lumped together and stated as an annual percentage of the share price or *expense ratio*.

In the past, it was difficult for investors to compare mutual fund fees, but today it is much easier because the SEC now requires every fund to report its fees clearly in a prospectus. According to Morningstar Research, the average expense ratio

Stock Funds (Capital Appreciation/Growth/Equity):

Aggressive Growth	Stocks selected for maximum growth.
Growth	Stock in companies with above-average growth rates.
Growth and Income	Stocks with solid dividends and increasing share values.
Equity Income	High-dividend stocks and bonds with emphasis on income.
Sector	Stocks of companies in one industry.
Small Cap/Mid-Cap	Stock selection based on company size.
Gold	Stocks of gold mining companies.
International	Stocks of foreign companies only.
Global	Stocks of U.S. and foreign companies.

Bond Funds (Income):

Bond	Corporate, municipal (tax-free), or government bonds.
High-Yield	Lower rated, higher yielding (junk) bonds.
International	Bonds issued by foreign companies and governments.
Global	Bonds issued by U.S. and foreign companies and governments.
Prime Rate Trusts	Collateralized corporate loans.

Funds with Both Stocks and Bonds:

Balanced	Conservative stocks and bonds in 40-60 mix.
Asset Allocation	Stocks, bonds, and cash in varying proportions.

Money Market Funds

(See page 188.) Because money market funds are a very different type of mutual fund, they are covered separately.

for U.S. stock funds is 1.39 percent, corporate bond funds average .9 percent, and municipal bond funds, .88 percent. International fund expenses average 1.79 percent because of the higher costs for trading and foreign-currency transactions.

Ways to Purchase Mutual Funds

Mutual funds, structured as either *open-end* or *closed-end*, are offered to investors in three different ways:

- Most funds are marketed through brokers associated with banks, brokerage firms, and insurance companies, all of whom charge commissions.

- Many funds market their shares directly to investors via the mail or telephone, charging little or no commission because marketing expenses are included in the annual fees paid by shareholders.

- Shares of some funds are publicly traded among investors, mostly on stock exchanges.

OPEN-END MUTUAL FUNDS

Most funds are *open-end*, which means there is no set limit to the number of shares. The total number of shares is always changing—new shares are created as money is invested, and shares are eliminated when sold (redeemed or liquidated).

Open-end mutual funds are highly liquid because managers are obligated to redeem shares within seven days of shareholder request. Funds *forward-price* both purchases and redemptions. That is, when a fund receives your purchase request, you pay the NAV calculated that day, plus the sales charge, if any; when you sell shares, you are paid the next NAV calculated. Newspapers quote offering prices and NAVs of funds for the previous market day.

When shareholder redemptions exceed purchases on a given day, the fund manager must sell securities if the fund's cash balance cannot cover the deficit. When share purchases exceed redemptions, the manager invests the money.

Open-end mutual funds require an initial investment of anywhere from $50 to $5,000.

Sales Loads

Most open-end mutual funds are marketed through commissioned brokers, but many advertise directly to investors. Generally speaking, funds that do not involve brokers are referred to as *no-load* or *low-load* funds. In no way does load factor indicate performance—all categories have their share of winners and lackluster performers. You can do the necessary homework to select funds or rely on the advice of brokers who market funds that charge commissions.

Many open-end funds offer a choice of how to pay sales charges. Depending on the class, investors pay a charge when they first invest, or when they sell shares, or sales charges may take the form of higher ongoing fees.

A Shares. The fund charges a *front-end* load that is deducted from the purchase price before shares are purchased, typically 2 to 5.75 percent of the share price. Class A shares are generally more cost-effective for larger purchases when held for a minimum of five years.

B Shares. The fund charges a *back-end* load at redemption called a *contingent deferred sales charge*. Back-end charges are typically reduced each year that shares are held, and usually disappear completely after 4 or 5 years. Class B shares charge higher annual fees, sometimes referred to as *12b-1* fees, to cover broker commissions. A potential advantage of Class B shares over Class A shares is that you can buy a greater number of shares initially. Class B shares are probably best suited for long-term investors who do not make large purchases.

C Shares. A *level* load, typically 1 percent, is charged annually, regardless of how long shares are held. Because Class C shares never convert to Class A shares, they are not the most cost-efficient when shares are held long-term.

D Shares. These shares incur a low annual fee like Class C shares, but may also charge a small front-end or back-end load.

Over a period of years, it does not make much difference which type of arrangement you choose. According to Chicago's Financial Research Corporation, the five-year total return for a $10,000 investment in a fund that averages a 10 percent annual gain is $15,713 for Class A shares, $15,694 for Class B shares, and $15,657 for Class C shares. Brokers may not explain all the different pricing options to you, and may make the choice for you.

Note . . . No-load funds do not impose sales charges but, like all funds, they do pass operating and management fees on to shareholders (although the SEC limits fees for any fund marketed as "no-load"). Over time, a load fund with low annual fees may be more cost-efficient than a no-load fund.

Breakpoints. A fund generally reduces sales charges for investors who meet specified higher investment levels called *breakpoints.* Some funds allow you to combine accounts to qualify for a breakpoint. For example, the shares bought in your IRA together with other accounts (perhaps even those of family members) may qualify for a higher breakpoint.

A *letter of intent* is a form you sign if you plan to invest a certain amount of funds within a 13-month period that qualifies you for a higher breakpoint. If you do not complete the purchase within the 13 months, you may remit the difference or redeem sufficient shares to pay the charge. Often the fund lets you backdate the letter up to 90 days after purchase.

Automatic Reinvestment. When purchasing shares, advise the fund to pay out all dividends and gains to you or to reinvest them in new shares. Nearly all funds allow automatic commission-free reinvestment of dividends and distributed capital gains in new shares at the NAV.

Mutual Fund Switching and Exchanges. Most mutual fund investment companies manage several different funds that form a "family." Shareholders benefit from this arrangement because, when their investment objectives change, they may *exchange* their shares (sell one fund and purchase another with the proceeds) with no commission. Because an exchange is always considered a sale, you should first consider the tax consequences.

CLOSED-END MUTUAL FUNDS

Unlike an open-end mutual fund with its constantly changing number of shares, a closed-end fund has a limited, fixed number of shares. While open-end share prices always reflect the

NAV, closed-end share prices reflect the supply/demand action of the market because the investment company does not promise to repurchase shares at the NAV.

Closed-end fund shares, which are usually listed on exchanges, may be purchased only from someone willing to sell their shares or sold to someone willing to purchase. These shares trade like common stocks with similar transaction expense. There is no minimum share purchase, but 100 share increments is typical.

Closed-end shares carry a different kind of market risk. Not only does the NAV fluctuate along with price changes of the fund's individual securities, but the fund's market price can trade higher or lower than the NAV. When the market price is lower than the NAV, the fund's shares trade at a *discount*; when the price is higher, the shares trade at a *premium*. For example, a bond fund with an NAV of $10.00 might be offered at $9.70—$10.00 worth of bonds may be purchased for $9.70. The *Wall Street Journal* reports the prices and NAVs of all exchange-listed closed-end funds once each week.

Initial Public Offerings. In the last few years, a flurry of newly issued closed-end mutual funds were created and offered through brokers (who are better compensated for these trades than for shares already trading). Some IPO fund shares were marketed as no-load, when in fact underwriting fees were 4 to 5 percent of the initial price. For a bond fund priced at $15 a share, for example, 75 cents might be deducted from proceeds and paid to brokers and underwriters, resulting in an NAV of $14.25. Without a significant decline in market interest rates, IPO share prices are likely to decline. Also, when you sell these shares, you must pay a commission—definitely not a no-load situation.

Although some investors purchased IPO shares as if they

were money market funds, there is no price guarantee. On the contrary—the longer maturities of the bonds, typically 20 years or longer, subject the funds to significant price volatility.

In 1992, the SEC voted to tighten disclosure rules on closed-end funds to prevent misrepresentation. If a broker recommends a closed-end bond fund on the offering, ask for the prospectus, and read the section covering fees. You may find the shares less attractive when the costs are considered. A better buy may be a closed-end fund trading at a discount that has a track record of paying dividends.

Leveraged Bond Funds. To boost yields to shareholders, the managers of some closed-end bond funds leverage their funds by borrowing against the funds' securities at a lower, short-term interest rate and using the proceeds to purchase a greater number of long-term, higher yielding bonds. Leveraged funds are riskier because they are even more vulnerable than other bond investments to a rise in interest rates. When interest rates spiked in early 1994, the market prices of many leveraged bond funds declined substantially. If you are risk-averse, avoid leveraged funds.

How to Select Mutual Funds

Mutual funds should be considered long-term investments and selected with care. With so many mutual funds from which to choose, however, the selection process can be confusing. Fortunately, the SEC requires that all mutual funds give investors a prospectus disclosing much of the needed information. The prospectus reports a fund's investment objectives, strategies, types of securities in which it may invest, risks, management fees, and commissions. Rather than acting solely on a fund's advertising claims or a broker's recommendation, request a fund's prospectus and *read it thoroughly before investing.*

For even greater detail, request the Statement of Additional Information (Part B) as well as the annual report or last shareholder report for an explanation of how the fund's investment strategies have affected performance. Although these documents may be confusing, if you tackle a few, the task gets easier, and you are far less likely to choose a fund that will ultimately disappoint you.

Although it helps to read a variety of publications, do not make investment decisions based on mutual fund rankings in newspapers, magazines, and especially fund advertisements. With more than 100 different performance categories, many funds are able to claim the "number one" spot. Better to review research reports issued by Morningstar or Value Line, available at brokerage firms and libraries.

Evaluate Fund Type. Your most important consideration is the *type* of mutual fund. If you decide to purchase a stock fund, then you must decide what type of companies (larger, mature, smaller growth, foreign) as well as the management style (value, growth, aggressive growth, or equity income). Check a fund's largest holdings to see the kinds of companies or securities it purchases. To diversify, avoid funds heavily invested in only one or two industries or sectors, and select three or more funds with different strategies and investment styles.

Consider Performance. A fund's performance is important but past returns can be misleading. A fund that achieved two or three years of outstanding performance may have benefited from an investment style that could be out of favor in the months to come. The top-performing aggressive growth fund for three years running at the end of 1993 declined 35 percent in 1994!

Review a fund's total return performance covering a three- or five-year period. One year is too short and 10 years may be too long—many stellar funds were not around 10 years ago. Look at a fund's performance during bull markets, but give more weight to how it fared in bear markets (1981, 1987, and 1990), a more stringent test.

A good prospect is a top-performing aggressive growth fund that outperformed the S&P 500 index in good years and managed to weather down cycles with no greater loss than the S&P 500. For a more conservative selection, seek out a value fund that never suffered a significant loss in any calendar year.

Consider the Fund Family. You may want to participate in U.S. stocks now, but switch part of your money to foreign markets in the future. By choosing a well-integrated fund family, you can switch funds with just a phone call and without charge when your investment objectives change.

Consider Size. Very large stock funds may not be able to invest as they did when they were smaller. Perhaps a manager who gained a reputation for picking winners cannot duplicate his earlier performance as his fund grows. While it may be time to move out of an equity fund when it doubles or triples, bond funds might offer better performance as they expand. Because expenses reduce bond fund yields, economies of scale might dictate higher returns for larger bond funds than smaller ones.

Open-End versus Closed-End. Although some closed-end funds are star performers, a significant disadvantage is that you cannot switch to another fund without incurring a brokerage commission, unlike an open-end fund.

A potential disadvantage of all open-end bond funds concerns the dividend. As interest rates decline, the fund's dividend tends to decline. The fund manager is obliged to purchase more bonds as new money is invested, adding lower yielding bonds to the portfolio. Even though you may have invested when rates were higher, your shares are diluted with new shares. Because there is less chance of dilution with closed-end funds, their dividends are less likely to be reduced.

Bond Funds versus CDs. To pay higher yields, most bond funds invest in long-term issues; the longer the maturities, the greater the market risk. All interest earned could be offset by a loss of principal if rates rise only one point.

As interest rates declined over the last few years, many investors took their money out of CDs and money markets to invest in bond funds. Accustomed to CDs with stable values, investors were unpleasantly surprised when their share values deteriorated as market interest rates shot up in 1994. A far safer way to earn more than CDs is to purchase short-term, high-quality bonds.

Dollar-Cost Averaging. The systematic investment of a set dollar amount at regular intervals is a defensive strategy called *dollar-cost averaging*. Share prices will vary, but by regularly investing the same dollar amount, you purchase more shares when prices are low and fewer shares when prices are high, thereby lowering the average price paid.

Dollar-cost averaging also helps protect you from investing all your money at what could be the worst time—for instance, just before a crash or bear market. Rather than contribute $2,000 all at once to your IRA, deposit $166 each month to purchase shares in a mutual fund. If a market correction occurs, accelerate your contributions and share purchase.

Tax Implications

Whenever you sell mutual fund shares, even to switch to another fund in the family, a taxable event occurs. If you sell shares at a profit, you owe tax on the gain. If you sell at a loss, you may deduct it. If selling only part of your shares for a profit, you can minimize the tax liability by indicating at the time of sale that you are selling shares purchased at the highest price or the IRS assumes that you sold the ones bought first—*first in/first out* (FIFO).

For tax purposes, mutual fund returns fall into several categories: long-term capital gains, short-term capital gains, taxable dividends, non-taxable dividends, federally taxed dividends, and dividends subject only to state taxes. Some funds make *return of capital* distributions that are not taxed but must be subtracted from the shareholder's *basis* (cost). Shareholders are sent 1099 forms indicating how dividends and capital gains are reported to the IRS.

You are liable for taxes on a fund's capital gains whether reinvested or distributed by the fund, even though you may not have owned the shares at the time the gains actually occurred. Most funds declare and distribute gains toward the end of the calendar year, so if you're buying a fund outside a tax-exempt account near the end of the year, consider postponing the purchase until after the capital gains *record* date.

Unless purchased in a tax-exempt account, you need to keep records of fund shares bought or sold, noting dates and prices. Avoid writing checks to access cash from mutual fund accounts—you may be creating a tax nightmare. Every check requires shares to be sold, which triggers a taxable event, so write checks as infrequently as possible.

UNIT INVESTMENT TRUSTS

A *unit investment trust* is a portfolio of stocks or bonds selected to achieve specific investment objectives within a limited period.

UITs, created and sponsored by financial firms, are offered to investors in increments of $1,000 (face value) with terms from 3 to 25 years. Similar to closed-end mutual funds, UITs provide benefits small investors would not otherwise achieve—diversification, professional selection of assets, and perhaps monthly income. Although tax implications, risks, and criteria for purchase are very similar to those of mutual funds, there are significant differences.

- A UIT is created with a set number of shares called *units*, and new units are never created.

- UITs are not actively managed but rather supervised by their sponsors. Portfolios are changed only if something goes really wrong, such as a company declaring bankruptcy or defaulting on a bond. In that event, the sponsor is likely to liquidate the security and either reinvest the proceeds or distribute them to unit holders.

- Unlike a mutual fund, a UIT has a specified, finite life that terminates when assets mature. The proceeds are then distributed to unit holders.

- Distributions are paid to unit holders monthly or quarterly, and dividend reinvestment is rarely offered.

- There are no ongoing management fees.

Examples of UITs are

- Portfolios of corporate, municipal, or government bonds that provide monthly or quarterly income payments.

- A portfolio composed of shares in many different utility companies, providing diversification and income.

- A portfolio of European companies, diversified by country and industry group.

- A portfolio composed of several companies in the telecommunications industry.

Commissions and Trading. When initially offered, investors pay the net asset value plus the markup, typically 4 to 5 percent, or slightly less when units are purchased in the secondary market. Sponsors agree to purchase units from unit holders who want to sell. Sellers are paid the NAV with no commission charged.

The following is an example of a Municipal Investment Trust (MIT) unit:

Price:	$1,018.93	
Par Value:	$1,000.00	
Accrued Interest:	$3.17	} per unit
Annual Income:	$60.00	
Monthly Check:	$5.01	
Sales Charge:	4.50%	

Current Yield: 5.9%   Long-Term Yield: 5.89%

Average Life: 29 years   Quality: AAA Insured
Diversification: 13 issues, 10 states

Note . . . The true yield of a bond UIT might not be easily determined when the portfolio holds many different bonds. The SEC has ruled that sponsors must quote the *long-term yield* (which might be lower than the current yield) of any newly issued trust, but they are not required to do so for trusts traded in the secondary market.

Before purchasing a bond UIT, check the portfolio for call provisions to avoid paying a 4 percent commission for a UIT that holds bonds callable within a short time.

Individual Bonds versus Bond Funds and UITs

To have better control over costs and market risk, you are probably better off buying individual bonds than funds and trusts, but only if you learn to purchase them safely. Although there are costs to purchase individual bonds, if you shop around and get respectable prices, you might lock in higher yields than you can get in a fund or trust, and you avoid annual management fees that reduce interest payments.

By building a portfolio of individual bonds, you can select issues with varying maturities, some short-term. That way, if you need to cash out during a down market, you can sell only your short-term bonds, which are subject to minimal market risk. However, if you are not willing to take the time to analyze each individual purchase, investing in funds and trusts may be the best alternative. The following are comparisons of your options.

Guaranteed Principal. Individual bonds and unit investment trusts pay bondholders the face value upon maturity, but there is no such guaranteed repayment with mutual funds because they never mature. When you cash out of a mutual fund, the sale price may be higher or lower than your purchase price. Market prices of all fixed-income investments are influenced by interest-rate fluctuations, but unlike mutual funds, individual bonds and UITs promise to return principal upon maturity.

In *Beating the Street*, author Peter Lynch warns "a bond fund offers no protection against higher interest rates, which is by far the greatest danger in owning a long-term IOU. When rates go higher, a bond fund loses value as quickly as an individual bond with a similar maturity." Since most bond funds hold long-term issues, they are subject to substantial market risk and are especially inadvisable when interest rates are low and likely to rise.

Fees. Longer term, individual bonds may cost less to purchase than mutual funds because their interest payments are not reduced by annual management fees and costs to purchase may be lower.

Dividends. If interest rates decline after you invest, a mutual fund's dividends are also likely to be reduced, but this does not generally occur with individual bonds and unit trusts. As interest rates fell during the 1980s, mutual funds reduced their dividends while individual bond and UIT payments remained stable. Additionally, some bond fund managers employ strategies to boost dividends that may erode share values.

Bond funds and unit trusts usually pay dividends monthly or quarterly; most individual bonds pay semiannually.

Minimum Purchase. Mutual funds and UITs may be purchased with less money than individual bonds, often for less than $1,000.

Note . . . Most sophisticated bond investors build portfolios of individual bonds of varying maturities and avoid trusts and funds.

Ways to Purchase Bonds

	Advantages	Disadvantages
Individual Bonds Minimum Investment: $5,000–$10,000 Interest Payments: Semiannual Markup/Commission: .5% to 3% Annual Fee: None	• Promised return of principal • Interest rate locked in • Less vulnerable to market risk if short-term, high-quality • No annual fees to reduce yield • Low commission	• No professional management • No diversification • No reinvestment
Open-End Mutual Funds Minimum Investment: $50–$1000 Payments: Monthly, quarterly Commission: 0% to 6% Annual Fee: .75% to 1%	• Active professional management • Dividend reinvestment • Diversification	• No promised return of principal • Annual fee and/or commission reduces yield • Greater market risk if bonds are long-term • Yields fluctuate and may decline as they are subject to dilution
Closed-End Mutual Funds Minimum Investment: $1,000–1,500 Payments: Monthly Commission: .5% to 2% (New offering: 3% to 5%) Annual Fee: .75% to 1%	• Active professional management • Dividend reinvestment • More stable yield than open-end fund • Diversification	• No promised return of principal • Shares can trade at discount or premium to NAV • Commission cost, trades like stock • Greater market risk if bonds are long-term
Unit Investment Trusts Minimum Investment: $1,000 Payments: Monthly Dealer Underwriting Fee: 3% to 5%	• Promised return of principal • Professional selection and surveillance • Yield locked in • No annual fees to reduce yield • Diversification	• No reinvestment • Greater market risk if bonds are long-term • No fund switching

*Happiness seems to require a
modicum of external prosperity.*

Nicomachean Ethics
Aristotle

MANAGED ACCOUNTS

Although there are hundreds of good mutual funds, if you
have the means, you may consider engaging a professional adviser to manage your account. Indeed, most of the nation's
large pension-fund trustees hire professional investment advisers rather than invest their pension money in mutual funds
or trusts.

Like mutual funds, an individually managed account gives
you access to expert investors. The difference between the two
types of accounts lies in the size of the account and the
way it is structured. In fact, the same adviser may be managing both a mutual fund and individual accounts.

A simple rule of thumb in deciding between mutual funds
and individually managed accounts is *stick with funds if your
account is less than $100,000.* There are two reasons. First, the
better advisers, who manage millions of client dollars, often
have a minimum requirement of $1 million. Second, an ac-
count of less than $100,000 may not provide for sufficient
diversification.

Selecting an Adviser

When you establish an individually managed account, you relinquish control by written contract to an adviser who makes all investment decisions on your behalf. An adviser may be anyone in the business of advising clients on how to invest their money.

The SEC requires investment advisers, often called portfolio or money managers, to be registered and to disclose basic information about their finances and education. Investment advisers are not generally licensed brokers, although a broker may be a registered adviser. At this time, the SEC oversees about 20,000 registered advisers who manage assets totalling $9.6 trillion. This is up from only 4,000 advisers in 1980.

Although the SEC regulates the activities of registered advisers, individual inspection is spotty. Your challenge is to engage an expert, ethical adviser who does not operate alone but with an entire support staff. The following case illustrates the ramifications of selecting an unscrupulous adviser:

> *In September 1992, investment adviser Steven D. Wymer pleaded guilty in federal court to defrauding clients of $174 million. Wymer, the former president and sole shareholder of Institutional Treasury Management of Irvine, California, admitted luring clients with false promises of profits. He then proceeded to lose their money in speculative securities trading. He also squandered much of his customers' money on luxury items for himself.*
>
> *Wymer covered up his losses by sending out false statements and confirmations to his clients who did not learn the true status of their accounts for many*

years. Although authorities investigated his firm three separate times in the late 1980s, Wymer had been able to placate their auditors with elaborate phony documentation.

Wymer's fraud was finally uncovered when SEC examiners found irregularities in one of his client's accounts. Wymer was found guilty and sentenced to 15 years in federal prison. This high-profile case spurred the SEC to increase its scrutiny and regulation of all investment advisers.

Of course, many advisers are both honest and competent. The nation's large pension fund trustees would hardly engage investment advisers if they were not convinced of their merit. Indeed, many investors, such as the one below, have their advisers to thank for their accumulated wealth.

In 1983, George Tomkin, age 40, met with his broker to discuss investments for his pension plan. The broker recommended that Tomkin allocate 75 percent of his pension assets to stocks and 25 percent to bonds. His broker conducted a "manager search" for a professional adviser, whom Tomkin hired to select and manage his pension's stock investments. In addition to his monthly statement, the brokerage firm sent Tomkin quarterly reports on his portfolio's performance.

Although there were several minor market setbacks, Tomkin's stock account grew in value. Everything was going smoothly until suddenly, on October 19, 1987, the stock market crashed. When Tomkin's business partner panicked and immediately sold off his entire stock portfolio and mutual fund shares,

Tomkin called his adviser to ask if he should be selling too.

Despite the one-day, 508-point drop in the Dow, the adviser counseled his client to commit additional *money to stocks and he submitted specific recommendations. It took great courage to act amidst all the uncertainty and pessimism, but Tomkin agreed and bought several stocks at the lower prices. The new shares turned out to be the most profitable investments he ever made.*

Tomkin's partner never got back into the market, and his portfolio did not recover its losses for many years. Tomkin's stocks, however, have nearly tripled in value in the decade he remained invested.

The Broker/Consultant

Some brokers will help you select an adviser and help monitor your account's performance. They identify several top-performing advisers whose investment style and philosophy are compatible with your risk profile and investment goals. With access to third-party, unbiased analyses of advisers, consultants and brokerage firms probably offer the best scrutiny of advisers for small investors and trustees of small pension funds than anything else available to them at a relatively low cost.

A broker has no conflict of interest when his client's account is managed by a professional adviser. The only way the adviser and the broker can increase their fees is to increase the value of the account—the best possible outcome for their client as well. While a consultant guides you through the managed account process, the selection of adviser is ultimately your decision and your responsibility.

Write an *investment policy statement* covering your financial goals, risk parameters, and targeted annual returns. Both you and your broker are then positioned to detect any deviation from stated policy, and will have a standard against which to judge your account's performance.

Custodial Arrangements

Regardless of whether you engage a broker to help you select an adviser, you should always have your securities held in custody at a trust company or brokerage firm. When depositing money, always make your check payable to this third-party custodian. *Never make a check out directly to the investment adviser.* Custodians of adviser-managed accounts must report to clients at least quarterly on all their holdings, which prevents advisers from hiding losses for any significant time.

Fees

Total costs for individually managed accounts are marginally higher than total annual expenses for most mutual funds, but the extra benefits may be worth the extra cost. No fees are charged to get in or out of the service, which may be terminated at any time.

Managed-account expense is twofold: The adviser's annual fee is typically 1 percent or less of the account value, and transaction costs are either charged for each individual transaction or covered by quarterly *wrap* fees.

Wrap is a method of payment based on account market values rather than transaction activity. The service generally offers other benefits such as manager search and ongoing performance monitoring. Wrap fees for stock accounts are typically .5 to 2 percent of the account value, with larger accounts paying a lower percentage than smaller accounts. Wrap fees eliminate conflict-of-interest concerns because the predictable known cost of all transactional activity allows the broker/consultant to serve with objectivity.

Managed Accounts versus Mutual Funds

Individually managed accounts may offer several advantages over mutual funds.

Market Timing. A mutual fund manager acts at the mercy of thousands of shareholders. During market corrections, many shareholders panic and sell *after* stock prices have dropped. To meet massive redemptions, the fund's manager is forced to become a net seller when prices are down, typically locking in the worst possible prices. Investors also tend to invest in mutual funds at market peaks. These are the exact opposite of the optimal times to buy and sell. An individually managed account affords greater control.

Quality. To meet massive redemptions during market corrections, a mutual fund manager may sell the higher quality companies that have performed best, leaving the lower quality holdings in the portfolio. There is no reason for this to occur in a managed account.

Better Selection. A mutual fund typically holds a large percentage of securities that have been owned for a long time, and they may not be those a manager would buy with new money. When you start an individually managed account, the adviser purchases stocks he believes are the most attractive at that time.

Customization. Advisers can tailor your portfolio to fit your personal objectives and risk tolerance. For example, you can restrict an adviser from purchasing certain stocks, such as tobacco and defense companies.

Tax Advantages. You may incur lower taxes with your own account. When mutual fund shares are purchased prior to the capital gains ex-dividend date, you may be taxed on gains you did not earn, but this cannot occur in your own account. Also, you can implement tax planning by offsetting losses with gains.

Better Executions. Because they trade such large positions, mutual fund managers cannot always buy or sell as efficiently as independent advisers to get the best prices.

Third-Party Monitor. One of the services provided to individually managed accounts, but not to mutual funds shareholders, is the quarterly unbiased, third-party performance monitor. This report compares the managed account's performance with the S&P 500 index as well as with the performance of hundreds of other large portfolio managers.

Personal Attention. Many investment advisers communicate valuable information to clients. For instance, some advisers provide a written rationale for new positions as they are added. Most important, many advisers communicate with nervous clients during rough markets to keep them from exiting at the worst possible times and counsel clients to invest additional funds after market corrections.

Greater Accountability. Under ERISA (Employee Retirement Income Security Act of 1974, the federal law governing pension accounts), anyone handling pension fund assets is a fiduciary. As such, all plan trustees are subject to rules pertaining to written investment guidelines as well as diligence in selecting and monitoring their investment advisers, who are also fiduciaries. Mutual fund companies are not fiduciaries and are not required to comply with ERISA. Because trustees are *personally* liable as fiduciaries, they should take every precaution in their selection of adviser by employing consultants to guide them.

Summary

Even the most sophisticated investor with years of experience in stock picking should consider managed investments. With professional management, your holdings are scrutinized daily, a task busy investors rarely have time for. Mutual funds are efficient vehicles for switching money among various asset classes as well as markets. If you have more than $100,000 to invest in stocks, consider engaging an adviser to help you remain objective when markets flounder. Because the choice of investment adviser is critical, you are well-advised to employ consultants to help select and monitor your adviser, a service that rarely adds to the cost.

PORTFOLIO MANAGEMENT STYLES

Professional investors typically espouse one or more of the following investment styles.

Top-Down versus Bottom-Up

To determine the appropriate allocation for portfolio assets among stocks, bonds, and cash, *top-down* managers focus first on macroeconomic issues such as inflation and the direction of interest rates. Next, they target sectors the economic environment will favor to identify superior-performing industries before selecting specific securities.

Bottom-up managers take a microeconomic approach —they focus on the fundamental merits of particular companies first and foremost, and the economic environment second.

Sector Rotator

The *sector rotator* is a top-down investor who bases stock selection on anticipated economic, political, demographic, and social trends. The sector rotator attempts to identify market changes as early as possible to choose stocks from those sectors positioned to benefit most.

The most common rotation is by economic sector and industry. Market history demonstrates that stocks of companies within similar industries tend to rise and fall together. In a strong economic environment, capital goods, basic industry, technology, and other economically sensitive sectors are emphasized. When the economy is weak, utilities, drugs, foods, and other recession-resistant sectors are stressed.

Growth Versus Value

The two basic styles of individual stock selection are growth and value. While both styles claim to capitalize on rising prices and to avoid overvalued stocks, there are basic differences between the two.

The *growth* manager seeks companies with sustained rates of earnings growth that typically exceed 15 percent per year whether they are mature, blue-chip companies or small, younger companies. Growth companies usually trade at higher price/earnings multiples than value companies and are more often found in the technology, communications, and entertainment sectors. With little or no dividends and higher P/Es, growth stocks tend to be more volatile and vulnerable to market corrections.

The *value* manager analyzes a universe of stocks and identifies those that may be undervalued, or inexpensive, relative to a variety of fundamental and/or technical criteria. Value managers tend to stress companies with strong management, healthy balance sheets, sound dividend payouts, low P/E ratios, low price/book ratios, and high cash flows. Value stocks tend to populate the financial, utility, and basic-industry sectors. Value managers, who tend to be patient with longer term outlooks, sell shares as they become fairly recognized by the market.

Value investing outperforms growth investing in some market cycles and lags in others, but the two styles tend to produce similar returns over long periods.

Asset Allocator

Asset allocators believe that investing optimally among the various classes of stocks, bonds, and cash is a much more critical determinant of portfolio performance than individual security selection. Following a top-down approach, they are concerned with the economy, liquidity, and monetary policy, as well as indicators such as investor sentiment. Individual stock selection carries less weight to the asset allocator who may use value, growth, or some other style.

Contrarian Investing

Contrarians invest in out-of-favor stocks. They are the consummate value investors, buying stocks trading at large discounts to their perceived values, based on company fundamentals. In the extreme, the contrarian manager may even buy a bankrupt company, betting on a rebound.

Income/Yield

Taking the bottom-up approach, *income* managers concentrate on selecting stocks with high dividend yields and below-average P/E ratios. This style tends to be the least volatile of the equity styles.

Small-Cap Versus Large-Cap

Public companies are often described and differentiated by size, and advisers tend to specialize in either the large mature companies or small, newer ones. Companies with market capitalization (share price multiplied by number of shares outstanding) below $750 million are generally considered *small-cap*; between $750 million and $3 billion are referred to as *mid-cap*; companies above $3 billion are *large-cap*.

Everybody needs to have some money readily available for emergencies and unexpected, but essential, expenditures. Finding a safe place for "rainy day insurance" is an important part of planning your cash management. However, while money market funds and bank CDs can accommodate your liquidity needs, they are not risk-free, despite what you may have heard.

Chapter **10**

Cash Management

*"The lack of money is
the root of all evil."*

George Bernard Shaw

Capital markets, the focus of preceding chapters, bring together borrowers seeking long-term capital with investors who have money to lend. The nation's *money markets* and banks accommodate governments and companies who need to borrow large sums of money for a very short term as well as investors who need liquidity but want their money to earn a respectable yield.

MONEY MARKET FUNDS

A money market fund is a highly liquid mutual fund that allows for deposits and withdrawals of cash at a constant share price of $1.00.

Money market fund interest fluctuates and accrues daily, and is credited to shareholders monthly. Because they pay higher yields than traditional savings accounts, money market funds have become increasingly popular. At the end of 1987, they held about $255 billion in deposits. In 1995, more than 1,000 funds held in excess of $700 billion.

Categories

Most money market funds invest in a variety of financial debt instruments, although some limit themselves to certain types of loans to provide particular benefits. The four basic types of money market funds are

- **Generic.** Composed of *commercial paper* (short-term, unsecured loans), *certificates of deposit* (loans to large banks), *bankers acceptance* (bank loans to exporters and importers to finance international transactions), *repurchase agreements* (contracts to repurchase financial assets), and municipal and Treasury securities, these funds generally pay the highest rates.

- **Government.** Limited to government-guaranteed and/or agency issues, these funds are subject to the least credit risk.

- **Municipal.** Limited to municipal loans that pay interest exempt from federal taxation and sometimes state and local taxation, these funds may offer the highest after-tax yields for investors in high tax brackets.

- **Foreign Currency.** Invested in loans denominated in foreign currencies, these funds may offer higher yields but are subject to currency risk.

Risks

Money market funds are subject to the risks of the debt instruments they hold, namely *credit* risk and *market* risk. Although money market funds guarantee that shareholders will always get back $1.00 for every share redeemed, the guarantee is only as good as the assets or sponsor backing it. With the recent problems encountered by money market funds, it is prudent to address *management risk* as well.

Credit Risk. Money market funds generally invest in only the safest, highest rated instruments. Some fund managers, however, hard-pressed by the low interest rate environment, have compromised the safety of their funds in attempts to boost fund yields by purchasing lower quality issues.

In 1989, a large company defaulted on $1 billion in commercial paper, some of which was held by two money market funds. Fortunately, no shareholder lost money because the sponsors were able to bail out their funds by purchasing the defaulted issues from the portfolio at face value.

Market Risk. Money market share prices (NAVs) actually fluctuate above or below $1.00 as prices of the debt instruments in the portfolio fluctuate. To protect investors, regulators restrict money market funds from purchasing financial instruments with maturities longer than 13 months, and a fund's average maturity must not exceed 90 days (although fund averages are currently much shorter).

Some fund managers compromise safety and assume greater market risk when they allow their fund's average maturity to extend longer than that of most other funds. As long as interest rates are stable or declining, these funds continue to pay higher yields. If market rates rise suddenly, however, their yields may not be competitive and shareholders might flood the funds with redemptions. Such an event may require a fund to sell its holdings at depressed prices, thereby jeopardizing the $1.00 share price.

Management Risk. Although the investing public feels that money market deposits are very safe, a few funds have encountered problems that should alter that perception. When interest rates climbed steadily in 1994, a number of large funds that were managed aggressively suffered their greatest losses ever. Several fund sponsors had to infuse their funds with private capital to avoid shareholder losses. One of the country's largest banks pumped $67 million into one of its funds.

In 1994, a small institutional money market fund that served several banks, not individual investors, failed to guarantee the $1.00 share price. After paying out only 94 cents per share, a 6 percent loss to shareholders, the fund was liquidated. Although this was an isolated situation, it illustrates what can happen. Should any large fund fail, a run to redeem shares might cause real chaos in the bond market and cause shareholder losses. Therefore, you must scrutinize your money market investment just as you would any other.

How to Limit Risk

Selecting a money market fund with the highest yield is definitely not prudent. If a fund's yield is higher than most, you can assume that the fund is taking more risks. It is not easy for you as an individual investor to analyze the integrity of money market funds because fund managers are not likely to divulge the risks they take in prospectuses and annual reports, although regulators may some day mandate such disclosure.

The safest funds are those that never invest in derivatives and invest only in government-guaranteed instruments with shorter maturities. Although the yields may be lower, they may be exempt from state and local taxation. Call the fund management to determine if they purchase derivatives.

The shorter a money market fund's average maturity and the higher the quality of its holdings, the safer it is; however, yields will probably be lower.

Note . . . When an institution advertises that it offers insurance on your account, it is not referring to the *market value* of your securities or money market fund shares. Insurance covers only security *certificates* against loss, theft, or damage.

CERTIFICATES OF DEPOSIT

A *certificate of deposit* (or time deposit) is a loan made to a bank or savings and loan that states a specified rate of interest to be paid for an agreed-upon period. Most CDs are issued in increments of $1,000 and pay interest semiannually.

Comparing Rates

Most investors shop around for a bank that offers favorable CD rates. Comparing CD rates used to be confusing, but new regulations imposed by the Federal Reserve require banks to compute and advertise CD rates uniformly using the *annual percentage yield*. The APY is calculated by compounding the stated rate of interest on the entire balance on a daily basis.

If you roll over a CD into another one when it matures, the interest rate could be adjusted higher or lower. (Most banks automatically reinvest matured CDs in retirement accounts, paying the adjusted rate, unless instructed otherwise before the stated deadline.)

Penalties for Early Withdrawal

If you liquidate a CD before it matures, you incur an early withdrawal penalty. When the interest earned amounts to less than the penalty, you end up owing the bank money, which is taken from your principal.

Before purchasing CDs, always ask what the penalty is for early withdrawal. Consider purchasing smaller increments so that the penalty is lower if you need to withdraw some of your money before the maturity date.

Note . . . Because Treasury bills are exempt from state and local taxes, they may offer higher after-tax yields than CDs with no greater risk. (See page 129 to calculate the *taxable equivalent yield*.)

Federal Deposit Insurance

When you purchase a CD, the bank invests your money in a variety of ways, seeking to earn more than it pays you for the use of your money. If the bank's investments are not sufficiently profitable, it could lose all or part of its depositors' money.

When a bank fails, it is taken over by either another bank or the FDIC. When a bank is taken over by another bank, the FDIC must pay the contracted rate of interest on deposits up to the date of the bank's closing, but the new bank may reduce the rate after the account is transferred.

When a bank is taken over by the FDIC, accounts are paid off with accrued interest. Some depositors, however, have earned less interest than originally promised while waiting for the FDIC to pay off their account. So far, the FDIC, which is funded by insurance premiums paid by banks and S&Ls, has been able to cover nearly all losses incurred to date, but there are misconceptions about how much the FDIC covers.

The FDIC insures individual deposits of $100,000, including accrued interest. This applies to all branches—you can no longer allocate deposits to separate branches or juggle names on accounts to get around this limitation.

Your retirement accounts, which are covered separately from all single ownership accounts, are added together and insured for no more than $100,000 per participant. Joint accounts are insured separately, but they are construed to be equally owned. For example, if husband and wife have three joint accounts totaling $300,000 in branches of the same bank, their insurance is limited to $200,000, $100,000 for each of them, leaving $100,000 uninsured.

Could Your Bank Fail?

Prior to the 1980s, the nation's banks suffered two periods of major failures. The first occurred in the 1890s, the second in the 1930s, both during severe economic depressions. During the Great Depression, more than 9,000 banks failed. Immediately following his inauguration in 1933, President Franklin Roosevelt closed all banks to prevent runs (mass depositor withdrawals). That year, Congress passed legislation that established the Federal Deposit Insurance Corporation. Initially, insurance coverage was limited to deposits of $5,000.

The reason for creating deposit insurance was not to eliminate bank failures, but to bolster the public's confidence in the banking system. The strategy worked, and deposits to

Some bank personnel have inadvertently advised depositors that accounts are insured separately. This is not true. Taking deposits that exceed $100,000 under false pretenses costs banks nothing, which gives them little incentive for educating their staff to give accurate information. If your bank fails, you no longer deal with the bank's management but with the FDIC. If your money is not covered according to its rules, you lose it. If you need more information, call the FDIC at (800) 934-3342 to request their pamphlet *Your Insured Deposits*.

Credit Unions

An estimated 60 million Americans save with credit unions that offer CDs in addition to a full range of financial services. Unfortunately, many credit unions are experiencing nearly the

banks and S&Ls grew dramatically as insurance coverage expanded to $40,000 per account.

Things started to go wrong in 1979 when the Federal Reserve raised interest rates to slow inflation. Banks and S&Ls were forced to pay higher rates than they earned on the home mortgages they held. The higher cost of money pressured profit margins, causing the "squeeze" that precipitated what came to be known as the *S&L crisis*.

To give them some relief, Congress began to allow banks and S&Ls to make investments other than home mortgages and it increased insurance coverage from $40,000 to $100,000. In the decade that followed, billions were loaned out for risky ventures that ultimately could not be retrieved. When collapsing oil prices caused a plunge in real estate values, many banks were left holding the bag.

identical problems of banks and S&Ls from aggressive, risky investing such as using significant leverage to increase rates to attract depositors. The General Accounting Office, a Congressional watchdog agency, reported that 40 corporate credit unions had total losses of about $600 million at the end of 1994. Some losses exceeded 40 percent of the institution's total capital.

In early 1995, regulators seized control of one of the nation's largest "umbrella" credit unions, which served approximately 500 individual credit unions. The institution had suffered losses of $100 million from derivative investments that soured when interest rates rose. Fortunately, deposits of $100,000 or less were insured. You must be just as cautious depositing money to credit unions as to other financial institutions.

Throughout the 1980s, banks and S&Ls failed in record numbers because of the economic environment, the depressed real estate market, lack of regulation and monitoring, reduced net worth requirements, aggressive accounting practices, and soured junk bond holdings. The government responded by changing accounting rules that allowed failing institutions to appear solvent on paper. Losses mounted when regulators failed to close insolvent institutions promptly, and by 1990, problem loans hit a post-World War II high.

Deposit insurance was (and still may be) the culprit for granting substandard institutions AAA ratings on deposits— rarely do bank customers question how their deposits are invested because they are insured. As long as they stood to profit from risking depositor money with seemingly nothing to lose, greedy bank and S&L managers failed to measure risk and reward responsibly. The appalling lack of oversight by federal

Banking Tips

- Never deposit more than $100,000 per person in a single FDIC-insured institution, including all branches. If accrued interest causes your account value to exceed $100,000, withdraw the excess immediately.

- Compare CD interest rates using the annual percentage yield but be suspicious of institutions paying the highest rates. Banks and S&Ls advertising higher yields probably assume greater risks in their investments, and these institutions may be next in line to fail. Depositors are not in a position to analyze a bank's solvency, and they are rarely warned about an impending bank failure. If bad news leaks out, depositors will withdraw funds as quickly

regulators and the deregulation of an already federally pampered industry intensified the severity of the crisis.

Although low interest rates have helped the banking industry recover, profits may not reflect more efficient operations or better management but rather the huge spreads between interest rates customers pay to borrow and the rates banks pay depositors. Higher interest rates might reverse the trend. Some bank portfolios are still loaded with unprofitable real estate, and the commercial real estate market in certain areas may not fully recover for several years. Even so, the crisis appears to have been resolved, at least on the surface.

Savvy investors generally find better vehicles for investing their savings than those offered by banks and S&Ls. However, if CDs are your choice, at least make sure that you adhere to FDIC limitations on insurance coverage.

as possible, causing a run that could be the finishing blow to a marginally healthy bank.

- Consider purchasing CDs in smaller increments to reduce the penalty if you need to withdraw funds prematurely.

- Consider purchasing CDs from brokerage firms. Brokered CDs do not have early withdrawal penalties because they trade like bonds—you do not have to sell the entire CD, but may sell off part of it. If interest rates decrease, you might sell a brokered CD for a profit. If interest rates rise, you may need to offer a discount to sell your CD; however, the discount may still be less than a withdrawal penalty.

Note . . . Surveys show that many bank customers incorrectly believe that mutual funds purchased at banks are FDIC insured. Mutual funds are *never* insured. Moreover, some bank customers are unaware that banks charge commissions for mutual fund shares. Regardless of where you invest, read the section on fees and risks in a mutual fund's prospectus.

Summary

As investments, money market funds and bank CDs rarely make sense because after taxes and inflation, the buying power of your money erodes. However, these funds are good for parking cash that you may need to spend in the next few months. Be suspicious of banks and money markets offering the highest rates, and invest only in money market funds with short average maturities and no derivatives.

Innternational investing was once considered exotic, an area where only the most sophisticated and adventurous investors feared to tread. With the increased globalization of market economies, however, foreign securities may make sense for any investment portfolio.

Chapter **11**

International Investing

*"No one would remember the Good
Samaritan if he'd only had good
intentions. He had money as well."*

Margaret Thatcher

According to the Securities Industry Association, U.S. investors purchased a record $128 billion of foreign securities in 1993, more than they bought during the entire decade of the 1980s. U.S. pension funds have been allocating a much greater portion of their portfolios to foreign assets. Their decision is only partly based on the desire to exploit better performing markets—they also seek to lower portfolio risk.

FOREIGN STOCKS

In the aftermath of World War II, the U.S. got a healthy start toward becoming the world's largest producer of goods. In the last 20 years, however, the U.S. has lost more than half its share of the global market.

Although U.S. public companies still represent about one third of the world's stock market capitalization, the U.S. has only nine of the world's 100 largest banks; 18 of the 50 largest insurance companies; seven of the 10 largest automobile companies; and only six of the 10 largest food companies.

Interdependence of world economies has strengthened nearly all markets worldwide. For example, the unification of Europe offers superior companies opportunities to dominate a larger market. Communications capability coupled with powerful new political changes promote much greater economic expansion. Former communist countries are adopting capitalistic principles, and the movement away from socialism will increase privatization around the world. With fewer isolated economies and the trend toward less government intervention of business, free-market activity is far greater today than ever before in history.

Performance

When it comes to performance, not only has the U.S. stock market failed to place first in more than a decade, it has placed among the top five performing markets only twice. In 1993, the U.S. market was one of the worst performers, while each market of four other countries delivered more than 68 percent to investors.

Top Performing Stock Markets

1983	Norway +82	Denmark +69	Australia +56	Sweden +50	Netherlands +38
1984	Hong Kong +47	Spain +42	Japan +17	Belgium +13	Netherlands +12
1985	Austria +177	Germany +136	Italy +134	Switzerland +107	France +83
1986	Spain +123	Italy +109	Japan +100	Belgium +81	France +79
1987	Japan +43	Spain +38	UK +35	Canada +15	Denmark +14
1988	Belgium +55	Denmark +54	Sweden +49	Norway +46	France +39
1989	Austria +105	Germany +47	Norway +46	Denmark +45	Sing/Malaysia +42
1990	UK +10	Hong Kong +9	Austria +7	Norway +1	Denmark 0
1991	Hong Kong +50	Australia +36	U.S. +31	Sing/Mal +25	N Zealand +21
1992	Hong Kong +32	Switzerland +18	U.S. +7	Sing/Mal +6	Netherlands +3
1993	Hong Kong +117	Finland +83	New Zealand +70	Sing/Mal +68	Switzerland +47
1994	Finland +52.47	Norway +24.07	Japan +21.62	Sweden +18.8	Ireland +14.5

Stock Indexes (including dividends):

	1986	1987	1988	1989	1990	1991	1992	1993	1994
U.S.*	18.6	5.2	16.5	31.4	−3.1	30.5	7.6	10.1	1.5
EAFE**	69.9	24.9	28.6	10.8	−23.2	12.5	−11.8	32.8	7.9

* S&P 500 Index
** Morgan Stanley Index for Europe, Australia, Far East

U.S. stocks appreciated 325 percent during the 1980s, but eight other markets performed even better. British stocks grew 431 percent and the markets of Japan and Sweden soared an astounding 1,100 percent. The total value of all U.S. stocks in 1973 was about $700 billion. By 1993, however, the market had grown 620 percent to $4.4 trillion. This seems impressive when taken alone, but when compared with some other markets it is not that staggering. In the same 20-year period, foreign stock capitalization increased more than 1,800 percent, from $400 billion to almost $7.2 trillion, nearly three times as fast as the U.S. market! And the trend shows no signs of reversing. Below are the global markets annualized returns from December 1974 through December 1994.

Major Global Stock Markets	
Market	**% Return in U.S. Currency**
Hong Kong	23.6
Netherlands	20.0
United Kingdom	19.8
Singapore	17.7
Japan	17.4
Sweden	16.9
Belgium	16.2
Switzerland	15.4
France	15.2
Australia	14.4
United States	14.1

Morgan Stanley Capital International

Diversification

The case for global investing goes beyond any economic forecast. Although all market economies are influenced by other markets, their business cycles rarely experience the same peaks and valleys. When the U.S. economy and stock market are stagnating, other markets could be booming. All markets correct from time to time, but there are almost always a few rising stock markets somewhere.

Furthermore, indexes around the world have been beating out the U.S. market. In 1987, the year of the U.S. market crash, U.S. stocks finished the year 5.24 percent higher (as measured by the S&P 500 index); however, the markets of Europe, Australia, and the Far East rose 24.9 percent (as measured by the MSCI EAFE, the global index).

Combining U.S. and foreign investments cushions against the impact of weak markets. When you consider performance, diversification, and the fact that U. S. citizens represent only 5 percent of the global population, a compelling case emerges for seeking investment opportunities beyond our borders.

Emerging Markets. The markets of Mexico, Brazil, Argentina, the Philippines, India, Chile, Turkey, Greece, Korea, Thailand, and Portugal have exploded, but many analysts believe their major growth will occur in the next decade. Approximately 85 percent of the world's population occupies the emerging market countries yet they represent only 12 percent of total global stock capitalization.

According to the World Bank, emerging markets are projected to grow 6.5 percent annually (versus 2.5 percent growth in the more mature markets) because of improved literacy rates, an expanding middle class, cheaper labor costs, growing export rates, and evolving market systems. Although it took 1,000 years for the living standard of these countries to double, in the next 20 years it could double again. (Between 1951 and 1973, Japan, which had been considered an emerging market, expanded by 2,933 percent.)

Pacific Rim. The markets of Japan, Hong Kong, South Korea, Taiwan, Thailand, Singapore, Indonesia, Malaysia, and Australia have doubled in the last decade and now represent nearly 40 percent of global market capital. This region, which now holds nearly half the world's population, is a $3 trillion market growing at $3 billion a week.

Risk

While the opportunity for profits abounds in foreign territory, the risks are significantly greater. Chief among them is *political risk*—leaders can be overthrown, governments toppled. The less developed the country, the greater the risk of political upheaval and government intervention in the marketplace.

Foreign companies are more difficult to analyze because they do not disclose the same financial data as U.S. corporations nor do they follow the same stringent accounting principles. Corporate financial analysis is often reported several months after the fact, and it may be less reliable because it is typically conducted in-house rather than by independent accountants.

Many foreign stock markets are far less evolved than ours and potentially more volatile. Transaction costs may be significantly higher, and there are also additional costs associated with currency conversion. Many foreign markets are less regulated for investor protection, and access to up-to-the-minute stock quotes is difficult.

When you purchase a foreign security, your dollars are converted to the foreign currency in which the security is based. Such currency conversion subjects your investment to *currency risk*, a risk generally not associated with fundamental issues, that comes from the rise and fall of the dollar compared with the currency in which your investment is based.

When the U.S. dollar rises against a foreign currency, your investment in that currency decreases in value. For example, in 1994, the fall of the Mexico peso more than wiped out the substantial gains that investors had enjoyed from owning Mexican stocks in prior months. Conversely, when the U.S. dollar falls against a foreign currency, investment denominated in that currency benefits. A few foreign currencies, such as those of Hong Kong and South Korea, tend to trade in a tight range with the U.S. dollar, but most provide either a hedge for a weak dollar or pose risk for a strong dollar.

To give you a sense of currency risk, the chart below compares annualized returns of emerging markets from December 1987 through December 1994 in local currency versus U.S. dollars.

	Local Currency	**U.S. Dollars**
Brazil	1474.18	32.96
Argentina	318.26	41.58
Turkey	70.36	1.32
Mexico	55.14	38.33
Chile	49.55	38.19
Indonesia	30.07	24.85
Philippines	29.59	26.67
Thailand	27.85	27.73
Greece	22.18	11.43
Malaysia	19.21	18.09
Taiwan	17.04	18.43
Jordan	9.63	−1.31

American Depository Receipts

Stocks of more than 1,300 foreign companies can be purchased as *American Depository Receipts*, or ADRs, negotiable receipts issued by U.S. banks representing actual shares held in their custody or a foreign custodian bank. The primary advantage of ADRs is the reduced hassle and expense associated with local foreign shares called *ordinary* shares.

ADRs trade like U.S. shares with the same dividend payment schedules, and they may be custodied at U.S. brokerage firms or held in certificate form. In contrast, some firms charge more than $200 to issue certificates for ordinary shares. When ADRs are listed on U.S. exchanges, the companies must provide financial reports in the same form as U.S. public companies. Although they trade in U.S. dollars, ADRs are still subject to currency risk.

Foreign Stock Mutual Funds

Analyzing foreign companies and markets can be difficult, but individual investors can purchase shares in mutual funds to take advantage of both professional management and diversification. An *international* mutual fund invests exclusively in foreign companies; a *global* fund can invest anywhere in the world, including the U.S.

An *emerging markets* fund focuses on less-developed, faster growing markets. *Pacific* funds invest exclusively in Pacific Rim countries. Single-country funds have a major drawback because the managers do not have the option to invest elsewhere when the outlook for that market is negative.

Indexes

Dow Jones World Stock Index. In 1993, Dow Jones & Company introduced a world stock index that now includes about 3,000 foreign companies in 28 markets located in three geographic regions—Pacific Rim, Europe, and the Americas. Each country's index is calculated in both its own currency and the U.S. dollar.

The index categorizes within nine broad sectors such as basic materials, utilities, consumer, and financial. You can assess the political, economic, and financial forces affecting the global markets, and also gauge how an individual issue has performed against its peers on a global, regional, or national basis. For example, you can look at the auto manufacturing industry in just the U.S., in Europe, the Far East, or around the world.

MSCI EAFE. The Morgan Stanley Capital International index represents 20 markets located in Europe, Australia, Asia, and the Far East. It is used as a benchmark to compare *international* equity portfolios.

MSCI World. The Morgan Stanley Capital International index includes the EAFE markets as well as the U.S. and Canada. It is used as a benchmark to compare *global* equity portfolios.

Foreign Stock Exchanges and Indexes

Exchange	Index
Tokyo	Nikkei Average
London	FT 100-Share
Frankfurt	DAX
Paris	CAC-40
Toronto	300 Composite
Brussels	Bel 20
Zurich	Swiss Market
Milan	MIBtel
Amsterdam	ANP-CBS General
Stockholm	Affarsvariden
Australia	All Ordinaries
Hong Kong	Hang Seng
Singapore	Straits Times
Johannesburg	J'burg Gold
Taiwan	D J Equity Mkt
Madrid	General Index
Mexico	I.P.C.

FOREIGN BONDS

In 1970, bonds denominated in U.S. dollars represented 65 percent of all bonds traded worldwide, but today they account for less than 44 percent. Whether investors can profit more from purchasing foreign bonds than U.S. bonds depends on yields and currency fluctuations.

Foreign entities issue two basic types of bonds: *dollar-denominated* and *nondollar-denominated*. If the primary trading market is the U.S., they are called *Yankee bonds*; *Eurobonds* trade mostly outside the U.S.

Foreign bonds are traded over-the-counter with brokers handling currency conversions as part of the transactions. They are more expensive to trade than U.S. bonds because of higher markups, larger spreads between buy and sell prices, and currency conversion.

Risk

In addition to credit risk and market risk, foreign bonds are subject to currency risk. Although some foreign bonds offer higher yields than U.S. bonds, the extra returns for U.S. investors could easily be wiped out by falling currencies.

Many mutual funds have been created to make it easier to participate in higher yielding foreign bonds. Some fund managers attempt to protect the U.S. dollar value of fund shares by engaging in various hedging techniques to "insure" their portfolios against currency losses. To do this, the manager uses a part of the fund's income, which reduces the dividends. Because hedging currency risk is expensive, mutual fund managers may opt to assume the risk rather than reduce fund yields.

During the European currency crisis in 1992, a number of foreign bond funds lost market value because they were not adequately hedged. While some funds generated total returns of 7 percent or more in local foreign currencies, they sustained losses of 10 percent in U.S. dollar terms. In 1994, many foreign bond funds suffered the consequences of the emerging markets' debt crisis. Certain short-term funds had been touted as low risk, but sudden currency shifts extracted an unfortunate toll on share prices which caused shareholder losses.

With the cost of hedging and management fees, the potential for earning more than you could with U.S. bonds is greatly diminished. Many analysts today suggest that foreign bond investing makes little sense—the limited potential for higher yields simply cannot compensate for the risks.

"For better or for worse, since the collapse of the Bretton Woods international monetary order, currency traders provide the only financial discipline the world knows."

The Vandals Crown; How Rebel Currency
Traders Overthrew the World's Central Banks.
Gregory J. Millman

CURRENCY TRADING

Currency markets, not central banks and finance ministries, decide currency-exchange rates. The globalization of trade and finance has spawned highly computerized communications networks that interconnect currency traders 24 hours a day. Traders tend to make instant judgments about fact and rumor, and even the slightest hint of rising inflation or political instability may spur the trading that moves currency markets. Currency trading volume exceeds $200 trillion a year—more than 10 times the value of the entire annual production of the Western industrialized nations.

A currency is evaluated in the global marketplace in much the same way a company is evaluated—on the nation's ability and willingness to produce and pay its bills. Factors that strengthen a nation's currency are

- stable government,
- credible political leadership,
- sound fiscal and monetary policies,
- low inflation rate,
- noninflationary economic growth,
- attractive interest rates, and
- trade surplus.

Booming emerging markets are extremely vulnerable to currency devaluation that results from inflationary pressures. The amazing 1,117 percent increase in Brazil's markets in 1992 was actually only a 5 percent increase in terms of the U.S. dollar because of Brazil's extremely weak currency, a consequence of its high inflation.

The currency of one country may be strong against the currency of another but weak against that of a third. Because an appreciating currency converts into more units of a foreign currency than it did previously, it can purchase more foreign goods and services. Conversely, a depreciating or cheaper currency converts into fewer units of a foreign currency, causing price increases for imported goods. However, a cheaper currency may improve a nation's trade balance because it stimulates foreign sales of its exports.

As an individual investor, protecting the value of your assets from currency risk (hedging) is impractical, but you should understand how currency fluctuations impact your investments outside U.S. borders so that you can diversify your foreign holdings.

Tax Implications

Although most foreign countries do not impose capital gains taxes on profits, they do tax stock dividends and bond interest payments, and withhold a percentage of each payment. U.S. investors incur taxes on income and gains from all securities, both foreign and domestic, and may be able to take tax credits for foreign taxes paid.

Just as you wouldn't place all your money in a single industry or company, it may not be prudent to invest in only one country. The investment environment today is a global one, offering investors ultimate diversification for their savings. The array of global markets permits investors to exploit value wherever it may be found. By investing globally, you can move money into markets where high interest rates and recessions have taken a toll and stock prices are cheap. Whether you are looking for fast-growing companies or great values in established companies, you may find more of what you seek by expanding your investment horizons globally.

*I*f you had a crystal ball that revealed exactly where rates of inflation and interest were headed, you could make very profitable investment decisions. In fact, forming such judgments constitutes the most significant activity of many professional investors. Inflation and interest rates are sure to affect your financial life, and therefore, no study of investing would be complete without exploring their roles.

Chapter **12**

Inflation and Interest Rates

"A nickel ain't worth a dime anymore."

Yogi Berra

Money is a medium of exchange that is measured by what it can purchase, and its value has been shrinking rather steadily for more than a half century. This event, which we call *inflation*, influences the cost of borrowing money, or *interest*. As all successful investors know,

Rates of interest and inflation, which cannot be separated, influence the return on any investment.

INFLATION

While we experience inflation simply as rising prices, it is more accurately a monetary event caused by a population having too many dollars to purchase a finite supply of goods and services. High inflation can wreak economic havoc: it has been responsible for ravaging the economies of many nations, undermining the political structure and causing the overthrow of leaders.

The mere anticipation of higher inflation can affect you personally in a number of ways, both long and short term. For example, currency traders might sell U.S. dollars if they expect inflation to rise. This raises prices on any imported products that you purchase. A rise in inflation can push interest rates higher, which might increase your monthly mortgage payment. Inflation generates higher tax revenues to government coffers. Because of ''bracket creep,'' as our incomes rise, we pay higher taxes, although we may be no richer. In the long term, inflation erodes the buying power of your savings, which might leave you with insufficient funds to maintain a desired standard of living when you retire.

Effects of Inflation on Investment

You can make better investment decisions once you understand and appreciate how inflation can impact an investment favorably or erode its market value. In some cases, inflation is a double-edged sword, as it creates both beneficial and detrimental consequences.

Real Estate and Hard Assets. An investment that is expected to increase in value in line with inflation is called an *inflation hedge*. Traditionally, assets such as real estate, commodities, precious metals, fine art, and collectibles have been considered inflation hedges, but the market value of many such assets has failed to keep pace with the rate of inflation in recent years.

The higher interest rates caused by higher inflation make real estate more expensive to purchase because it is typically bought with borrowed funds. Conversely, lower rates stimulate the real estate market by making it less expensive to purchase and own. Nevertheless, during some cycles, inflation has enhanced the value of real estate as a hard asset inflation hedge.

Common Stocks. Lower inflation (and the accompanying low interest rates) encourages higher stock prices because investors are less likely to accept the low returns of bonds and CDs. Furthermore, lower interest rates tend to stimulate economic growth and corporate profits which support higher stock prices.

The higher interest rates from rising inflation hurt stocks in the short term because investors tend to favor higher yielding bonds and CDs, effectively eroding the demand for stocks. Also, high rates make it harder for businesses to profit. Over the long term, however, inflation can help stocks because it forces companies to raise prices, which proportionately increases corporate revenues and profits on which the stock price is based. In fact, quality common stocks have proved to be a very reliable hedge against normal inflation.

Bonds. Of all investments, bonds are the most acutely sensitive to inflation because of its impact on interest rates and buying power: Declining interest rates cause bond prices to rise; rising interest rates cause bond prices to fall.

Rising inflation hurts bonds because, not only does it cause higher interest rates that reduce a bond's market value, inflation also erodes the buying power of a bond's interest payments and the proceeds received when the bond matures. Unless a bond's yield exceeds the inflation rate and the taxes due on the interest earned, the bondholder secures no *real* return.

Effects of Inflation on Savings

Even when it is managed judiciously by the government, we still have inflation, however low it might be. Careful financial planning requires that you anticipate inflation because, over time, it takes a significant toll on even the most prudent investments. Although you may believe your savings and investments are on track, if you are not factoring in inflation, you could be way off your goal when you retire.

The dollar amount you need today to sustain your desired living standard could more than double if you retire in 15

Table 12-1. Effect of Inflation on Savings								
	Inflation Rate							
Years	3%	4%	5%	6%	7%	8%	9%	10%
5	1.16	1.22	1.28	1.34	1.40	1.47	1.54	1.61
10	1.34	1.48	1.63	1.79	1.97	2.16	2.37	2.59
15	1.56	1.80	2.08	2.40	2.76	3.17	3.64	4.18
20	1.81	2.19	2.65	3.21	3.87	4.66	5.60	6.73

Example: If inflation averages 5% for 10 years, multiply your present income by a factor of 1.63.

years, or triple if you retire in 25 years. For example, as Table 12-1 illustrates, if inflation averages 4 percent, in 10 years you will need 48 percent more income just to keep pace with the buying power of today's dollars—$44,400 to purchase what $30,000 buys today ($30,000 x 1.48).

Inflation Terms

Deflation. *Deflation* is a decrease in the prices of goods, services, and hard assets. During deflationary cycles, cash becomes "king" because high unemployment and weak demand for goods and services generally stabilize or increase a currency's buying power.

While it is not uncommon for one or two commodities to periodically experience price declines, widespread deflation is rare. The only period in this century when the U.S. suffered general deflation was during the Great Depression in the 1930s.

Economists generally agree that when debt is incurred for current consumption rather than for long-term investment to expand the creation of goods and services, higher inflation can result over the short term. Over prolonged periods, however, high debt ratios may eventually crush the economy and lead to a collapse of price structure—deflation.

Although a sluggish economy causes hard times for many people, it is the best possible scenario for government bonds, which hedge deflation better than any other investment. As demand for goods and services decline, so do borrowing and interest rates, resulting in higher bond prices.

Disinflation. A declining rate of inflation is referred to as *disinflation*, a condition prevalent in the U.S. throughout the 1980s.

Hyperinflation. When accelerating rates of inflation are so severe that people try to get rid of their currency before its value plummets even further, the condition is one of *hyperinflation*. In Germany in the 1920s, a wheelbarrow full of cash was required to buy a small bag of groceries. Brazil has experienced hyperinflation in more recent times.

Stagflation. Decreased demand for goods and services in a normal business cycle generally lowers the inflation rate, but sometimes prices rise or remain relatively high despite a sluggish economy. Such *stagflation* may be the result of shortages or inefficient productivity of goods. The U.S. experienced stagflation in the 1970s when gasoline shortages were prevalent. Russia has been experiencing stagflation—its economy is depressed but the prices of goods continue to rise.

Economic Indicators

The following indexes gauge rates of inflation/deflation:

The Commodities Research Bureau Index. The CRB futures index, based on prices of 22 different unprocessed commodities, tracks inflation at the most basic level. The CRB index may have inherent distortions. For example, it is dominated by food prices, which often say more about the weather than about demand.

The Federal Reserve Board looks at many indicators, including the CRB, for a succinct statement of the effects of its monetary policies. When the CRB remains relatively stable, it may indicate that the supply of credit is adequate to maintain economic growth without creating undue inflationary pressure. If the CRB index rises significantly, the Fed may tighten credit to slow the economy.

Consumer Price Index. Researched and compiled by the U.S. Bureau of Labor Statistics, the CPI measures price levels for food, housing, transportation, medical care, clothing, entertainment, and services to track the average U.S. citizen's cost of living. Table 12-2 tracks the CPI index from 1987 to 1994.

Table 12-2. The Consumer Price Index		
Year	CPI Index	Annual Change %
1987	115.4	4.4
1988	120.5	4.4
1989	126.1	4.6
1990	133.8	6.1
1991	137.9	3.1
1992	141.9	2.9
1993	145.8	2.7
1994	149.7	2.7

The Producer Price Index. The PPI tracks changes in wholesale price levels of raw materials.

Note . . . The cost of wheat is part of the CRB, the cost of wheat flour is part of the PPI, and the cost of a loaf of bread is part of the CPI. The CPI and the PPI are reported monthly in *The Wall Street Journal* when the figures are released by the government; the CRB is reported daily in the commodities section.

Consumer Confidence Index. The government measures consumer attitudes toward the job market, the economy, and their personal financial situations. The CCI is considered an important indicator because consumers account for two thirds of economic activity, and their savings, spending, and borrowing practices affect interest-rate levels.

Other Economic Indicators. Professional investors also monitor indicators such as retail sales, housing starts, orders for durable goods, unemployment, oil prices, industrial production, inventories, to name a few.

"The stock market opened lower this morning responding to the drop of the dollar, but rallied when Germany lowered its prime rate. By noon, traders realized that higher interest rates would cause the economy to slow and stock prices fell back, but by the close, prices soared when the dollar traded higher . . ."

"The monetary climate—primarily the trend in interest rates and Federal Reserve policy—is the dominant factor in determining the stock market's major direction."

Winning on Wall Street
Martin Zweig

INTEREST RATES

Over the years, I have known individuals who resisted buying stocks and bonds because they believed interest rates would rise. They based their projections solely on the fact that interest rates had been higher once and were therefore likely to rise again. Regrettably, they missed the bull market in stocks and bonds entirely, and many continue to park their cash in money market funds and CDs that rarely keep pace with inflation. While they did not lose money, their money lost buying power, which amounts to the same thing.

No one can always accurately forecast the direction of interest rates, not even the most focused economists—there are far too many variables. Nevertheless, you should be able to form practical "guess-timates" once you understand the key components that govern interest-rate levels: inflation expectations, the interaction of supply and demand for capital, and the role of the Federal Reserve Bank.

Inflation Expectations

When you lend out your money, its buying power is diminished by the inflation rate. Your *real* return is the rate of interest earned minus the inflation rate. For example, if you lend $10,000 at a rate of 8 percent for five years, and the inflation rate averages 5 percent, your real return is roughly 3 percent annually because the buying power of your original $10,000 principal is diminished by 5 percent.

When lenders expect higher inflation, which is generally more prevalent during times of economic expansion, they require higher rates of return to compensate for the potential loss of buying power. Conversely, when inflation is expected to remain low or decline (during periods of economic slack, for example), lenders charge less for the use of their money. Inflation expectations depend on the prospects for the economy, the outlook for the U.S. dollar, and recent inflation experience, to name a few.

Capital Supplies versus Demand

Competition for available capital influences the cost of borrowing. The supply of capital comes from private and corporate savings, government-created credit, and foreign inflows. Demand is created by the spending and borrowing of federal and municipal governments, corporations, and consumers. When borrowers and spenders exhibit less need for capital, interest rates tend to drop; when the competition for capital increases, interest rates rise.

When the rate at which the citizenry saves money does not keep pace with the demand for borrowing, interest rates tend to rise. The more we save, the more we invest in fixed-income investments such as bonds, which tends to raise their prices and lower their yields. With "baby boomers" entering their high savings years, analysts project a rise in the nation's savings rate, which could help keep interest rates relatively low (compared with historical interest-rate cycles).

U.S. Government. For many years, the U.S. government has not generated sufficient tax revenues to cover what it spends. The shortfall is called a *deficit*. As budget deficits rise, the government is forced to borrow. The more it borrows, the higher the interest rates it might pay because it competes with the corporate and private sectors for the nation's finite savings supply.

Corporations. When the economic outlook is negative, businesses borrow less. This reduces competition for available funds and tends to lower interest rates. Conversely, businesses are more inclined to borrow for expansion when the outlook is positive, which increases competition for capital and tends to push interest rates higher.

Consumer. The spending of U.S. citizens greatly influences economic activity as well as the demand for capital. When the population feels pressured financially or is worried about employment, it spends and borrows less. The reduced demand for capital typically lowers interest rates. Conversely, when consumers increase their spending and borrowing levels, the economy strengthens, causing higher rates of inflation and interest.

Market Competition. As the markets compete for investor dollars, yields of certain core investments influence the returns of other investments. For example, when Treasury bond yields rise, banks and businesses are forced to pay even higher rates to attract depositors and lenders because they must compete with the government's status as the most creditworthy borrower.

The stock and bond markets are always competing for your money. During the 1970s, for example, investors sold their stocks to buy higher yielding bonds. As economies become more closely linked, interest rates of some countries influence rates of other countries.

Role of the Federal Reserve Bank

Two major concerns of U.S. citizens are employment and the buying power of their money. The problem is that when jobs are plentiful, inflation tends to rise, eroding the dollar's buying power. In fact, most economists believe that full employment for all citizens is possible only during periods of rising inflation. Although the government issues policies to keep inflation in check and the economy growing to provide jobs, it's a difficult balancing act. The government assigns the task of steering the economy to the Federal Reserve Bank.

Established by Congress in 1913, the Federal Reserve Bank (aka the "Fed") regulates the U.S. banking system, acting as agent of the U.S. Treasury Department in a totally independent capacity. Attuned to the delicate balance of the economy, the Fed exercises its powers by intervening with countercyclical policies, endeavoring to keep the economy growing at an optimal pace without unacceptable inflation.

The Federal Reserve influences economic activity by creating an elastic supply of credit for consumers and businesses to spend. The aggregate of credit or liquidity in the system, the *money supply*, includes funds on deposit in banks and money market funds. Over the years, various measurements have been used to define liquidity in the financial system. However, with so much money pouring into mutual funds and with several newer, alternative methods of obtaining credit, not counted as part of the money supply aggregate, traditional measurement may be less reliable.

Note . . . Do not confuse money supply with the amount of bills printed and coins minted. Currency constitutes only a fraction of the total money supply.

The Fed considers the ideal rate of economic growth to be one that is consistent with the economy's long-term potential to grow—faster growth may cause an unacceptable rate of inflation and slower growth may lead to higher unemployment.

> *As long as the Fed maintains money-supply growth at a pace that can be absorbed by the demand for goods and services, inflation does not generally result.*

To determine the health of the economy, the Fed measures the increase or decrease in the *gross domestic product*, the dollar value of goods and services produced in the U.S. (GDP is considered a more accurate measure of the country's output than the *gross national product*, because it does not include goods produced by U.S. companies in other countries.)

When the economy threatens to overheat during periods of accelerated growth, inflation concerns may prompt the Fed to take a preemptive strike to slow the economy to a soft landing, taking care to avert a recession, which would increase unemployment. (As a rule of thumb, the economy is considered to be in recession when GDP growth drops to zero or below for two consecutive quarters.) Conversely, when a sluggish economy threatens to lapse into recession, the Fed acts to stimulate the economy by lowering interest rates.

The Fed's three chief strategies for influencing the economy, short-term interest rates, and ultimately the value of your money are

- decreasing or increasing reserve requirements for the nation's banks;
- raising or lowering the discount rate; and
- manipulating the money supply and the *federal funds rate* through open market securities transactions.

Bank Reserves. The Fed influences interest rates by changing the reserve ratio member banks are required to hold against deposits. When the Fed decreases reserve requirements, banks have more money to lend and, with sufficient loan demand, the economy expands. Money is "created" as commercial banks loan it out because, once borrowed, it "expands"—each dollar in the system may change hands a number of times during the year. (In recent years, the Fed has not targeted bank reserves as a means of controlling interest rates. After Chairman Paul Volcker was appointed in 1979, the focus switched to manipulation of the federal funds rate.)

Discount Rate. The Fed controls short-term interest rates when it adjusts the *discount rate*, the interest rate the Fed charges member banks when it lends them capital to replenish reserves. Banks in turn must raise or lower the rates they charge their customers. (In recent times, banks rarely borrowed from the Federal Reserve Bank because lower rates were available elsewhere.)

Open Market Operations. The federal funds rate, the benchmark for short-term interest rates in the U.S., is the rate commercial banks charge other banks for overnight use of their funds. The Fed does not mandate the federal funds rate, but rather manipulates it in the desired direction by buying or selling Treasury securities in the open market.

Expanding business activity increases the demand for money and puts pressure on bank reserves. To slow the economy by making borrowing more expensive and more difficult, the Fed *sells* Treasury securities to drain money from the system ("tighten" credit).

Conversely, when economic activity slackens, loan demand dries up. To stimulate the economy, the Fed *buys* Treasury securities from the private sector in the open market. The sale proceeds generally end up in banks, expanding their reserves and allowing them to lend out more money ("loosen" credit). If and when bank customers borrow and spend the money, the activity stimulates the economy.

> *"You mean to tell me that the success*
> *of the program and my reelection hinges*
> *on the Federal Reserve and a bunch of*
> *f----- bond traders?"*
>
> The Agenda: Inside the Clinton White House
> Bob Woodward

THE BOND TRADERS

Years ago, the Fed routinely accommodated the Congress' fiscal agenda with little concern for the reaction of the financial markets. The large institutional holders and traders of bonds, who dominate the credit markets, expect the Fed to act responsibly. Indeed, these "vigilantes" have become so sophisticated that they react to even the slightest suspicion of Fed action that might depress bond prices.

No one gets nervous when the Fed allows the money supply to expand to accommodate the growth of goods and services; however, any Fed move deemed inflationary might prompt traders to sell bonds, which results in higher interest rates. So, despite its intention to lower interest rates, a Fed directive could backfire!

When the Treasury sells securities to the public to finance the government, it removes money from the system and gives it to the government to spend. This does not create additional purchasing power but merely transfers it from one sector to another.

In the 1970s, however, the Fed simply *credited* the Treasury's account with money to spend by increasing the Fed's holdings of Treasury securities without requiring any payment. Purchasing power was not transferred but was actually *created* with no offsetting increase in goods or services. Such *monetizing* of government debt was responsible for the high inflation prevalent in the 1970s.

Unlike the central banks of fiscally irresponsible countries, the Fed has resisted monetizing for many years. It is probably safe to assume that our market disciplines, to a large degree, force the Fed to refrain from taking any action that would create havoc in the credit markets.

Summary

An understanding of the significance of interest rates and inflation is vital to profitable investing, not because it increases your profits so much as it helps you avoid losses and erosion of buying power. Your challenge is to accumulate wealth by selecting investments that outpace inflation.

Who hasn't been tantalized by the thought of getting rich quickly and effortlessly? Indeed, it is this temptation that has led even sophisticated investors into ruinous financial situations. Yet every good investment involves a certain amount of risk. The chances are that at some point in your financial life you will be approached by someone soliciting your investment, so you must be able to tell the difference between prudent risk and pure folly.

Chapter **13**

Risk or Rip-Off?

"Be not penny-wise; riches have wings; sometimes they fly away of themselves, and sometimes they must be set flying to bring in more."

Francis Bacon

RISK

One investment "fact of life" that all successful investors recognize is:

You cannot operate in the financial arena without encountering risk.

"Riskless investment" is an oxymoron to be forever banned from your vocabulary. The good news is that, instead of buying into a dream (or a nightmare), you can learn how to assume investment risk intelligently.

Although investments such as CDs and Treasury bills may appear to be free of risk, these investments—which typically yield little more than the rates of inflation—generally deliver a negative return after inflation and taxes take their toll. Thus, with the certainty of inflation, you must assume prudent investment risk just to offset a potential loss of buying power.

By assuming or retaining all the risk of an investment, you are positioned to capture the greatest reward. The stock market is a perfect example of the risk/reward phenomenon. I have been asked so many times, "Isn't investing in stocks just gambling?" Whether it is a gamble or not depends on the quality of the information with which you operate. As Michael Milken put it, "Risk is a function of knowledge." One of the most astute investors, financier John Pierpont Morgan, said, "I never gamble." Perhaps Morgan was so sure of his ability to gather accurate information that he believed he left nothing to chance.

Investor projections are often based on historical perspective. For example, if a company's earnings have been growing steadily for several years and it is maintaining its franchise or market share with little or no apparent threat to its customer base, purchasing the company's stock could be profitable. On the other hand, sometimes a company has no profit history but has developed new technology that would fulfill a public need, a speculation more difficult to analyze.

As an investor, you live the "what if" life. What if interest rates rise? What if rates decline? What if I need my money back quickly? What if another company's technology is superior?

Successful investors not only recognize that there is no financial reward without risk, they accept the possibility that risk may be lowest when others see it as greatest—and vice versa. It's no coincidence that individuals who make the greatest efforts to scrutinize their investment options achieve the greatest returns. To succeed in the investment arena, you must operate with the most accurate and timely data possible, or hire those who do.

How To Reduce Risk

Prudent investing generally requires that you take steps to reduce risk with the help of proven strategies.

Diversification. The best way to reduce risk is to diversify your investment portfolio's holdings. Diversification encourages a variety of asset classes such as stocks, bonds, funds, money markets, and real estate. Diversification lessens the impact of investments that lose money because the losses are offset by gains in other investments. Do not however, diversify to the point at which you do not have the time to effectively manage your portfolio.

An *equity* mutual fund may be well-diversified if it holds shares in many public companies spread among several industries. A *balanced* mutual fund with both stocks and bonds is further diversified. For ultimate diversification, you can participate in several markets worldwide.

Asset Allocation/Market Timing. You can reduce the risk in your portfolio by investing in certain asset classes at propitious times. Although asset-allocation decisions may be more difficult to make than diversification decisions, they have greater impact on your portfolio's performance.

To decide what percentage of your portfolio to allocate to each asset class at any given time, you will have to pay close attention to market indicators and cycles. When stocks are expected to outperform bonds, allocation may call for 60 percent stocks, 30 percent bonds, and 10 percent money markets or cash.

Many analysts and financial firms publish asset-allocation recommendations for their customers based on their prognosis of the overall investment environment, but you should also base your portfolio's allocation on your age, income, risk tolerance, liquidity needs, and investment goals.

Dollar-Cost Averaging. Probably the most practical way to reduce investment risk is through *dollar-cost averaging*. By consistently investing the same dollar amount, you buy more shares when prices are low and fewer shares when prices are high. The strategy not only results in lower average share prices, it also protects you from investing all your money at the worst possible time, like just before a severe market correction.

Dollar-cost averaging works optimally with mutual fund shares, but you can also apply it to the purchase of common stock. For example, you may consistently invest retirement plan contributions in shares of a carefully selected company each year. Dollar-cost averaging disciplines you to invest consistently, regardless of the investment climate—a proven wealth-building practice.

Constant-Dollar Plan. A defensive technique, the *constant-dollar plan*, is a strategy that forces you to buy when prices are cheaper and sell when they are higher. If a stock portfolio is valued at $100,000, each month that its value dips below that amount, you invest enough cash to bring the level back up to $100,000. If the level rises to $110,000, you sell enough shares to bring the level back to $100,000. This conservative strategy takes advantage of lower prices and helps protect profits.

How To Transfer Risk

There are ways to transfer risk to eliminate it entirely. One is to purchase life or disability insurance whereby you transfer financial risk to an insurance company in exchange for paying a premium. You can transfer the risk of owning stock by buying put options. Entire stock and bond portfolios may be protected with option contracts.

Transferring risk may be the most important financial decision you can make. If you are the only wage earner in your family, your family's economic survival may depend on your investment in a life insurance policy.

How To Measure Risk

Market risk refers to the fluctuation of an investment's price volatility or potential loss in market value at the time you need to liquidate. Wall Street has found a way to actually measure the risk of certain investments in terms of price volatility.

Alpha. With this measure, you can gauge how much better an investment or portfolio performs, given its risk. Alpha is the return over and above the market average, as measured by the S&P 500 index. An alpha of "0" means you are being adequately compensated for risk taken; a higher number reflects better than expected performance.

Beta. With this measure, you can gauge a security's price volatility relative to the overall market. Theoretically, a portfolio or security with a beta of 1.00 moves in line with the S&P 500 index. A beta higher than 1.00 denotes greater price volatility than the overall market; a beta lower than 1.00 denotes lower volatility than the market. A beta of 1.3, for example, reflects volatility 30 percent greater than the market; a beta of .94 is 6 percent lower volatility than the market. A high beta may be good during a rising market because it implies higher returns, but when the market is falling, a high beta implies greater potential for losses.

The safer an investment, the lower your potential return; the greater your risk, the higher your potential return.

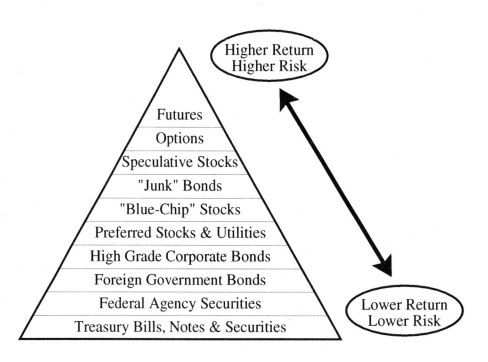

Types of Risk

Market Risk	An asset may lose market value because of economic and other swings in the overall market or conditions affecting the asset itself.
Credit Risk	The borrower may fail to repay principal.
Inflation Risk	The currency in which an asset is based may lose purchasing power.
Liquidity Risk	An asset may lose market value because it is difficult to sell. Examples are limited partnerships and certain junk bonds.
Interest-Rate Risk	The market value of a fixed-income investment moves opposite to market interest rates.
Reinvestment Risk	When reinvesting a bond's principal and interest proceeds, you might not get as high a rate because market interest rates have declined.
Currency Risk	An asset denominated in foreign currency may lose value when the U.S. dollar strengthens.
Manager/Adviser Risk	You might incur a financial loss because of mismanagement on the part of the individual or institution engaged to select and/or oversee your investment.

RIPOFF

Financially illiterate people are magnets for con artists, and countless investment scams flourish amid financially gullible populations. If you have money, you may be a target and, if you lack investment knowledge, you are vulnerable.

There are many types of investment fraud. One type, the *Ponzi scheme*, may or may not involve any legitimate underlying investment. The scheme works because the promoter starts paying a high return to investors, whose faith grows stronger with each payment. Although the enterprise fails to generate any profits or income, the promoter takes money from new investors to pay prior investors, pocketing what money he can.

Charles Ponzi was an immigrant from Italy, who came to the U.S. in 1903 at age 21. He traveled about the U.S. and Canada, working mostly odd jobs, before settling in Boston. Ponzi discovered that some international postal-reply coupons that enabled correspondents to prepay return postage for letters sent abroad could be redeemed in the U.S. for significantly more than their cost, because of variances in currency-exchange rates. With the pretense of investing in the coupons, he presented this as an investment opportunity to unsuspecting victims.

Here's how the scheme worked: Ponzi borrowed money by writing promissory notes for $10, redeemable in 90 days, contracting to pay investors 50 percent interest (more than 200 percent annually). To expand his scheme, he paid his agents 10 percent commission for brokering the notes. Ponzi repaid the loans with new money coming in from subsequent investors who swallowed the story about his postal-coupon business.

Initially, Ponzi preyed on only a few uneducated Italian immigrants but, as these investors were repaid their loans with outrageously high interest, many more were lured into the scheme. Abetted by press coverage throughout New England, it wasn't long before Ponzi was taking in thousands of dollars each day. Within months, more than 30,000 investors, including many successful, reputable professionals, had funded Ponzi's scheme to the tune of more than $15 million.

Despite scrutiny by postal authorities, the state's attorney general, and the Boston police, no irregularities were found. Many interpreted the lack of indictment as proof that the operation was legitimate. When a reputable credit-analysis firm pronounced his operation financially sound, Ponzi was hailed a hero.

A reporter for the *Boston Post* suspected the truth—Ponzi was paying the interest solely from funds taken in from investors. The *Post* suggested that Ponzi's "business" of handling international postal-reply coupons could not possibly be as profitable as his operation indicated. It was odd, the editorials pointed out, that Ponzi deposited his money in a bank where it earned only 5 percent while he paid out much higher rates of return. Ponzi sued the *Post* for libel.

Not until the *Post* revealed that Ponzi had been convicted of forgery in Canada, for which he had served two years in jail, did the financial manipulation finally end. Ironically, many investors were furious with authorities for killing their "golden goose" when Ponzi was convicted and sent to prison. He was released in 1934 at the age of 52 and deported to Italy.

Modern Scams

The practice of "robbing Peter to pay Paul" has flourished ever since Ponzi's remarkable enterprise, and such scams are likely to continue as long as there are investors who believe they can make a quick buck with little or no risk.

Swindlers who appear legitimate operate in the same places you find legitimate investment offerings. The elderly are favorite targets because they tend to have the most available cash. With interest rates low, as they have been recently, investors are more willing to listen to pitches about all sorts of higher yielding opportunities.

Scam artists promote their wares mostly via the telephone, but many have raised millions through seminars and infomercials. It has become increasingly difficult to differentiate between infomercials and objective advice. Many solicitations are presented within a talk-show format, which gives them more credence because listeners assume that regulators would not allow falsehoods to air.

Television. In March 1993, a scam advertised to investors on a financial cable-TV station took California investors for $90 million. Through a securities underwriting that paid brokers 8 percent commission, a real estate developer raised the money to build homes on vacant desert, promising investors a 15 percent annual return to start paying immediately. Prospective investors, mostly elderly and retired people, were escorted by the developer on a tour of a few model homes.

Though the company was never profitable, monthly interest payments to the 5,000 investors continued to be paid. The developer was actually paying them out of the funds coming in from new investors. When new investment revenues were insufficient to cover the payments, the company folded.

The sponsors of this project may not have intended anything fraudulent, but they failed to *orally* disclose the substantial risks of their operation. Had investors read the prospectus, they would have been advised that the investment made sense only for "persons who have other adequate resources and are in a position to bear the loss of part or all of their investments." Prospectuses for all such securities contain similar disclaimers to reduce the liability of general partners and sponsors.

The more financially naive the population, the more outrageous the scams. In 1994, thousands of Russian investors bought shares in a type of fund operated as a pyramid scheme named "MMM." For about six months, the operators advertised the fund on television to investors who were paid healthy returns for a time. Although the Russian government warned the public to avoid the operation, citizens continued to hand over their money in hope of profit. When promoters could no longer cover all the payouts from new investors, the scheme crumbled, as all pyramids eventually do.

Telemarketing. A recent large-scale scam involved the sophisticated marketing of wireless communications investments. After learning that investors were bilked out of more than $30 million a month, regulators raided boiler-room operations in several states. Although the promoters had not actually produced anything tangible, thousands had invested on the promise of 600 percent returns over five years. The telemarketers had been paid up to 50 percent in sales commissions on money raised!

Radio. In 1995, a popular radio talk-show host, who dispensed investment advice, defrauded many listeners of millions of dollars. He enticed investors to put money in very risky deals, bordering on outright scams. After he was indicted, he fled the country.

Private Clubs. One of the most insidious operations is the "affinity fraud," through which con artists use affiliation in a professional or religious group to hook their victims. They introduce themselves as "fellow members," which often sways people who are not normally gullible to let down their guard.

Recovery Scam. One of the cleverest frauds perpetrated in modern times is the recovery scam. The victim receives a phone call from a company in the business of recovering money lost to con artists. Because the caller appears so knowledgeable regarding details of his worthless "investment," the victim trusts the caller to recoup his loss. Sometimes the very same swindler who scammed him originally returns with the recovery proposal. *There are no legitimate recovery services.*

Caveat Investor

If there is any easy money lying around, no one would force it into *your* pocket. If really great investment opportunities existed, who would care that *you* know about them? Only someone who stands to benefit would bother to solicit your investment.

Ponzi schemes, pyramid schemes, chain letters, and all other investment ploys have two things in common:

- Naive individuals who invest despite the lack of evidence to support the viability of the enterprise.

- A con artist who makes a good living by preying on gullible investors. He is typically an engaging individual who may truly believe he is acting ethically—a persuasion that appears to enhance his talent for duping others.

Most individuals believe they are too smart to be scammed, but the billions of dollars lost to investment schemes each year is overwhelming evidence that many are vulnerable. Lists of unfortunate investors often include names of celebrities with access to the best financial advisers, some of whom were taken in as well.

The Department of Corporations in your state cannot possibly police the thousands of companies that submit applications to sell securities or some other type of investment, nor do regulators routinely spot potential scams.

The authorities cannot prevent you from being victimized —they can prosecute the criminal only after you have been had and your money is gone forever. No matter how sophisticated you are, you may be a mark. It is strictly up to you to protect yourself by following these due diligence rules:

- Check out the quality of any investment advice, and scrutinize all recommended investments thoroughly. Never sign anything you do not read and understand.

- Develop the habit of thoroughly reading all written marketing material presented with investments. Read, then reread, prospectuses.

- Ask questions until you understand *how* an enterprise will generate profits, and then quantify the risks. Remember, there are few if any guarantees in the investment arena.

- Never invest in anything you do not understand. If an investment is so complicated that you cannot understand it, it is probably inappropriate for you.

- Check the credentials of anyone who tries to sell you any type of investment. Be especially wary of telephone solicitations and recommendations on penny stocks. Deal only with reputable, established firms.

- Treat every investment as a business deal. If you are not comfortable making an investment, don't make it. When you need more information, get it.

- Never invest when you hear the words "sure thing," and be skeptical of promises of quick profits.

- Limit riskier investments to a certain percentage of your net worth.

Remember, there's always free cheese in a mousetrap:

Any investment offering a return substantially greater than the market is either very risky or not legitimate. The bigger the promised payoff, the greater your risk.

Summary

Once you decide to invest your money, you need to bite the bullet and take appropriate risk. How well you can match risk with reward determines how comfortable you will be with your decisions. Your ultimate success depends on how well you assess, analyze, and assume the risks necessary to achieve your financial goals.

*C*ommon stocks are not the only way to participate in growth investments. Wall Street also created professionally managed portfolios of real estate as well as a variety of other types of enterprises. Structured as limited partnerships and real estate investment trusts, these are some of the more difficult investments to analyze. Private mortgages (trust deeds) can be very risky for investors who fail to exercise certain precautions.

Chapter **14**

Partnerships, REITs, and Private Mortgages

"Education is when you read the fine print.
Experience is what you get when you don't."

Pete Seger

LIMITED PARTNERSHIPS

A *limited partnership* is a legal investment contract in which two or more people arrange, for their mutual benefit, to finance, create, and maintain a business enterprise.

In concept, the partnership structure is sound because it affords small investors access to large-scale investment opportunities in which they could not otherwise participate. Most partnerships involve ownership of hard assets, such as real estate, cable-TV properties, and oil and gas which offer investors one or more of the following:

- **Income.** Cash payments to the partners.
- **Growth.** Appreciation in the value of partnership assets.
- **Tax Benefits.** Opportunities to reduce current income tax liability.

In a *general* partnership, the partners share equally in the obligations and liabilities. In a *limited* partnership, however, a general partner develops and manages an enterprise; the limited partners finance the enterprise and share in the profits and losses.

The general partner is directly responsible for the day-to-day management of the enterprise and its ultimate success, and reports to the limited partners on the progress of the enterprise. Limited partners neither make decisions nor otherwise participate in management.

The qualifier "limited" refers to the limited partners' liability, which is limited to their cash investments. In contrast, a general partner's liability is unlimited. A partnership's life is also limited—ultimately, assets are sold and proceeds are distributed to the partners.

Note . . . A *private* limited partnership, which is restricted to a small number of wealthy individuals, is not required to be registered with the SEC. A *public* partnership, marketed to an unlimited number of investors, must register and provide prospectuses and other disclosures to investors.

A partnership's profitability depends on the

- expertise and integrity of the general partner,
- timing or feasibility of the purchase of assets, and
- program's structure for sharing the costs and profits.

Tax Advantages

A partnership generates tax deductions that result from asset depreciation as well as taxes, loan interest, and various other fees and expenses, all of which are passed through to the limited partners. With LPs, there is no double taxation of income. Although the partners pay taxes on income, the partnership itself is not taxed. In contrast, public companies pay taxes on their earnings before paying dividends to shareholders, who are also liable for taxes. The general partner sends limited partners annual *K-1 reports* that provide data required for their tax returns.

The Tax Reform Act of 1986 reduced the tax benefits of LPs considerably, redefining personal income categories as

- **Active.** Income from salaries, commissions, and bonuses.
- **Portfolio.** Income and capital gains from financial assets like stocks and bonds.
- **Passive.** Income received from a business or activity in which the taxpayer does not materially participate, such as a limited partnership.

The new legislation essentially eliminated the "deep shelter" deals that generated large tax deductions to offset all types of income, because it changed how losses and deductions impact each income category. Write-offs generated by passive business activities could no longer offset active and portfolio income, only income received from passive business activities.

If passive losses exceed the passive income earned in a calendar year, the excess may be carried forward to subsequent years. Passive losses carried forward may offset active and portfolio income when an investor sells his partnership units or when the partnership is liquidated.

Note . . . If borrowed funds supplement the partners' invested capital, such leveraging augments tax benefits and potential income and profits, but it also increases financial risk. A partnership that is financed totally by investors with no borrowed funds (*non-leveraged*) is considered safer. Also, tax-exempt accounts may be subject to UBTI, *Unrelated Business Taxable Income*, generated from leveraged partnership investments, which might create a taxable event.

Liquidity

Partnerships are generally *self-liquidating*—the assets are eventually sold and the general partner shares the proceeds with the limited partners. Until then, unlike most other financial assets, limited partnerships are mostly illiquid investments, which is a major drawback for many investors.

However, if a limited partnership offers a current return of 8 percent or more per year that is partially tax sheltered, and your alternative is to earn less than 7 percent (taxable) in a safe, liquid investment, you may decide that earning 33 percent greater after-tax income is worth the forfeiture of liquidity.

Evaluating a Limited Partnership

Sponsors of limited partnerships typically solicit your investment with attractive marketing brochures describing the potential benefits of the enterprise. Although sponsors are required by securities regulations to furnish potential investors with a lengthy prospectus describing the risks, these documents are so mystifying and tedious that investors rarely read them thoroughly. Despite the difficulty, you should read the prospectus carefully.

Do not rely on what a broker or sponsor advises if the information is not consistent with the prospectus. Fewer investors would invest in limited partnerships if they took the time to digest the entire prospectus. Prospectuses typically contain disclaimers intended to absolve the sponsors and the general partner of almost anything that could go wrong.

The following checklist will help you analyze a limited partnership:

- ☐ Read the prospectus and all marketing materials thoroughly.
- ☐ Discuss the investment with reputable financial advisers.
- ☐ Determine a worst-case scenario based on various economic environments.
- ☐ Research the experience and track record of the general partner.
- ☐ Determine if the fees and leverage are appropriate, and if the timing of the venture is in line with your views regarding the future economic environment.

☐ Verify that partnership assets have been appraised by a reputable independent appraiser, and that the appraised value is not less than the purchase price.

☐ Do not invest in partnerships that do not guarantee a preferred return to limited partners; limited partners should be paid income and capital gains before the general partner.

☐ Beware of *blind pools*, LPs that do not identify specific properties. Make sure you know exactly how your money is being spent. New construction is always riskier because more can go wrong.

☐ Limit illiquid investments to less than 15 percent of your portfolio and, unless you are prepared to lock up funds

Public Partnerships: A Rocky History

In the 1970s and 1980s, more than $100 billion was raised to fund limited partnerships to develop and manage real estate, finance oil and gas exploration, and speculate in cattle ranches, media properties, and various other enterprises. These asset classes had been enjoying a bull market, and partnerships were created to accommodate the small investor. But when the economic environment turned dramatically, these assets failed to keep pace with inflation, and some even declined in value.

The first thing to go wrong was a plunge in the price of oil. As a consequence, many of Wall Street's energy programs failed to deliver any income to investors. Collapsing oil prices

for the entire term—six to 12 years or even longer—avoid partnership investments altogether.

☐ Ascertain that the potential risk falls within your tolerance, and that benefits justify having a non-liquid investment.

☐ Have the general partner demonstrate the channel through which the partnership is purchasing the asset(s). Avoid inside deals in which properties are purchased from parties connected with the partnership, because this conflict of interest may lead to higher purchase prices.

☐ Beware of "rollups" (reorganized partnership offerings) by general partners who may be taking more than their fair share of the completed programs.

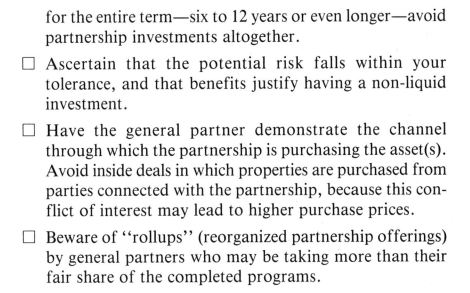

also devastated real estate values throughout the "oil patch" areas of the country.

The situation worsened when, in 1986, a major tax reform law restricted or reduced many deductions generated by these investments. Many properties had been purchased for inflated prices that were rarely questioned by investors who were mesmerized by the very attractive tax writeoffs.

Some programs were leveraged with debt that obligated investors to deposit more cash each year, even though the programs appeared to be losers. Investors found they were stuck in illiquid securities for which there was no market at any price. Today it is nearly impossible to identify a public partnership with a market value higher than the original investment.

Minimum Investment. Public offerings of limited partnerships generally require a minimum investment of $5,000, although some may be purchased in an IRA for $2,000. Certain private programs require a minimum of $50,000.

Suitability Requirements. Most states require that investors meet minimum income and net worth requirements before they invest in limited partnerships. Investors generally must earn at least $30,000 to $60,000 annually and have a net worth of $100,000. Some offerings require an annual income of $200,000 and a net worth of $1 million, excluding personal residences.

Fees and Profit Participation. Some local developers, acting as general partners in private LPs, often require investors to put up all the money while they take between 35 and 50 percent of the profits but none of the risks. Although public limited partnerships are often criticized for their high fees, often as much as 20 percent of the funds raised, they generally give investors 80 to 90 percent of the income and profits with no payments to the general partner until investors have recouped at least double their original investment.

Secondary Market. No efficient market currently exists for liquidating partnership interests. Brokerage firms used to match clients who wished to sell their units with buyers within their client base. Starting in 1991, however, the SEC required securities firms to maintain current prospectuses on programs brokered in the secondary market. Because they deemed it too expensive to comply, the firms suspended their internal matching services.

There are companies specializing in the resale partnership business that assist limited partners in liquidating their units, but questionable valuations and thin markets produce bids as low as 20 to 50 percent of original purchase prices. Some companies contact limited partners with offers to purchase their units at fire-sale prices, and resell them with high markups.

Some sponsors and other investment companies have offered to purchase units at somewhat higher prices than those available in the secondary market but substantially lower than their liquidation values. While limited partners such as probate estates are forced to sell, it is generally best to continue to hold units rather than accept the low prices offered.

A movement is underway to create a central pricing system for a more efficient secondary LP market. Trading might be done continuously or at weekly or monthly auctions. This could enhance unit prices, which would benefit holders who wish to sell. Buying units at depressed prices could be a wise strategy for well-informed investors.

Note . . . A *master limited partnership* is an LP that trades publicly on a stock exchange. Although MLPs are liquid, their risks are similar, so you should scrutinize an MLP as you would a public LP.

REAL ESTATE INVESTMENT TRUSTS

A real estate investment trust, commonly referred to as a REIT (pronounced "reet"), is a corporation that owns and manages a portfolio of real estate properties and/or mortgages. Like a closed-end mutual fund, a REIT has a limited number of shares.

REITs have become extremely popular in the last several years. In 1993 alone, more money was raised for new REIT offerings than in the previous 32 years combined! More than 175 REITs, representing billions of dollars of real estate, are publicly traded.

The REIT explosion may be the result of the real estate slump suffered across the United States in the 1980s, which threatened to derail the entire financial system. As a consequence of sustaining massive losses, traditional institutional sources of financing for commercial real estate investment virtually dried up. The clear beneficiary of the dilemma has been the real estate investment trust instrument, which has successfully accommodated those who market all types of depressed real estate properties.

As investors surmised that the real estate sector had bottomed, their appetite for yield prompted unprecedented purchases of REITs. As REITs outperformed the S&P 500 index by a wide margin, Wall Street capitalized on the demand by underwriting many new offerings.

There are basically two types of REITs:

- **Equity** REITs own and/or develop real estate properties such as apartment buildings, office buildings, shopping centers, warehouses, hotels, and nursing homes.

- **Mortgage** REITs provide long-term mortgage loans and short-term construction loans. Shareholders receive the cash flow from interest-bearing mortgages.

Hybrid REITs invest in both real estate properties and mortgages. REITs generally offer investors:

- **Diversification.** Several different properties located in various geographic locations.

- **Income.** Quarterly dividends substantially sheltered from taxation.

- **Liquidity.** The only way to own real estate with instant liquidity.

- **Professional Management.** Real estate ownership without the work of managing it.

- **Small Capital Investment.** Participation in large real estate projects with relatively little cash outlay.

Tax Implications

As long as a REIT distributes 95 percent of its earnings to shareholders and meets other conditions, the REIT itself is not taxed. Dividends to shareholders are typically tax sheltered to some degree. When REITs pay *return of capital* distributions, which are not taxed, the cost basis (purchase price) of shares is reduced. When shares are sold, taxes may be due on *recaptured* gains.

Risks

The major risks of REIT investments are rising interest rates, real estate slumps, and poor management. Since many REITs rely heavily on adjustable-rate debt, rising interest rates might cause them to lose their yield advantage over competing fixed-income investments, which could depress share prices.

Some analysts caution that many newer REITs are loaded with debt and conflicts of interest. Unless you have the ability to understand complicated balance sheets, do not invest in REITs.

Evaluating a REIT

If you decide to invest in a REIT, you should know that even professional analysts have difficulty evaluating them. However, there are some things you can do to help reduce the risks:

☐ Examine the company's assets, liabilities, and cash flow to ensure that earnings are adequate for the REIT to pay its obligations as well as dividends to investors. Low levels of debt, 40 to 50 percent of total capitalization, and low exposure to floating interest rates are optimal.

☐ Do not opt merely for the highest dividend—many REITs paid healthy dividends before eliminating them entirely. Sometimes a REIT disguises problems by paying out an excessively high percentage of its cash flow. A payout above 90 percent is too high.

☐ Rather than focus on dividends, examine the *funds from operations*, the net income excluding gains or losses from property sales. The FFO is stated in a REIT's quarterly and annual reports.

☐ Consider only REITs whose management has established a positive reputation and track record for completing successful programs in specific geographic areas, ownership of at least 5 percent of the REIT, and a hands-on approach to major management functions.

☐ Avoid regions that are vulnerable to depressed economic cycles that might leave many buildings empty and unprofitable. During the last recession, prices of many REIT shares dropped 40 percent or more, and several were forced into bankruptcy. Several mortgage REITs repossessed properties when their owners defaulted on mortgages.

☐ Investigate the economic outlook for the REIT's holdings. Is there a glut of that type of property in that particular area? Have prices bottomed? While many REIT prices have greatly improved, some have become even more depressed. Some analysts project it could be years before the commercial real estate glut will be absorbed in certain major business centers.

☐ Watch out for inflated property appraisals and overly optimistic projections of rent increases. Avoid aging projects that might require rehabilitation. Investigate exactly what it is you are buying and cultivate a healthy skepticism regarding marketing claims.

☐ Read the entire prospectus, including the *Conflicts of Interest* section. A common abuse perpetrated by some outside management firms is to extract huge fees for expenses such as administration, commissions, and loan brokering. Generally speaking, these costs are lower when the REIT is operated by its employees.

- ☐ Never invest in inside deals in which management sells properties to a trust at inflated prices for its own profit.

- ☐ Be especially cautious regarding initial public offerings. Many are vehicles for institutional investors to cash out of their distressed holdings rather than to raise capital for quality properties. *Rollups* composed of failed limited partnerships may inherit the very problems that caused the failures.

- ☐ Avoid REITs that are selling at premiums to the market and be skeptical of those trading at a discount. Sorting out REITs that will survive and profit among those trading at depressed prices requires much analysis, and professional investors may have already bid up prices on the better performing REITs. Several REIT mutual funds are available that may be preferable if you do not want to analyze them yourself.

Comparison of Limited Partnerships and REITs

	Limited Partnership	*REIT*
Structure	Business formed for any purpose under a limited partnership act.	Corporation that holds, operates and/or sells real estate and/or mortgages.
Type of Ownership	Units shared among any number of limited and general partners	Common Stock
Limited liability	Yes	Yes
Professional management	Yes	Yes
Pooling of funds	Yes	Yes
Required distribution of income	No	Yes
Pass-through of income	Yes	Yes
Pass-through of losses	Yes	No
Ability to leverage without UBTI	No	Yes
Independent directors	No	Yes
Tax reporting	K-1	1099

*"I don't know anything about luck.
I've never banked on it, and I'm
afraid of people who do. Luck to
me is something else: hard work—
and realizing what is opportunity
and what isn't."*

Lucille Ball

PRIVATE MORTGAGE INVESTMENTS
(TRUST DEEDS)

A mortgage or trust deed is a legal loan arrangement used by
property owners who pledge real property as collateral for
money borrowed. If the borrower fails to meet the obligation
to pay either interest or principal on the loan, the lender's
recourse is to foreclose on the property, forcing the property's
sale to recover the investment.

When more than one mortgage is placed on a property, the
mortgages are ranked by priority of repayment. If your deed
or mortgage is recorded in the first position, you have a *first*
trust deed or mortgage that positions your claim first in line
to receive proceeds from a sale of the property. When the instrument is recorded in the second position, it is a *second* trust
deed or mortgage, and it is second in line to receive sale
proceeds.

Individuals usually invest through loan brokers rather than
shoulder the burden of finding a creditworthy borrower and
handling all the paperwork themselves. In some states, you
must use the services of a licensed loan broker to ensure that
the interest rate is not usurious (above the lawful rate). Private
mortgage investments are *not* securities, and therefore are
rarely offered by securities brokers.

Risks

Many investors consider private mortgages to be safe, conservative investments that offer high monthly income. Actually, there is considerable credit risk. Will the borrower repay your loan and the interest owed? Although the process to ensure a safe investment is very involved, the risks can be reduced significantly if you take the required precautions. Neglect even one, and the risks may be considerable.

Mortgage scams exist because investors, attracted to the high yields, fail to scrutinize the investments. In California, regulators claim that their primary problem is fraudulent investments in second mortgages. Even a company that operates ethically may get into trouble and cause customers to lose money. The following is only one of many such cases.

Property Mortgage Corporation had invested more than $200 million of investors' money in mortgage loans, paying them returns as high as 15 percent for more than 25 years. Unexpectedly, in early 1991, the company stopped paying interest payments and filed for bankruptcy protection.

When PMC was scrutinized by investigators, they discovered that the company's income from operations had not been sufficient to meet the interest payments due investors for several years. PMC's principals had been covering the shortfall with money from new investors in a type of Ponzi scheme.

Because investors continued to receive payments, they were unaware of the company's insolvency or lack of ethics. Many investors had even increased their contributions, and several retirees had lost their entire life savings. Investors recovered only a small fraction of their money, and most fear that what's left will be spent on lawyers in their attempts to recover more.

While many loan brokers are reputable, a few are active scam artists who use phony property appraisals. Another abusive practice is to make several loans on the same property while representing to lenders that the property offers adequate collateral. A subsequent foreclosure sale reveals many investors' loans were not secured at all, often not even recorded. When sale proceeds cover only the first mortgage, all the others lose out. Sometimes a foreclosure does not produce sufficient funds to cover even the first mortgage and the overdue property taxes.

How To Reduce Risk

Whether or not you invest in private mortgages through a licensed mortgage broker, you should do the following to properly secure your investment:

☐ NEVER INVEST IN ANY TYPE OF MORTGAGE POOL OR LIMITED PARTNERSHIP! Be wary of any company or broker that recommends such an investment. Make sure the deed of trust or mortgage, title policy, promissory note, and all assignments or endorsements are in *your name*. Many scam artists enlist investors in pooled deals that provide investors with no real collateral. Even legitimate operations that pool their customers get into trouble, so keep your investments segregated.

☐ Have the property appraised by an honest, accredited appraiser. Because comparable property prices may have recently declined, make sure the appraisal is current. Ask for a copy of the appraiser's resume with at least three references and *physically inspect the property yourself.* Keep in mind that appraisers are more likely to accommodate the interests of brokers because brokers are their greatest source of referrals. Unethical appraisers exaggerate property values, and some even write up evaluations on properties they never bother to inspect.

☐ Ask to see the borrower's credit report, financial statement, and employment record. There should be evidence confirming the borrower's ability to make monthly payments as well as return the principal when due.

☐ Secure a lender's policy of title insurance (ALTA or CLTA), and file it in a safe place. A property's title must not be encumbered by any unpaid taxes, mechanics' liens, or other encumbrances. The title company is responsible for thoroughly researching the property's title, and it becomes liable for any problems that may result from reporting errors and other discrepancies.

☐ Have the borrower provide *guarantee replacement* insurance coverage, and have your name included in the policy as *loss payee* or *mortgagee.* Make sure the property is adequately and continuously insured against fire and water damage. In some areas, earthquake coverage is recommended, but it is expensive. File a copy of the policy in a safe place and instruct the insurer to notify you if the borrower misses a premium payment.

☐ Have the transaction handled by an escrow company (preferably not the broker's own escrow company) or an appropriate third-party professional who handles such transactions in your state.

☐ Immediately upon closing, make sure the trust deed or mortgage is recorded either by you, the escrow company, or title company. If you delay, a deed or lien might record prior to yours, relegating your position to a lower status in the event of foreclosure. (If you are buying an existing instrument, make sure the assignment is recorded and a proper endorsement added to the title policy.)

☐ Never allow mortgage investments to exceed 25 percent of your net worth excluding home, cars, furnishings, and immediate short-term spending money.

Collateral. The safety of a mortgage or trust deed investment depends primarily on the collateral. Be very selective in accepting a property, and lend no more than 60 percent of its appraised value, minus all existing liens against it.

Avoid making a loan behind a large first mortgage or trust deed. Do not invest in instruments other than the first position unless you have sufficient capital to make monthly payments on all loans recorded prior to yours. If a foreclosed property's proceeds are not sufficient to cover your loan, you might forfeit your entire investment. By making payments on loans prior to yours, however, you ensure that the sale of the foreclosed property covers all prior debts including your loan, provided sales proceeds are sufficient.

Avoid lending money to people you know, particularly friends and relatives, because they may take advantage of you, knowing you would be reluctant to foreclose to recover your investment. Avoid nonprofit organizations, especially religious institutions. Courts are sometimes unsympathetic to those who would foreclose on such debtors.

Avoid commercial properties because they are more complex and incur potentially higher legal costs when problems arise. Never lend on raw land, unless it is directly in the path of nearby development and your exposure is less than 50 percent of the appraised value.

Often the safest properties to accept as collateral are single-family homes in areas of population growth. Even "starter" homes owned by first-time buyers may be viable collateral, especially if the homeowner has substantial equity in the property. The neighborhood should host a diverse working population representative of several different industries.

Liquidity. One drawback of the trust deed mortgage investment is the lack of liquidity. Cashing out generally requires discounting the price to attract a buyer. Liquidity and sales price depend on the mortgage's security and yield. You may need to engage the services of a licensed mortgage broker and it might take as long as 30 days to get your money. Broker commissions may run 5 to 10 percent (*points*) of note balances, and there may be other charges.

Note . . . Private mortgage investments are not good for speculation, and should be bought only by investors with knowledge of real estate investing who plan to keep them until paid off.

Summary

While some limited partnerships and REITs have been outstanding investments for income as well as growth, overall there appear to be more losers than winners. Because limited partnerships are illiquid—you are stuck for the duration—they should be researched thoroughly. Fees may consume a high percentage of funds invested.

Private mortgage investments are typically loans to individuals who cannot qualify to borrow from commercial lenders, so you need to be especially cautious. Do not compromise on the quality of borrower or property or neglect any steps in the due diligence process—the one you skip could cost you dearly.

To compete for investor dollars, many of the nation's 2,000-plus insurance companies have created investment products that provide benefits other than financial protection against death, illness, and catastrophe. Insurance companies today offer conservative tax-deferred savings contracts called annuities.

Annuities

"Wealth is well known to be a great comforter."

The Republic
Plato

An *annuity* is a savings contract between an investor and an insurance company.

Traditionally associated with the older generation and ultra-conservative investors, annuities accommodate any savings program when the goal is to finance a long-range need such as retirement. Although the annuity concept is uncomplicated, there is more to the selection process than merely finding an insurance company that pays a good rate.

Annuities fall into two very distinct categories, *deferred* and *immediate*. Although both types of contracts are offered by insurance companies, they serve different financial needs: If your objective was to save for the future, you would choose a deferred annuity. You would invest in an immediate annuity only if you need current income.

DEFERRED ANNUITIES

A *deferred* annuity is an investment contract with an insurance company that provides a *tax-deferred* savings program. Deferred annuities function like large, nondeductible IRAs, and make sense as long-term savings vehicles for future income needs.

The two major benefits of investing in an annuity are

- tax-deferred accumulation of savings, and
- proceeds that can be passed to beneficiaries without the delay or cost of probate.

The first benefit is the most attractive feature of a deferred annuity. Taxes are deferred on all income and capital gains that accrue, a tax advantage granted by Congress many years ago to encourage Americans to save for retirement. "Tax-deferred," however, is not "tax-free." Someday the annuity's income and gains will be fully taxed, but compounded growth is enhanced when taxes are deferred.

Minimum Investment. Most annuities require a minimum deposit of $5,000 (*Single Premium Deferred Annuities*, or *SPDAs*), although some contracts allow you to invest smaller amounts on a flexible timetable.

Unlimited Deposits. While all qualified retirement plans carry many restrictions, few are placed on annuities. Contributions to retirement accounts are limited, but you may invest as much as you wish in annuities. Also, annuities require no mandatory distributions starting at age 70½, so you may defer taxes on income and gains indefinitely.

Distributions. All distributions are fully taxed until nothing is left in the annuity except the original principal (first in, last out).

An annuity is *not* a viable way to save if you need to take distributions before 59½ because the IRS imposes a 10 percent penalty in addition to the income taxes. (If a contract predates August 14, 1982, when the law was changed, the first distributions are not taxed because they are considered return of principal, and the 10 percent penalty is not imposed.)

Note . . . Although many brokers recommend annuities for IRAs and pension accounts, they are generally not a good choice. Investments in qualified retirement accounts grow on a tax-deferred basis, so paying extra fees for an annuity may decrease returns. Before investing in any annuity, make sure you have maximally funded all tax-exempt retirement accounts for which you qualify, because they may offer tax deductions in the amount of your contributions—annuities do not.

Surrender Charges. Deferred annuities are always liquid because you may cash out at any time. Although there are no up-front, out-of-pocket charges when you invest, surrender charges, starting at around 6 or 7 percent, are imposed on distributions above the allowed maximum for the first several years. However, most contracts impose no surrender charge for distributions of income or gains that have been credited to the contract, and many contracts allow for annual penalty-free withdrawals of 10 percent of contract values, even if they contain principal.

10-Day Review. After purchasing an annuity, you will receive a contract from the insurance company explaining the terms, conditions, and rate guarantees. Investors are granted a minimum of 10 days (some states mandate 30 days) to review their new contracts. If a contract is rejected within that period, the company is required to return all the investor's money.

Before investing, ask questions until you fully understand the contract. If your questions are not answered by your broker to your satisfaction, contact the company directly. If you still do not receive satisfactory answers, or if you believe the contract will not meet your needs, return it within 10 days for a full refund.

Participants

Although the terms of annuity contracts differ, there are always five parties designated by the investor: The *contract owner*, the *annuitant*, the *payor* (typically these three are the investor), the *beneficiary*, and the *insurance company*.

- **Owner.** The owner, who is generally the investor, controls the annuity and retains the right to transfer it to another party, liquidate it, and take distributions or assign them to another party. The owner may be an individual, married couple, partnership, corporation, or trust.

  Note . . . Because tax implications are affected by designation of ownership, consult a professional for tax advice before purchase. For example, joint ownership is not generally recommended.

- **Annuitant.** The annuitant is the individual upon whose life the annuity is "measured." Although he has no control, the contract remains in force until the annuitant dies, at which time it matures. At any time, the annuitant, who is usually the owner, may be changed to any other person who was alive when the annuity was originally purchased.

- **Payor.** All cash payments are distributed to the payor.

- **Beneficiary.** When the annuitant dies, the annuity's accumulation value is paid to the beneficiary, bypassing probate. Any number of beneficiaries may be designated, including estates and charities, and changes may be made at any time.

- **Insurance Company.** Because the contract is issued and guaranteed by the insurance company, invest only with top-rated companies.

How to Evaluate the Safety of Insurance Companies

Before investing in any annuity, you should know about recent problems within the insurance industry. (See page 274.) Although there have been positive changes, you still need to scrutinize the financial strength of any insurance company before investing.

The most reliable credit evaluations are furnished by S&P and Moody's. The largest, most familiar sounding companies are not always the most fiscally sound, but at least 100 companies have been granted very high ratings. The company you select should have ratings no lower than AA− from S&P and A1 from Moody's. (See credit rating chart, page 104.) Ratings are available from the insurance companies, libraries, and insurance agents and brokers.

Fixed versus Variable

Deferred annuities are either *fixed* or *variable.*

A *fixed* annuity is a tax-deferred savings contract in which the insurance company guarantees a rate of return as well as repayment of principal when the owner requests it. The insurance company invests your deposits in bonds mostly, and bears all the investment risk. Periodically, the company credits you interest, according to the terms of your contract. In a *variable* annuity, you, as the investor, bear all the investment risk by allocating your deposits to one or more of the contract's mutual fund *subaccounts.*

You should choose a contract that fits your risk tolerance and investment goals. If interest rates are high, you may prefer to lock in a steady guaranteed return; however, if rates are low, a variable contract may offer significantly higher returns for your long-term savings, albeit with greater risk. The average return for variable equity funds for the last five years was substantially higher than fixed-rate yields.

Selecting a Fixed Annuity

Because the insurance company is the guarantor of a fixed annuity, you must first examine the company's financial strength as reflected in the ratings assigned it by S&P and Moody's. You may also call your state's insurance department or commissioner to check on a company's performance.

Next, ask how the insurance company invests your money —some take more risk to pay higher yields. Nearly all insurance companies hold high-yielding bonds and unprofitable real estate to a degree, but some have more exposure than others. Ask the broker for a breakdown of a company's assets, and consider only those that invest conservatively.

When recommending a particular annuity, the broker may show you an *illustration* that projects the future life of a contract, given an assumed rate of investment return. Be sure to question the broker as to what is guaranteed and what is merely projected.

Comparing Rates. Most fixed annuities offer a guaranteed rate for one year or more. When the guarantee period ends, the contract rate is reset to reflect current market levels. Most contracts guarantee that the rate will not fall below a stipulated *floor* rate, which for most contracts today is about 4 percent.

Because you cannot withdraw all your money for several years without a penalty, consider all aspects of the annuity contract, not just the first-year rate. A company might guarantee a rather high rate for the first year, but fail to offer a competitive rate in subsequent years. Companies most likely to reduce their rates are those offering unusually high first-year rates. It may be preferable to choose a guaranteed three-year rate unless there is a very good reason to expect market rates will rise.

It is never prudent to select an annuity or any other investment solely on the basis of high yield—the amount of extra return may not be worth the added risks. Generally speaking, if you want less risk, you must be satisfied with lower yields.

Market Value Adjustment. Some fixed annuities include provisions that pass on interest-rate risk to the investor if distribution of principal is taken prematurely. The *market value* *adjustment* results in higher surrender charges when interest rates have increased and lower charges when rates have declined. Therefore, the MVA feature is more attractive when rates are high and expected to decline, but you should avoid MVA contracts when rates are expected to rise.

Fees. For fixed annuities, the quoted rate of return is net with no fees charged against the contract. The insurance company advances commission to the broker, which is eventually recouped from annual contract fees.

Selecting a Variable Annuity

Investing in a variable annuity is similar to selecting a mutual fund. Because a variable's subaccounts are always custodied at a bank or trust company, separate from the insurance company's assets, your investment is always protected from any insurance company liquidation or bankruptcy. With safety not subject to the insurance company's financial strength, you can base your choice of contract on the performance of its investment subaccounts.

Subaccounts. Variable contracts offer stock and bond funds, a money market fund, and perhaps a foreign stock or real estate fund. The insurance company generally engages an investment advisory firm to manage the subaccounts. If you are investing for many years without the need for current distributions, consider equity funds rather than bond or fixed subaccounts. For greater diversification, purchase contracts that offer international equity funds.

When your deposit is allocated to a subaccount, shares are purchased at the *accumulation unit value*, similar to the net asset value of a mutual fund. With just a phone call, you may

		Annualized Return		
Subaccounts		3 Years	5 Years	10 Years
Assets ($MM)	Type of Fund	%	%	%
8,694.8	Agressive Growth	23.72	26.26	14.86
32,080.0	Growth	15.68	15.45	12.78
30,728.3	Balanced	8.89	10.85	10.51
9,838.7	Corporate Bonds	5.31	8.03	7.95
3,703.0	High Yield Bonds	9.21	13.85	8.81
16,398.3	International Equity	10.90	6.13	--

Variable Annuity Returns
(through August 1995)

Morningstar, Inc.

switch your money among the variable's subaccounts without incurring any extra fees or tax liability on any income or gains.

Insured Benefits. Most annuity contracts are insured in the sense that, if the annuitant dies, beneficiaries never receive less than the original deposits, even if contract values have declined. Declining values are not a concern for fixed annuities, but the possibility always exists that a variable contract's value might drop below the original amount invested. To limit this risk, the company may guarantee an *estate benefit* equal to the investor's original deposit.

Some contracts guarantee beneficiaries a minimum return, perhaps 5 percent, for each year the annuity remains in force until its value has doubled, regardless of contract performance. Some variable contracts offer a *step-up* provision that limits the downside of contract values. For example, a contract that increases 60 percent in value by the fifth year may pay out that amount to beneficiaries upon the death of the annuitant, regardless of any decline in value after the fifth year.

Fees. For variable annuities, many company expenses are passed on to contract holders and deducted from contract values. *Mortality and expense* (M&E) fees, which average 1.4 percent annually, pay for the guaranteed death benefit. Advisory fees, ranging from .5 percent for money market accounts to more than 1 percent for international accounts, are also charged. A flat administration charge from $25 to $40 is imposed annually to cover services such as mutual fund switching. All this adds up to around 2.5 percent annually, about 1 percent more than fees charged for mutual funds, which may be a fair trade-off for tax-deferral and a guaranteed principal death benefit.

Note . . . Because they contain mutual fund subaccounts, variable annuities are subject to both SEC and insurance regulation, and the broker must be securities licensed.

Why You Must Review Credit Ratings

In the late 1970s and early 1980s, the insurance industry, along with many other financial institutions, experienced a unique period of double-digit inflation and interest rates. Many investment decisions reflected the belief that these high rates would prevail indefinitely. As inflation and interest rates fell to record low levels, insurance companies' profitability suffered.

When the real estate market weakened, many insurance companies repossessed unprofitable real estate through foreclosure. Compounding the situation, the junk-bond market started to decline in the fall of 1989. To disguise heavy losses, many failing companies manipulated their financial reporting.

Comparing Contracts. For each recommended contract, ask the broker

- *What are the investment choices offered and what are their three- and five-year performance figures?*

- *What are the fees for taking distributions? What percentage of funds can I withdraw each year without charge?*

- *What is the guaranteed death benefit?*

Dollar-Cost Averaging. To reduce the risk of investing your entire deposit right before a market correction, consider *dollar-cost averaging* your deposits over the first six months to a year (see page 232). Your deposit may be allocated initially to the money market or fixed account, with scheduled transfers to a stock fund each month.

A major insurance company, Executive Life, had been backing its contracts with a high percentage of junk bonds. When the value of the bonds plummeted, the company was forced into receivership. Although all death benefits were paid, some of Executive Life's annuity contracts underperformed, and investors were not able to cash out.

In 1990, a record 29 insurance companies became insolvent compared with 10 in 1988 and the annual average of five during the 1970s. Since 1991, regulators have seized six large insurance companies that have been reorganized or sold to other insurance companies. Many annuity contract holders were not able to access their funds for more than two years, and some contracted benefits were never delivered. Unlike bank deposits, there is no federal insurance that covers deposits made to insurance companies. Although each state has a guaranty

Maintaining Your Annuity

After you invest in a deferred annuity, establish a separate file for storing annuity contracts and annual statements, and inform the company if you change your mailing address.

Review your contracts at least once each year. Insurance companies send out statements annually that indicate a contract's current status, including income and gains credited and current account values. A good time to review your contract is when you receive your annual statement.

Check the insurance company's current credit rating, and determine if the contract is earning a competitive rate. If you own a variable annuity, compare its performance with that of other annuities. If your annuity is lagging, consider transferring the funds to a better performing contract with a 1035 exchange.

---

fund to cover some losses, total policy cash values are not guaranteed.

In 1992, insurance regulators mandated new capital standards for insurance companies. Prior standards required all companies, regardless of size, to have $5 million in capital, but now they are required to maintain minimum capital levels that are based on the risk of their investments and operations.

The new regulations give insurance companies incentive to divest riskier assets such as junk bonds and unprofitable real estate. Also, insurance companies had not been required to state the market value of their assets, but now balance sheets must reflect paper losses when asset values decline. Regulators now have more effective oversight and the power to close down marginally healthy companies *before* they become insolvent, which offers more protection to annuity investors.

1035 Exchange. You can exchange your annuity contract for another company's contract without incurring a tax by implementing a *1035 exchange*. The purpose of an exchange is to *legally defer taxation* on a contract's accumulated income or gains, and to continue *earning on a tax-deferred basis*. The 1035 exchange abides by IRS regulation; it is not merely an insurance company policy.

To process a 1035 exchange, contact the insurance company representative for the necessary forms. If the existing carrier imposes a surrender penalty that reduces the cash amount to be transferred, it may be better to wait until the surrender period has elapsed.

Annuitization. At some point after purchase, deferred annuities accommodate the need for current income payments through *annuitization*. When you elect to annuitize, the insurance company begins to make a series of monthly fixed-dollar payments for a period of years until all principal and accumulated growth has been completely distributed. Most companies offer a variety of options that include regular payments for a specified period, your entire life, or your life plus the life of another. Before annuitization, you can withdraw part of your annuity's cash value.

Some insurance companies impose annuitization when the annuitant reaches a certain age, typically 90. This is not an IRS ruling but company policy, so if you do not want to annuitize, you may process a 1035 exchange to another company that allows for indefinite tax-deferred accumulation.

When the Annuitant Dies. Upon the death of the annuitant, contract proceeds are paid directly to the beneficiary(s), bypassing probate. No taxable event occurs if the beneficiary is the annuitant's spouse as long as the spouse takes no distributions. All other beneficiaries are taxed on the contract's accumulated pretax earnings. For example, if an annuity was purchased for $50,000 and the payout to the beneficiary is $100,000, $50,000 is taxed as income. Although the entire $100,000 bypasses probate, it is included in the annuity owner's estate and may be subject to estate taxes.

IMMEDIATE ANNUITIES

Investors who need income might consider an *immediate* annuity, a contract that guarantees a certain number of equal monthly or quarterly payments that begin immediately. Here's how it works: You give your money to the insurance company and it agrees to give it back to you in monthly installments with interest. Most immediate annuities make payments to the annuitant for a specified number of years or his entire lifetime, but some continue to make payments to heirs when the annuitant dies within a certain period.

Immediate annuities provide tax-advantaged income because payments include both the credited interest (taxable) and partial return of your principal (not taxable).

Note . . . Because you lock in a rate of return for the entire term, immediate annuities are better investments when interest rates are high, and less attractive when rates are low.

Selecting an Immediate Annuity

Once purchased, immediate annuity contracts are irrevocable (they cannot be changed). Therefore, it is critical that you select them with the greatest care. First, eliminate all insurance companies except those with the highest credit ratings. Then, compare the monthly payments each company guarantees as well as *all* other elements and terms of the contracts. Are payments for life or a specified number of years? If I die, will payments go to my beneficiary?

To determine how much a contract earns, add all payments to be made over the life of the contract and subtract the annuity's original cost. Once you have this figure, compare its return to that of other immediate annuities as well as other investments. (Immediate annuities typically do not offer as high total returns as certain alternative conservative investments.)

When you receive the contract, you have at least 10 days to scrutinize it. If you are not convinced the contract meets your needs, return the contract for a full refund.

Split Annuity. By purchasing both a deferred annuity and an immediate annuity, you can generate monthly income that is partially tax-free. When the *split annuity* is properly structured, the immediate annuity is fully paid out by the time the deferred annuity has grown back to the original investment.

Summary

Historically, tax-deferred annuities have served as effective retirement savings vehicles. Variable annuities allow you to move money among various markets and sectors with no current tax. Select contracts with care and discrimination, and deal only with brokers who represent several different insurance companies that invest conservatively. Before investing in an annuity, make sure you have funded all your qualified tax-exempt retirement accounts.

*L*ife insurance may be the most important investment you ever make if another person's welfare depends on your support. For decades, this unique type of financial protection has sustained millions of dependents after the death of a family breadwinner. Although it may seem less intimidating than other types of investment, insurance is sufficiently complex and unique to warrant some study.

Chapter **16**

Life Insurance

"You never see the bus that hits you."

Anonymous

Life insurance is a contract with an insurance company that promises to pay a cash *death benefit* to one or more beneficiaries upon the death of the insured in exchange for a sum of money, or *premium*.

The principle governing life insurance is simple: Insurance companies determine approximately how long a group of people will live and estimate the premium revenues they must collect to insure them as a group and still be profitable.

Some people question the need for life insurance, especially younger families who do not want to be saddled with additional ongoing expenses. If you have dependents, you really should have the protection that insurance offers—the question you should be asking is not should I have it, but how much should I have and what kind.

Determining Coverage

To determine how much coverage you need, first consider funds required at the time of death such as medical expenses, burial costs, estate taxes, and funds for a readjustment period. Then estimate how much your dependents will need for ongoing monthly living expenses, day-care costs, college tuition, and retirement. Be sure to factor in inflation. As a rule of thumb, most families need between five to eight times their current annual income. Subtract from this total any coverage offered by your employer.

Although life insurance is often used to help with financial goals such as retirement and education expenses, its primary purpose is the financial protection of dependents to cover living expenses when a breadwinner dies. The purchase of coverage for any person who is a financial liability (such as a dependent child or parent) may be a waste of money. But if you decide you want it, sometimes it is more economical to add a *family rider* to your own policy. A better plan still is to invest the money in stocks, bonds, and mutual funds—you will undoubtedly need more money if your dependent lives.

Once you determine how much life insurance you need, the next step is to determine what kind will best meet your needs. Term life and whole life are the more traditional forms, but in the mid-1970s, the insurance industry created universal life and variable life to offer greater flexibility.

Note . . . Beneficiaries receive death-benefit proceeds from life insurance *income* tax-free. Section 101(a)(1) of the *Internal Revenue Code* states that proceeds paid "by reason of the death of the insured" are excluded from gross income. Benefits received, however, are not free from *estate* taxation. To avoid estate tax liability, someone other than the insured must own the contract, or you must establish an irrevocable trust. Before purchasing life insurance, read Chapter 22 on estate planning.

Finding an Insurance Company and Agent/Broker

Your liaison with the insurance company is a licensed insurance broker. An insurance broker can wear one of many hats including stockbroker, financial planner, or some other investment professional. Once you decide on the coverage you need, your next step is to contact one or two brokers who represent several high-quality insurance companies, and advise them that you want to receive quotes for insurance coverage. The broker/agent you engage should be able to offer you a choice of companies.

Nearly every year, a number of insurance companies file bankruptcy, which is certain to adversely affect many policyholders. You must therefore address the financial strength of any insurance company with which you choose to do business by checking its ratings from the two major credit rating services (page 104). Do not select any company with an S&P rating lower than AA – or a Moody's rating lower than A1.

The broker will ask you questions regarding the amount of

coverage you need, your age, lifestyle, and health history. Answer all questions truthfully and carefully. Most insurance companies require the insured to be physically examined by one of their licensed medical professionals. Ideally, your broker will explain your options and help you shop for coverage that accommodates your individual needs at the most efficient cost.

Your broker's questions will also help determine the cost of your insurance coverage. Insurance companies compare your responses to actuarial tables of historical data. The cost of your coverage is based on your age, sex, and health, as well as your behavior—do you use tobacco, sky dive, bungee jump?

Healthy persons who maintain healthful lifestyles may be categorized as a *preferred risk*, which allows for lower premiums. If you have a chronic illness, you may be charged higher premiums. A company decides to insure your life only after reviewing your application. If you do not tell the truth, the company may cancel the policy or refuse to pay a claim.

Purchasing Tips

When you purchase any insurance policy, there are several important things to consider. First, always make your check payable to the insurance company, *never* to the broker, and ask for a receipt.

Second, when you receive your new policy from the insurance company, read it very carefully. You have 10 days (or more in some states) from the time you receive the policy to change your mind. If you decide not to keep the policy, cancel it immediately and ask for a refund.

Third, you will be paying a commission that is not disclosed. Most insurance companies advance commissions to brokers, which are eventually recouped from contract expenses. That is why policies that offer cash values have little or no value in the first or second year after the policy is issued.

TERM LIFE

Term life insurance protects against financial loss that results from death during a specified period. Term pays out a death benefit only if you die during the contracted period. At the end of the period, the protection ceases. You can usually extend coverage by paying renewal premiums that may increase each year as you age.

Term is the least complicated insurance coverage because it does not provide for any investment account or cash value. The greatest advantage of term insurance is that you can purchase greater coverage at a younger age when the need for protection is generally greatest. However, in later years, term can be too expensive to continue. In fact, insurance companies pay out death benefits on term insurance only about three percent of the time because most people discontinue term coverage when it becomes expensive. Once they decide to reenter, they are either too old or too unhealthy to get affordable coverage. Many term policies can be converted into some form of permanent life insurance without further medical examination or other evidence of insurability.

Who Should Buy Term Insurance?

Term insurance is generally more appropriate for young

families with limited incomes because it costs less, at least in the short term (fewer than 10 years). Term is the best choice for coverage that is needed for only a short period.

How To Purchase Term Insurance

The first thing to do when considering a proposal or quote is to check the company's credit rating so that you can narrow your selection to companies with acceptable ratings. Then, for each proposal, ask the broker the following questions:

- *Is the quoted premium rate* current *or* guaranteed? *What is the cost difference between the current and guaranteed premiums over the life of the contract?* Current rates may be lower initially, but they may be increased if the company's actual expenses exceed projected expenses. To prevent term insurance from becoming too expensive, most companies offer a *guaranteed* rate, the maximum rate they can charge. Although it may be more expensive initially, a guaranteed-rate policy may be safer in the long run because there are no rate-hike surprises.

- *For how many years is the rate guaranteed?* Because of recent legislation, there is an industry trend for shorter guarantee periods.

- *For how many years can I renew the term policy, and what are the conditions of renewal?* Some contracts are more flexible than others.

- *Under what circumstances may I convert the term policy to a permanent policy? Will there be any credit available to apply toward a permanent contract?* You may have to requalify with another medical examination, or the company may not offer any upgrade to permanent coverage.

WHOLE LIFE

Whole life—also known as straight, ordinary, or permanent life—offers protection at a level premium for the entire lifetime of the insured by combining protection with an investment program. Whole life policies are generally the highest quality coverage with the most predictable costs. The advantages are guaranteed death benefit (face amount), guaranteed fixed or level premiums, and guaranteed *cash surrender value*. By paying a premium that does not change for the life of the contract, your cost of insurance is averaged out over your lifetime.

Cash Surrender Value. Whole life is more expensive than term life because the higher premiums provide the company with extra money to establish a *cash value* account. These funds continue to generate earnings that pay for the rising costs of coverage. The CSV represents cash to be returned to the policyholder if the policy is cashed in (surrendered) before the death benefit is paid. It is based on the company's investment returns, its expenses, and mortality costs. You may access your policy's cash value for low-cost, tax-free loans. *As long as your policy stays in force, no tax is incurred on any interest or dividends credited to the policy.*

Dividends. Some whole life policies offer dividends, based on company profits, that are not guaranteed. Often policyholders use the dividends to enhance their policy values or pay future premiums.

Accidental Death Rider. Some policies provide for additional benefit as a result of accidental death of the insured.

Limited Pay. By paying a higher premium for a period of years, some policies become paid in full. For example, you may pay premiums for 20 years, at which time the policy is guaranteed to be paid up. The insurance remains in effect to age 100 without additional premiums. When you reach age 100, the policy pays out the death benefit.

Single Premium Whole Life. *SPWL* is a hybrid of an annuity contract and a term insurance contract. As its name suggests, a single premium creates an immediate cash value that earns income to pay for a death benefit. All SPWL earnings accumulate tax-free, but they become taxable if the policy is cashed in. (For policies purchased before June 21, 1988, loans may be made without income tax or penalties, regardless of age. Tax-free withdrawals are allowed on contracts purchased after that date only if they are properly structured to meet strict guidelines.)

The main distinctions between an SPWL and an annuity are

- Annuities typically offer no death benefits. SPWL contracts always do.

- Some SPWL contracts offer tax-free borrowing. Annuities rarely do.

- Cash values generally accrue more slowly in an SPWL than an annuity because costs for term insurance reduce the growth of account balances.

- The SPWL death benefit passes income-tax-free to beneficiaries, but annuity distributions are taxable.

Who Should Buy Whole Life?

Generally speaking, life insurance should be bought for its

death benefit, not as an investment. Unlike term policies, whole life policies offer cash value accounts. If you anticipate the need for coverage for 20 years or more, a cash value whole life policy will probably be less expensive than term coverage in the long run, although more expensive initially.

How To Purchase Whole Life Insurance

Proposals for whole life insurance typically take the form of *illustrations*, computer printouts of a policy's projected year-by-year performance. An illustration is not a legal document —the company's legal obligations are spelled out in the policy, not the illustration.

Note . . . Illustrations are generally based on a set of assumptions that reflect only one year of guarantees, but the costs of coverage might rise and interest rates could fall, producing a much different outcome. Because these components are rarely guaranteed for the life of the contract, count on them to change over the years.

Theoretically, all illustrations should be quite similar, but in reality they often vary substantially. The National Association of Insurance Commissioners may someday restrict brokers from making any projections that are not guaranteed. To get a sense of what could occur if interest rates fall and insurance costs rise, request an illustration based on a return that is 1 to 2 percent lower than the projected rate.

After you eliminate companies with unacceptable ratings, you must compare the insurance costs and death benefits of various policies by seeking answers to the following questions:

- *Do I qualify for preferred rates?* Some companies grant

a preferred rate for an individual they consider a better-than-average risk, based on such factors as health, lifestyle, and family history. However, although *you* may believe your health is terrific, an insurance company's criteria may be too stringent to grant you preferred rates.

- *What are the premiums and when are they due? Under what circumstances may the premiums be increased? Are the illustrated premiums sufficient to guarantee protection for my entire life?* In comparing costs of coverage, make sure that you compare similar contract specifications such as the death benefit and period covered.

- *What is the crediting rate on which the illustration is based?* The crediting rate is never guaranteed for the life of the contract but adjusts to market conditions.

- *Does this contract pay any dividends?* If so, ask to see its 20-year dividend history.

- *Which figures in the illustration are guaranteed and which are not? Will I be notified if they change?* An illustration's appreciation of tax-deferred compounded growth over a long period may be seductive, and brokers are often able to manipulate the numbers to look enticing. Investors rarely scrutinize and interpret the material carefully, and often miss important disclaimers. Regardless of what the illustration suggests, if rates decline, the company will probably require payment of additional premiums to keep the policy in force, a fact many brokers fail to clarify. Therefore, it is important to determine what is guaranteed and what is merely projected.

- *Is the death benefit guaranteed or could it change depending on interest rates or other factors?*

- *What happens to the policy if I cannot make a required payment because of financial hardship? Does this policy offer the option to reduce the annual premium? If so, how would this affect the overall policy performance?* Policies generally allow some of the options provided on page 299.

- *Does the contract include any* term rider *reflecting a degree of pure term coverage?* The greater the amount of term insurance in a policy, the lower the cost initially but the greater the chance of higher rates over time. To compare contract costs effectively, you must know what percentage of the coverage is term.

- *Does the contract allow for loans? If so, what are the limits and the costs?* Policy loans generally cost less than commercial loans.

UNIVERSAL LIFE

The innovative *universal life* insurance contract was created in 1979 and has since become the industry's fastest growing product. When double-digit investment returns were common in the 1980s, consumers became dissatisfied with the low cash surrender values of traditional whole life contracts. UL, which is a way to purchase permanent term insurance, was created to accommodate consumer demand for greater investment returns, flexibility, and more affordable coverage than whole life offers. A more apt name for this type of policy might be "flexible premium adjustable term life" because universal life offers

- flexibility in the amount and frequency of the premiums to be paid,
- adjustment of the death benefit up or down over the course of the contract,
- tax-deferred accumulation of income and gains, and
- tax-favored borrowing against policy equity.

Universal life builds a fund from premium deposits that generates income to pay for all or part of the term insurance and contract expenses. Each month the insurance company accesses this fund to cover contract expenses. As long as the investment account and paid-in premiums cover expenses, the contract remains in force. Any excess funds remain in the account and draw interest. If the investment account does not earn enough, the company bills the policyholder for additional premiums.

Disadvantages of universal life coverage include a lack of guarantees and the need for close monitoring—the rate of current interest credited to the contract is not guaranteed and the cost of insurance may rise. For the last several years, companies have increased their costs of insurance as market interest rates declined, requiring many policyholders to pay more than they had expected to keep their policies in force.

Who Should Buy Universal Life?

Individuals who need permanent coverage with flexibility in payment of premiums may find UL preferable to whole life or straight term insurance.

How To Purchase Universal Life Insurance

In addition to the questions you ask for whole life, ask the following questions:

- *Are there any guarantees in the contract, and if so, what are they?*

- *What is the minimum premium to keep the policy in force to age 100 (or some other age) at the guaranteed interest rate and guaranteed insurance cost? What is the difference between the policy's current cost of insurance and its guaranteed cost? What conditions must be met before I can stop paying premiums and still keep the policy in force?* Many agents fail to disclose the potential costs of a contract. If you ask for a proposal to show the guaranteed costs, you will find them higher than the current costs. When comparing contracts you want to know how high the cost of coverage could rise.

- *What are the flexible features of the contract? How are changes made and how often may I make them? Are there any charges for these services or new medical requirements in making changes?* To make viable comparisons, you need to know as much about each policy's terms as possible.

- *Is the cash account included in the death benefit or will it be paid separately to the beneficiary?* Some contracts pay the death benefit in addition to the cash account (which should be higher); some don't.

- *Does the policy pay periodic interest bonuses? Under what circumstances? Are they guaranteed?*

VARIABLE LIFE

With a conventional whole life or universal life contract, the company invests your premium payments within its general portfolio and makes certain guarantees regarding crediting of annual interest. With a *variable* life contract, however, you (as policyholder) decide how your premiums are invested among several investment subaccounts the insurance company provides. Unlike a fixed-rate contract, a variable policy positions your premiums to achieve potentially higher returns, but with higher risk.

The investment subaccounts, which typically include at least one bond fund and an equity fund, are managed either in-house or by an independent advisory firm. Investment performance has a direct impact on the policy's death benefit and cash value. Good investment results may increase the policy's death benefit and cash value; poor performance may decrease the death benefit and cash value.

While dividends and crediting rates on conventional whole life and universal life policies have been decreasing since the mid-1980s, several equity-based variable policies have performed very well.

Fees. Because variable life contracts involve investment options, policy expenses include investment charges in addition to the usual fees. Many investors believe the extra fees are justified because of the potentially higher returns. With respectable performance, these contracts can provide coverage at a lower premium cost than any other type of insurance, but there are no guarantees.

Fixed Spreads. Though investment returns are not guaranteed, the insurer must guarantee a fixed spread between what the account earns and what it credits. For example, if the separate account earns 10 percent and the spread (policy expense) is 1.5 percent, the company must credit 8.5 percent to the policy. (In a conventional policy, an insurer might earn 8 percent in the general account but credit only 5 percent to the policy.)

Safeguards. A variable contract's assets are always kept separate from the company's general funds and are therefore not vulnerable to losses that may result from the insolvency of an insurance company. (In a conventional policy, there might be some loss to policyholders if the company files for bankruptcy.) As a security-type investment, variable life insurance is regulated by the SEC as well as by insurance regulators, and brokers must be licensed to sell both securities and insurance.

Who Should Buy Variable Life?

Variable life contracts could be the least expensive coverage if the financial markets cooperate. Some years the investment account will more than cover the costs of coverage, other years it may fall short. As long as the policyholder is able to pay in premiums to cover any shortfall, variable life may be the best choice.

Variable contracts are especially appropriate when both retirement funding and life insurance are needed. Also, a variable policy may be appropriate for survivorship coverage when used to prefund estate taxes or long-term insurance coverage.

How To Purchase Variable Insurance

After checking the insurance company's credit rating and the basic contractual features of the policy, ask the following questions:

- *What has been the performance of the investment subaccounts for the last five years and who manages the funds?* Compare the performance of a contract's accounts with the major market indexes as well as with the performance of other available contracts.

- *What are the guaranteed features?* Make sure you understand how the contract is structured—no two contracts are identical.

- *What are the total fees, including the funds' management fees and cost of insurance?* Insurance costs increase with age.

- *Are there any restrictions or fees for switching investment options?* Most contracts offer a fixed number of switches annually.

- *Is there a minimum guaranteed death benefit regardless of performance?* Some contracts guarantee a minimum, others pay according to contract performance.

SPECIAL COVERAGE

The insurance industry offers special coverage for financial and health needs. Two of the more popular options—survivorship life and living benefits—apply to many types of coverage.

Survivorship Life

Some companies offer contracts as *survivorship* packages, in which two people are insured but only one death benefit is paid, either at the death of the first person (a first-to-die plan) or the death of the second person (a second-to-die plan). The motivation for these plans is reduced cost. Many personal, estate, and business situations may be resolved more cost effectively with survivorship plans than single-life policies.

Some individuals in poor health who do not qualify for single-life policies may qualify for second-to-die policies. Because taxes are due on the estates of a married couple only after both have died, a survivorship policy is a less expensive way to ensure that funds will be available to pay estate taxes. A business owner may someday need to buy out a deceased owner's stock from his heirs. A first-to-die policy enables him to accomplish this when both he and the partner are insured.

Living Benefits

A relatively new type of rider requires the insurance company to pay all or part of the death-benefit proceeds prior to the demise of the insured for terminal or catastrophic illness. Some policies also cover the costs of nursing home confinement.

REVIEWING EXISTING POLICIES

Insurance policies are not investments to be tucked away and forgotten. All policies should be reviewed at least once every year. A good time to do this is when you receive your annual statement, which reports levels of death benefit coverage, current interest credited, expenses charged against the cash value, and current cash values. Upon request, the company will send you an *in force* illustration which provides an accurate picture of your contract's current performance based on interest rates and insurance costs.

Note . . . Always inform the insurance company of any address changes. Also, keep your policies safe and place a list of the policies in your safety-deposit box.

Changing or Canceling the Policy

Changes in your circumstances may call for changes in coverage. Perhaps you have a new baby or one of your children has graduated from college. Perhaps you have quit smoking, which entitles you to a premium reduction. If you want to change coverage for any reason, contact the insurance company to determine the current projections for your contract and ask how it might be restructured to accommodate your financial goals. If you have several small policies, it may be advantageous to exchange them for a single large policy with an equal or greater death benefit.

If a broker recommends collapsing a contract or borrowing from it to purchase more coverage, take no action without thoroughly examining all the ramifications—you may be facing an unwanted taxable event, surrender fees, or possibly the purchase of insurance you do not need.

Do not cash out a contract if the tax liability is high—a 1035 tax-free exchange to another contract is preferable because there is no taxable event. If you no longer need insurance coverage, transfer the contract's assets to an annuity with a 1035 exchange. Optimal restructuring can often be arranged by your insurance company without fees, charges, or taxes. If the broker is unwilling to help you, contact the company's customer-service representative who can advise you of your options.

Borrowing from Your Policy

Just about all cash value policies allow for policyholder loans that do not require repayment. Upon the death of the insured, the amount borrowed is deducted from the death benefit. Because borrowing may alter the contract terms, determine the ramifications before making a loan.

Resolving Cash-Flow Problems

Many policies bought in the last several years that offered "vanishing" premiums have underperformed original projections. With the decrease in interest rates and the increase in company expenses, many policyholders were required to pay additional premiums to keep their policies in force.

If you lack money to pay premiums, you are not forced to choose between canceling the policy or reducing coverage. Collapsing a policy not only means a loss of coverage, it may also result in a taxable event or even a loss of savings. All cash value insurance contracts offer one or more of the following options that might help relieve a temporary cash-flow crunch.

- You can use dividends to pay all or part of the premium when due.

- You may borrow from your policy to pay the premium. Borrowed funds must be repaid with interest or they are eventually deducted from the policy's death benefit.

- You can convert your policy to term insurance. By using cash values to purchase term insurance, the death benefit remains the same for a specified period.

- You can reduce coverage in some policies to convert to a paid-up status, which remains in effect indefinitely.

SALES TACTICS TO WATCH OUT FOR

The more you learn about insurance contracts, the less vulnerable you will be to shoddy sales practices. It is important for you to recognize that irregularities occur so that you can be on your guard. The following case should be food for thought.

In 1993, the managers of the the most profitable sales office for the country's largest seller of life insurance were found guilty by industry regulators of misleading the public. Because some of their agents had represented certain insurance products as retirement accounts, their customers had no idea they were actually purchasing life insurance.

Some of the agents had never before sold insurance, but were trained to memorize, word for word, detailed sales pitches in which they referred to their products as "retirement savings plans" and "investments," substituting the word "deposit" for "premium." Customers were led to believe their money would earn interest from the moment they invested, and that they could withdraw it at any time, but most of their first year's premiums were used to pay commissions. After the regulators moved in, the insurance company fired some employees and promised to refund money to thousands of customers.

This incident prompted regulators to investigate insurance sales tactics nationwide. They discovered that many agents employed by other insurance companies were also guilty of misrepresenting their contracts, and some even disguised the fact that they were insurance salespeople by calling themselves "financial advisers."

Unfortunately, some brokers persuade policyholders to exchange their perfectly good policies or borrow against them to purchase inferior ones. In some cases, an exchange is beneficial, but often the swap results in the purchase of excessive coverage and higher annual premiums. For example, if you no longer have need for life insurance, you may want to exchange your existing policy for one with a living benefit that pays for nursing home care or for an annuity. But remember that even when policies are swapped for better ones, commission charges may inhibit the new contract's cash value growth for 10 years or more.

A broker may advise you that your policy is not performing well when the lack of performance is solely the result of falling interest rates. Policyholders have been misled about how the new policies will be financed, and the truth is not discovered until after their original policies have been drained of value. Policyholders are generally unaware they are being churned (conned into buying a new policy so that the broker gets the commission) because they are not required to put up any new money.

Before making any exchange, have the broker get his company to examine your existing policy and state in writing how the recommended exchange would benefit you. Such requests have been known to make insurance agents quickly disappear. You should also consult your present carrier regarding the proposed exchange because a restructuring of your existing policy may be more beneficial and less costly. Second opinions are always a good idea anyway.

If you have a complaint about any insurance broker or company, contact its customer-service division. If you are still dissatisfied, contact your state insurance department or call the National Insurance Consumer Helpline, (800) 942-4242, sponsored by insurance industry trade associations.

Summary

The purchase of life insurance is one of the best ways to protect loved ones because the benefits make their lives more comfortable when you cannot be there for them. Many types of coverage are available at a range of prices. To select the most cost-efficient contract to meet your needs and pocketbook, deal only with licensed brokers who agree to help you compare policies offered by several high-rated companies.

Term Life _____

- Protection for a specified period
- Low initial premium that increases with age
- No cash value
- May be renewable and convertible to permanent policy

Whole Life _____

- Permanent protection
- Fixed premiums
- Fixed cash value
- Tax-deferred growth of policy values

Universal Life _____

- Permanent, flexible protection
- Flexible premiums
- Cash value reflects premiums paid and market conditions
- Tax-deferred growth of policy values

Variable Life _____

- Permanent, flexible protection
- Fixed or flexible premiums
- Policyholders control investment choices; market conditions dictate investment returns
- Death benefits and cash value vary
- Tax-deferred growth of policy values

*B*y now you understand the basic workings of the stock market. Perhaps you own some common stock and are patiently waiting for your long-term rewards. But part of you is saying, "Isn't there a faster way? I want to be much more aggressive and achieve potentially dazzling gains—even if it means taking greater risks."

On the other hand, you may be a very conservative investor who seeks to cushion any possible loss that might result from price declines in your stock portfolio. In either case, you may be ready to enter the many-faceted world of options.

Chapter **17**

Options and Other Derivatives

"Man is a gaming animal."

Charles Lamb

Derivatives typically refer to the riskier, complicated types of instruments, but the formal definition of a derivative is any instrument whose price depends on the price movement of an underlying investment. Wall Street has managed to create more than 1,200 different derivative contracts that enable parties to hedge or bet on the price of a stock, bond, index, currency, commodity, or just about anything that moves in the financial marketplace.

Nearly all large companies and institutions employ derivatives to cut financing costs, hedge currencies, or limit risk in their investment portfolios. Derivatives include CMOs, options, futures, swaps, and many of the newer, exotic products that trade on exchanges or privately among institutions.

The explosive growth of derivative trading is estimated to exceed $35 trillion worldwide. For the last three years, various equity derivatives traded on the American Stock Exchange represented 41 percent of total volume! It is estimated that the U.S. market for options and futures contracts has grown to over $14 trillion, more than double the capitalization of all the stocks traded on the New York Stock Exchange, the American Stock Exchange, and NASDAQ combined!

The derivative markets are so large that it warrants two chapters of coverage. The next chapter looks at futures; this chapter examines stock and index options.

STOCK OPTIONS

A *stock option* is a contract that confers either the right or the obligation to deliver or purchase stock. As the name "option" indicates, you are not actually buying or selling stock—you are securing the *opportunity* or contracting to the *obligation* to buy or sell stock within a set period at a predetermined price.

Stock options are highly standardized contracts stipulating very specific rights and obligations that have been traded in one form or another since the early 1800s. One option contract always covers *100 shares* of a public company. The stock price guaranteed by the contract is the *strike price*. Contract prices are referred to as *premiums*. The day on which a contract is scheduled to terminate is the *expiration date*, always the third

Saturday of a designated month, although trades are not accepted after 5:00 PM EST on the prior Friday.

The exchanges that trade stock and index options are the Chicago Board of Trade, the New York Stock Exchange, the American Stock Exchange, and certain regional exchanges. An exchange matches buyers with sellers in auction trading—for every contract bought, there is an offsetting sale of the identical contract. Options are not available on all companies, just those the exchanges deem marketable.

Stock options have symbols that identify the name of the company, the month in which the option expires, and the strike price. There might be several options on the same company with different expiration dates and strike prices. Brokers access prices (premiums) for options the same way they do stock prices.

Trading

Stock options, the most popular derivative instruments among individual investors, are traded for two reasons—to profit from speculation or to protect a stock investment. For the options market to operate, there must be two sides to every transaction, a purchase and a sale—one risky and the other conservative. These are opposite strategies: Conservative investors use options to protect their stock investments; speculators seek to earn substantial returns with little invested.

Leverage. A major feature of option contracts is the leverage. For example, a $50 stock might have an option costing under $1, allowing you to control a much larger number of shares with a limited outlay of cash. Because a 10 percent rise in the stock's price might double the option's market value, you can speculate for profit or "insure" a stock position against price declines with the substantial leverage that options provide.

Time Value. With stocks, you have unlimited time on your side, but with options, you are operating with a very limited amount of time. *Time*, in fact, is what you are buying—the right to purchase or sell a stock within a certain period. Therefore, each contract has what is known as *time value*—the option's market value decreases as the amount of time left decreases to reflect its shorter lifespan.

Calls and Puts

A newcomer to the options market can easily become confused and enter into a transaction that is in conflict with his investment goals. Navigating smoothly in the world of options requires an understanding of the various choices and strategies open to you.

Options fall into two categories—*calls* and *puts*. A call option confers the right or obligation to *buy* at a certain price; a put option confers the right or the obligation to *sell* at a certain price. You may have heard that options are very risky, but whether they are risky or conservative depends on which side of the transaction you take—there is a conservative side to every risky option.

Conservative	Risky	Very Risky
Selling Covered Calls Buying Puts	Buying Calls	Selling Uncovered Calls Selling Puts

Buying Call Options

Buying a call option is a speculative strategy that gives you the right to buy 100 shares of a company's stock at a fixed *strike* price during a specified period. Even though your option involves the shares of a superior growth company, you could lose *all* the money you invest.

When you buy a call option, you pay a nonrefundable premium in return for locking in a price for a company's stock that you believe is on the rise. You are not actually buying any stock—just the right to purchase the shares before a specified deadline. The more time you buy, the higher the premium, but your risk is limited to the premium paid.

At any time before the option expires, you may (1) sell the call for a profit or loss, or (2) *exercise* your call by purchasing the stock at the strike price. If the strike price is *not* reached by expiration, however, you must either sell your option at a loss, exercise it, or allow it to expire worthless. A call option is profitable only when the underlying stock's market price exceeds the strike price by more than the option's cost, before the option expires.

If you believe the strike price will not be reached, you may limit a loss by selling your call option before it expires. Or, if the option is profitable, you may want to sell (close out) the position rather than risk an adverse market move.

While they sometimes bring high returns, the purchase of call options is not for the risk-averse. To illustrate, consider this hypothetical case:

Mona Gibbons works for a major airline and has accumulated 500 shares of her company's stock, purchased at a discount through a company savings plan. Over the years, the stock's market value doubles. When it is rumored that the airline might be a target for takeover by a cartel headed by a well-known corporate "raider," some of her coworkers talk about buying "options." Gibbons has no idea what options are, so she calls a friend's broker.

Buying call options, the broker explains, will give her significant leverage that would allow her to participate in the future of thousands of shares rather than only 500. With a successful takeover, the options would be several times more profitable than her common shares. This sounds exciting and opportune to Gibbons, but she has no available cash to purchase options. When the broker suggests that she sell her shares to free up the cash, Gibbons agrees, sells her 500 shares, and uses the proceeds to purchase call options.

Unfortunately, the airline takeover fails. The price of the airline shares drops dramatically, with a consequent plunge in the value of the options. Within weeks, the options expire, worthless. Gibbons is very surprised and dismayed to discover that she has lost her entire investment. Worse yet, she no longer owns her original shares.

Of course, some traders do profit or options wouldn't be as popular as they are. Consider a profitable hypothetical case:

Steve Farber believes that the price of XYZ Corp. shares, currently trading at $91, is about to take off. Farber speculates by buying 10 of the XYZ $90 call options expiring in two months. The broker has advised Farber that the calls are offered at a premium *of $3.50 each. To buy the calls, Farber must pay 10 x $3.50 x 100 (shares per call) for a total of $3,500, plus commissions. The trade gives Farber the right to purchase 1,000 XYZ shares at a price of $90 per share at any time prior to the contract's expiration.*

XYZ's market price must rise to $93.50 for Farber to break even (the value of one share plus the cost of the option). As luck would have it, within two weeks, XYZ's price soars to $97, causing the calls to double in value. Just prior to expiration, XYZ's price reaches $100.50 per share, and Farber sells his calls for $10.50, a 200 percent profit (not including commissions)—all without owning even one share of stock.

When you buy a call option with a strike price lower than the stock's market price (like Farber did), the calls are *in the money* because they are more likely to generate proceeds. If your call option's strike price is higher than the stock's market price, the call is *out of the money*, because the stock's price has farther to rise before the call may generate any proceeds.

Selling Covered Call Options

Selling a covered call is generally done to protect an investment or to earn extra income. It involves contracting to sell stock you already own (hence the term "covered") if the stock's price reaches a certain level by a certain date. Selling call options earns premium income, but it limits your potential gain from share ownership because it obligates you to sell your stock for a fixed price even though the market price may be much higher.

Taking the other side of your contract is the call option buyer who pays a premium to wager that your stock's price will exceed the strike price. You and the buyer take opposite positions, but only one of you can be correct.

If your stock's market price exceeds the strike price by the expiration, the calls will be exercised (called away), requiring you to sell your shares at the strike price and pay a commission. But if the market price fails to reach the strike price, you keep your shares with no further obligation. Either way, you may keep the premium income. For example,

> In late October, John Hart believes the price of his 1,000 PDA shares currently trading at $89 will be flat for several months. He decides to earn extra income by selling PDA calls. The PDA January $90 calls are bid at a $1.50 premium. By selling (writing) 10 calls, Hart earns premiums totaling $1,500 (10 x 100 x $1.50), but he obligates himself to sell his 1,000 shares at $90.
>
> If PDA's market price exceeds the $90 strike price by the expiration date, Hart's calls will be exercised and he will have to sell his shares at $90 each. If PDA's market price begins to rise significantly and Hart decides to keep his shares, he will "close out" his position by purchasing back the call options at a higher premium. If PDA's price fails to reach $90 before the expiration, Hart's stock will not be called and he will profit by $1,500.

Selling a covered call is a conservative strategy because the premium income cushions any drop in your stock's market value, but you limit your potential profits as a shareholder. A successful covered call writing program earns stock dividends, option premiums, and capital gains on stock sales when calls are exercised.

A covered call option is generally sold (written) for a higher strike price than the stock's current market price (out of the money). That way, the stock is less likely to be called, but if it is called, a profit is locked in. When you sell a call option with a strike price below the stock's current market price (in the money), you earn a greater premium but your shares are more likely to be called.

Buying Put Options

Buying put options insures against loss. If you do not want to sell your stock but are concerned that its price may fall, a *put option* gives you the right to sell 100 shares of stock at the strike price before the expiration date, regardless of how low the share price falls.

The party selling the put options expects to profit by earning premium income for assuming the risk you want to avoid. As with other types of insurance, if the event you insure against fails to occur, you do not get back the premium you paid. Here's how it works:

> *Mary Willis owns 500 shares of ABC currently trading at $83. Concerned that ABC's price will weaken in the next three months, Willis purchases five ABC January 80 puts at $2 each. This gives her the right to sell (put) her 500 ABC shares at $80 anytime before the expiration date. Her cost for the "insurance" is $1,000 (5 calls x 100 shares x $2) plus commission.*

If ABC's price rises, the put options decline in value; if ABC's price declines, the puts rise in value. If ABC's share price falls below $80, Willis may (1) exercise her put options by selling her shares for $80, or (2) keep her shares and simply sell the puts for a profit. Either way, the put options cushion any decline in ABC's price below $80 during the period covered.

Selling Uncovered Calls

When you sell a covered call, you pledge stock you already own. But when you sell a "naked" or *uncovered* call, you contract to sell 100 shares of stock that you do not own. You expect to pocket the premium income without owning the shares pledged, but you may be obligated to purchase them at much higher prices, and possibly lose significantly more than you earned in premiums.

Selling an uncovered call has the potential for high profit, but your risk is *unlimited*. Although the call may be expiring in only a few weeks, there is no limit to how high the price of the stock may rise—stock you may have to purchase to comply with the option contract. However, if the stock's market price does not exceed the strike price before the expiration date, you have no further obligation. Either way, you keep the premiums earned. Here's how it works:

Roberta Kelly does not own any shares of RCA, but she speculates by selling five December $90 RCA calls at a price of $3. The trade nets her premium income of $1,500 (5 x 100 x $3), minus commission, but obligates her to deliver 500 shares of RCA if the stock exceeds $90 before the expiration date.

314   Invest without Stress

If RCA's price does not reach $90, the calls will not be exercised, and Kelly will have profited by $1,500. However, if RCA's price climbs to $92.50, Kelly will have to pay $2,500 to "close out" or "cover" her option position, $1,000 more than the premiums earned. If RCA's price goes to $95, it will cost Kelly $5,000 to cover her position, a net loss of $3,500, not including commissions. The higher RCA's price climbs, the more Kelly will lose.

Selling Put Options

Selling put options is potentially very profitable, but it is *very* risky. When you sell (write) a put option, you earn premium income for contracting to buy 100 shares of a stock if its market price falls below the strike price before the option expires. The put buyer taking the opposite side of the contract has protected his downside by obligating you, the seller, to purchase his shares if the price falls to a certain level. Although the terms "naked" or "uncovered" are rarely used to describe the writing of put options, the concept is the same—you do not own the stock that you might be required to purchase at a price higher than the market price.

As long as the stock's market price is higher than the put's strike price, you are not obligated to purchase the shares and you profit by the speculation. But if the stock's price falls below the strike price, you must (1) purchase the shares, not at their lower current market value, but at the higher strike price, or (2) close out your position by buying back the puts at higher premiums than you had received for selling them. Selling a put is risky business because your potential loss could greatly exceed the premiums you have earned. Here's how it works:

Stan Manley does not own any RPM shares but sells five RPM 80 put options to earn the $3 premium. He generates total premium income of $1,500 (5 x 100 x $3), minus commission. If RPM's price stays above $80, Manley will be able to keep the $1,500 with no further obligation.

If RPM shares trade below $80 per share before the options expire, Manley will have to (1) buy the shares at $80 (500 x $80 = $40,000), or (2) buy back the puts

---

DERIVATIVES: The Good, the Bad, the Ugly

Many argue that the capital markets are more efficient when participants can employ derivatives to identify and cover their risks. For the most part, derivatives behave exactly as designed, but they can be far more volatile than ordinary investments. While they might enable managers to scale back their portfolios' risk exposure in unprecedented ways, sometimes derivatives are used solely for speculation or to enhance portfolio yields.

The more esoteric derivatives are extremely synthetic securities, developed solely from complex (occasionally flawed) mathematical models; consequently, they may behave unpredictably in the real world. Even the professionals who design and market them cannot always predict how they could be influenced by atypical market conditions. With such unquantifiable downside risk, derivative prices could vaporize during periods of unfavorable market momentum.

for more than he earned from selling them, and pay commissions. The lower RPM's price falls, the more Manley will lose.

If you write put options before a market correction, your potential losses could be severe. Had you sold Tenneco 60 puts before the market crashed in 1987, for example, you would have lost 10 to 20 times what you made in premiums when the shares fell to $40 by the end of trading on October 19. You would have been obligated to purchase the shares at $60 even though you could not sell them for more than $40, and it took almost two years for the price to reach $60.

Some investors misinterpret high credit ratings on the underlying securities as a sign that certain derivatives are not risky. For example, some pension funds and insurance companies bought CMO *interest only* derivatives that plummeted in price when market interest rates declined, even though the underlying securities were backed by the U.S. government.

Most of the major problems encountered by various institutions and local governments resulted from their misuse of leverage, which often involved derivative speculation. In 1994, the manager of a hedge fund (unregulated private investment partnership) lost $600 million of his clients' money in what he had described as safe, "market-neutral" strategies involving mortgage derivatives. The same year, many money market and bond mutual funds with derivatives suffered enormous losses when interest rates rose. To quell shareholder lawsuits, some sponsors were obliged to bail out their funds by covering the losses with their own capital.

With ill-fated arrogance, corporate trustees and government

INDEX OPTIONS

A stock option covers the shares of only one company, but *index options* represent entire baskets of stocks, enabling investors to speculate on the direction of the overall stock market. Institutional investors, such as advisers of mutual funds and pension funds, frequently hedge their large stock portfolios with index options.

employees took outrageous risks with enormous sums of corporate and public funds in their quest for profits. When their bets backfired, derivative losses mounted, exacerbated by an unanticipated lack of liquidity in a previously untested marketplace.

Perhaps the most sensational fiasco caused by derivative trading involved the venerable 233-year-old British investment firm, Barings PLC, credited with financing the Louisiana Purchase and the Napoleonic Wars. Although widely regarded as one of the best managed firms in London, in 1995 it allowed a young employee trader to bet and lose its entire $1 billion capital base with futures contracts on a Japanese stock market index.

Derivatives have been somewhat incorrectly blamed for the Orange County, California, debacle that resulted from its bond

Index options trade very much like individual stock options, but they are never exercised for stock, only cash credits or debits. Options are available on several stock indexes.

Index	Symbol	Stocks in Index
S&P 500	SPX	500 large companies
S&P 100	OEX	100 large companies
Major Market	XMI	20 large companies
S&P Mid-Cap	MID	400 medium-size companies
NYSE Composite	NYA	All NYSE listed companies
Value Line	VLE	1,700 broad-based companies

trading speculation. Betting that interest rates would not rise, the county's treasurer leveraged Orange County's account by borrowing $12 billion to buy interest-sensitive investments, including long-term government bonds. Orange County would probably have been bankrupted even if no derivatives had been involved.

The lack of understanding of the full scope of risk exposure for certain "designer" derivatives concerns regulators who express misgivings about the potentially huge losses that might derail the financial markets and adversely impact the economy. Although many derivatives are currently unregulated, marketing standards may be imposed for institutions that more accurately reflect the risks of such transactions, and greater disclosure may be mandated for mutual funds that employ derivative strategies.

LEAPS

Stock and index options called *Long-Term Equity Anticipation Securities* are similar to other options in every way except they have expiration dates as far in the future as three years. LEAPS, which provide investors with extended control over the stock market's fortunes, are available on more than 150 stocks as well as several market indexes. Like options, LEAPS enable investors to speculate or hedge their portfolios against market corrections. Because of the longer periods covered, LEAPS' premiums are higher, but they may actually be more cost-efficient than trading several short-term options.

S&P Depository Receipts

SPDRs (pronounced "spiders") are a recent innovation that allow you to participate in the ownership of an entire basket of common stocks, selected to duplicate the S&P 500 index. Technically not derivatives, SPDRs represent ownership in a long-term investment trust. Investors who want to own an instantly diversified portfolio requiring a small investment might find SPDRs appealing.

SPDRs are listed on the American Stock Exchange under the symbol "SPY." Holders receive quarterly distributions corresponding to the accrued dividends minus the trust's expenses. SPDRs may be sold short and bought on margin. Because the price is based on supply and demand, SPDRs may trade at a discount from or premium to the trust's net asset value.

OPENING AN OPTIONS ACCOUNT

To trade options, you must open an account with a licensed broker. Because options are more speculative than most other investments, brokerage firms ask for assurances that you understand the risks involved. After giving you a booklet describing the risks, the firm requires you to sign certain documents. *Study the booklet and do not even consider option transactions until you thoroughly understand them.*

Where have all my assets gone,
my hard-earned savings,

Could have been a wealthy man
But options looked good,

Lost it all with that last bet,
Now I'm broke and deep in debt,

When will I ever learn?
When will I ever learn?

For trading uncovered options, brokerage firms require you to sign additional documentation, meet minimum net-worth standards, and perhaps have at least some investment experience. Moreover, these traders must maintain certain levels of equity in their accounts to protect firms against loss. Brokerage firms are more restrictive today because many were forced to cover huge uncovered option losses when the market crashed in 1987.

Note . . . You may unknowingly own derivatives. Ask your broker to check your bond and money market mutual fund holdings, including those in your firm's pension and profit sharing plans.

Summary

Because it's an arena only for the intrepid, you first need to determine if you can stand the heat. Before risking your money, consider a mock trading program by tracking hypothetical trades until you score profitably on paper. Test a broker's expertise by tracking his recommendations for awhile before acting on them. Factor in commissions because they are typically a high percentage of total funds invested. Do not risk more than you can comfortably lose. *Option speculation is as much a game of luck as one of expertise.*

We sometimes hear even prudent investments characterized disdainfully as gambling. However, there is one area of "investing" that would be hard to defend against that charge . . . commodity and financial futures.

Chapter **18**

Commodity and Financial Futures

*"The House doesn't beat a player.
It merely gives him the
opportunity to beat himself."*

Nick "The Greek"

The last chapter examined options, the most popular derivative contracts. Another class of derivatives—futures—is very similar to options, but futures are very different in some respects, and the underlying assets on which they are based include farm and agricultural products.

A *futures* contract is an agreement to either deliver or accept delivery of a commodity or asset at a later date for an agreed-upon price. A contract is either *long*, a buy position, or *short*, a sell position.

Participants in futures contracts agree to purchase or sell assets as much as a year or more down the road— hence, the term "futures." These instruments are highly standardized contracts for which the exchange and the clearing house act as counterpart to both buyer and seller, guaranteeing payment if either defaults.

Commodity futures contracts are written for agricultural products, metals, or raw materials. *Financial* futures cover stock indexes, foreign currencies, and instruments that are sensitive to interest-rate fluctuations.

Futures trading serves two vital functions for the marketplace—*risk transfer* and *price discovery*. The principle underlying futures trading is that cash prices and futures prices, being influenced by the same factors, move in tandem—not precisely, but close enough to minimize or transfer the risk inherent in a position by taking the opposite position in the futures market. The trading action of the futures market also facilitates price discovery, the benchmark pricing for determining the market value of a particular commodity or financial instrument at any given time.

COMMODITY FUTURES

Commodity markets date back to the Middle Ages when European merchants organized medieval fairs to promote and regulate commerce. In the 1700s, similar organizations existed in the American colonies, and by 1850, there were 1,600 such groups in the Midwest states alone.

In 1848, the Chicago Board of Trade was formed by 82 merchants as a centralized marketplace to facilitate the trading of grains and livestock. In 1898, dealers in butter and poultry products formed what later became the Chicago Mercantile

Exchange. These forums became the most successful institutions of their kind, perhaps because of Chicago's strategic location at the base of the Great Lakes, surrounded by the nation's most fertile farmlands. The exchanges exercised great influence over produce trade by creating innovative techniques for handling and storing large amounts of commodities.

Before the Civil War, commodity transactions were settled exclusively in cash. After the growing season, farmers would converge on the market all at once. Prices would plummet as supply overtook demand, forcing some to abandon or dump their unsold, hard-earned harvest. Yet each spring, shortages would again cause prices to soar.

Supply and demand imbalances and the problems presented by the transportation, storage, and delivery of agricultural products and livestock led to the logical development of a futures market. When the CBOT began trading futures contracts after the war, seasonal disparities evened out and commodity markets were dramatically altered. The earliest contract recorded was created on March 13, 1851, for 3,000 bushels of corn to be delivered the following June.

As an example of how commodity futures work, consider the farmer who grows soybeans. His profit depends on variables beyond his control, such as the price he gets when selling his crop. The farmer manages this risk by selling a futures contract. If soybean prices drop, the contract's profit offsets or cushions his loss.

The party taking the opposite side of the farmer's contract might be a soybean oil bottler whose profit margins are reduced when soybean prices rise. He hedges his risk by buying a futures contract to lock in prices. Farmers and other individuals who have vested interests in commodities view the futures market as a means of securing price protection.

FINANCIAL FUTURES

Until the 1970s, futures trading was limited to agricultural commodities, but a new financial era emerged as a result of major global events. Perhaps the most significant was the collapse in 1971 of the fixed exchange-rate system for converting world currencies. As currencies began trading on a supply/demand basis, there was a need for a flexible investment tool to hedge currency risk.

In May 1972, the Chicago Mercantile Exchange inaugurated the first-ever financial futures contracts based on seven foreign currencies. Their success stimulated the creation of interest-rate and stock index futures contracts. Today's modern futures market involves the entire spectrum of financial instruments that account for 80 percent of all future contracts traded. The most popular contracts, the Eurodollar, the S&P 500 stock index, and the U.S. Treasury bond futures contracts, are used routinely by pension fund and investment advisers, portfolio managers, corporate treasurers, and commercial banks.

Financial futures trading dwarfs commodity futures trading and has greatly altered the management of portfolios around the world. For pension and mutual fund managers, shifting billions around with *index futures* is easier and less costly than identifying and purchasing individual stocks. By selling futures equal to the value of his portfolio, a manager can insulate his portfolio from a correction in any market worldwide. Futures are also an efficient way for institutions to shift from stocks to bonds and from bonds to stocks when a manager changes his asset allocation.

Role of the Exchange

Most futures trading occurs on the two major U.S. exchanges, the Chicago Board of Trade and the Chicago Mercantile Exchange. In 1994, these forums traded a record 445 million contracts representing assets valued in the trillions. Another active exchange, the New York Mercantile, specializes in precious metals and energy futures contracts.

Futures exchanges are centralized forums that are similar in many ways to stock exchanges. They are membership organizations that neither set prices nor own or trade securities or contracts. Orders are transmitted by computer or telephone from brokers located anywhere in the world to the exchange's trading floor. They are then routed to the appropriate *pit* where they are traded in a process called *open outcry*.

Communicating with voice and hand signals, traders and floor brokers declare bids and offers in seeming chaos as they represent their interests or the interests of the clients of member firms. Wearing brightly colored jackets that distinguish their functions, they participate in one of the most dramatic demonstrations of free enterprise that arrives at the best possible prices at all times.

When a trade is consummated, it is recorded and entered into a computerized reporting system, which is accessible to investors and brokers around the world. Market orders typically take less than three minutes to process. Futures transactions are cleared and settled by the exchange's clearing house, which guarantees that traders fulfill their contract obligations. Violations can result in major penalties imposed by the exchange. Futures trading is not only governed by the exchanges but also federally regulated by the Commodities Futures and Trading Commission.

Trading Accounts

Individual investors trade futures contracts with registered commodity representatives. Before they may open an account, customers must meet substantial net-worth and income standards, and sign one or more legal documents. Make sure you deal with reputable brokers by first calling the industry hotline provided by the National Futures Association at (800) 676-4632. You will be advised of any formal disciplinary actions that have been taken against any registered personnel.

Margin. Futures traders generally participate with less than 10 percent of a contract's initial market value. With such aggressive leverage, a 10 percent decline in a contract's market value could result in losses that exceed your cash investment. To protect itself from the liability of covering a customer's losses, the commodity firm requires an initial "good faith" deposit, or *margin*, equal to a certain percentage of the contract's market value. Commodity firms' margin requirements normally exceed minimums set by exchanges.

Traders must also maintain a minimum *maintenance* margin. As futures contracts are repriced during market hours to reflect market prices, individual customer accounts are *marked to the market* to reflect profits and losses. When price moves cause account values to fall below certain minimum valuations, the firm issues a *margin call* requiring an additional deposit of cash or marginable securities. If the customer fails to comply, the firm is forced to close out the position. The customer is liable to the firm for any resulting deficit.

Delivery. A contract seller who wishes to make delivery or a buyer who wishes to take receipt may do so (for most contracts), but few actually do. Typically, contracts are offset in cash debits or credits.

Traders

There are two categories of futures traders: *hedgers* and *speculators*.

Hedgers. Traders who depend on the revenues of certain assets may take positions in the futures market to protect against price changes that could result in losses. A farmer can lock in grain and livestock prices; a portfolio manager may limit losses from stock-price declines or lock in profits. Futures contracts make it easier to plan business expenses because they essentially fix costs.

Speculators. Traders who have no vested interests in any commodity or financial asset may assume the risk transferred by hedgers strictly to capitalize on the volatility of the contracts themselves. While financial rewards may be substantial, so are the risks. The participation of speculators ensures a more stable and efficient market, and provides greater access to a broader range of trading interests.

Options on Futures

In 1982, the CME and the CBOT introduced a new dimension to the futures market—options on U.S. Treasury bond futures. Options on futures contracts, which function similarly to stock options, differ from futures in that they give buyers the right *but not the obligation* to buy or sell a specific amount of a specific asset or commodity within a specified period. By comparison, futures contracts *require* buyers and sellers to perform under the terms of the contracts if open positions are not offset before their expiration.

Most options do not subject buyers to margin calls, which enables them to maintain their positions despite adverse market moves without putting up additional funds. Also, the decision to exercise an option is entirely that of the buyer who, unlike the futures trader, can lose no more than the money invested.

Risks

Anything that might affect the supply and demand of a commodity or financial asset is sure to affect the value of a futures contract. Relatively small market moves may have a large and sudden impact on a position, resulting in sizable gains or losses.

A hedger's losses in the futures markets are offset by gains in the cash markets; losses in the cash markets are offset by gains in the futures market. For speculators, however, futures carry a high degree of risk. The potential for profit is proportional to the amount of risk assumed and the trader's success in forecasting price movement.

When prices move against you, your losses may not be limited solely to funds invested, and commissions and spreads offset your profits. You could lose your initial margin funds as well as any additional funds deposited in your account.

The futures market is populated mostly by professionals who are intimately familiar with their high-pressure environment, an arena in which novice traders rarely prevail. Sometimes, when an investor wins big with his initial trade, he gets caught up in the action, but subsequent losses may be sufficiently painful to get him out for good. I have never known an individual investor who speculated in futures for very long.

Caveat Investor

If you must play the futures market, recognize that profitable investing requires considerable concentration and study. Unless you become well-versed, you hardly stand a chance. Also, market conditions change rapidly, so you must have adequate time to follow them carefully.

Make sure you have a thorough understanding of the terms and risks of the contract traded as well as delivery specifications. Calculate the extent to which a contract's value must increase for it to be profitable, taking transaction costs into account. Develop a trading plan and place limits on losing positions.

Do not play with real money without first testing your skills in "paper trading." *Risk only a very small portion of your net worth, and never more than you can afford to lose.* Keep in mind that margin calls may be necessary to maintain a position.

To further minimize risk, consider managed participation.

Managed Programs

Futures transactions enable you to play either side of a market, with potential profits just as likely when markets correct. Therefore, introducing futures to an investment portfolio may enhance diversification. But rather than going it alone, you may be better off in managed participation that allows you to draw on the talents and experience of professional traders— after all, this is a professional's game. Despite higher fees and greater volatility than most stock mutual funds, a few managed futures programs have achieved remarkable returns.

Individual Managed Accounts. Investors with $100,000 to commit to futures trading may hire an adviser to make all trading decisions.

Private Pools and Public Funds. More than half of all managed futures are private pools that require a minimum investment of $25,000. Pools are usually structured as limited partnerships that require investors to meet stringent suitability standards. Admission or redemption is generally allowed on a monthly or quarterly basis. For investments of less than $25,000, you can participate in public funds, the futures counterpart of mutual funds.

Fees. Annual fees for managed futures are high, from 3 to 11 percent, and advisers take a percentage of profits for themselves. Investors receive updated disclosure documents explaining the fees, risks, adviser track record, and the maximum drop a fund has suffered since inception. Read the section of the disclosure document covering fees to determine the break-even threshold (how much the fund must rise before all fees are covered). Most licensed security brokers can make recommendations for futures managers, pools, and funds.

Summary

Futures trading is a very specialized type of speculation that requires more time and effort than most investors are willing to commit. Your chances of profiting may be slim, even if you understand the markets. Professional management may give you an edge, but advisers are sometimes hot and sometimes not, so if you are uncomfortable losing 30 to 50 percent or more over a short period, do not participate in any type of futures trading.

Some investments are not always what they seem, despite their glittering reputation.

Chapter **19**

Gold

*"A gold mine is a hole in the ground
with a liar standing next to it."*

Mark Twain

Five thousand years ago, the ancient Egyptians raised obelisks sheathed in a precious yellow metallic element. Their temple priests, pharaohs, and the wealthy used the metal to adorn edifices, clothing, and even their bodies. Ornaments fashioned in this metal thousands of years ago are as beautiful today as when they were first crafted. Indeed, for as long as gold has been mined, it has claimed an allure unlike any other.

The Babylonians were using pieces of gold as currency as early as 3000 B.C. Although gold is not the rarest or most expensive metal, because it is relatively rare, highly malleable, easily transported, and virtually indestructible, it has been a prime medium of exchange for millennia. Even when barter economies evolved into more sophisticated market systems, gold remained the one substance universally accepted as payment for goods and services.

Gold as an Investment

For more than a century, the U.S. dollar had been backed by gold stored in Fort Knox. As long as other major world currencies were pegged to the dollar, the price of gold remained very stable. Individuals who worried about political and economic situations that would devalue their currencies bought gold. These investors were not interested in speculating in gold; they merely sought to protect what they had.

As the price of gold accelerated throughout the 1970s, however, a new breed of investor emerged who was interested in gold strictly as a speculative vehicle. These "goldbugs" have attempted to forecast gold's price by monitoring indicators such as interest rates and the Commodities Research Bureau's index, which measures commodity price movements.

Gold and the U.S. Dollar

In 1787, the Constitution granted the U.S. government the exclusive right to coin money and to regulate its value. Five years later, Congress directed that all U.S. coins be made of gold, silver, or copper, and officially priced gold at $19.30 per ounce. A few private banks issued paper money that became easily inflated, but eventually the U.S. Treasury printed paper currency that was backed by either gold or silver reserves stored in Fort Knox. In 1834, the government raised the official price of gold to $20.67 per ounce, where it remained for the next 100 years.

The practice of issuing paper currency backed by metal

When the price of gold peaked in 1980 at $850 per ounce, financial assets such as stocks and bonds were not at all popular with investors. As inflation started to decline in the early 1980s, however, gold lost its appeal for more than a decade while stocks and bonds rallied vigorously. When gold hit a low of $326 per ounce in March 1993, the hottest investment for individual investors was bond mutual funds, but a year later, the price of gold had risen 18 percent as stocks and bonds gave back much of their gains.

Inflation Hedge

Historically, any event that might increase inflation, such as government spending, has been considered bullish for gold investment. But the reality is that gold's price has not paralleled

reserves, the *bimetallic standard*, or "gold standard," requires a nation's central bank to redeem its currency for metals upon demand. A currency's purchasing power tends to remain stable when backed by precious metals because constraints are placed on the liquidity of credit in the financial system.

In his bid for the Democratic presidential nomination in 1896, William Jennings Bryan urged the use of silver to back some of the nation's currency because it was more plentiful. His famous line " . . . you shall not crucify mankind upon this cross of gold" promoted a move considered radical at that time. Bryan lost the election, but fewer than 40 years later, a strict adherence to the gold standard contributed to turning what might have been a manageable economic downturn into the Great Depression.

The heavy costs of World War I had created extreme infla-

the inflation rate—by 1995, gold's price was less than half what it was at its peak 15 years earlier. The chart on page 340 gives you a sense of gold's erratic price movements.

When nations were less stable and paper money more precarious, no one was arguing about gold's role as an inflation hedge. Eventually, paper currency was pegged to gold to keep it as stable as possible. Since 1971, however, currencies have not been backed by gold but compete in modern financial markets. Consequently, gold has lost its status as an investment hedge to other investments like foreign securities and real estate. The goldbugs' appetites appear to be satisfied by the more speculative commodity and currency futures.

Even the stock market has proved to be a far superior inflation hedge. According to Lipper Analytical Services, gold mutual fund shares gained only 19 percent for the 10-year period ending March 31, 1993, in contrast to inflation's 45 percent rise and the U.S. stock market's return of 177 percent (as measured by the S&P 500 index).

tionary pressures worldwide, and by 1930, many economies could no longer afford to back their currencies with precious metals. It wasn't long before nearly all Western countries suffered their worst depressions in history. Some historians attribute the deflationary shock to world economies to the strict adherence to the gold standard rather than a policy that would allow money supplies to expand.

In 1934, to prevent speculation in gold that could exacerbate the already moribund U.S. economy, gold coins were withdrawn from circulation. Citizens were restricted from buying, selling, and owning gold except in the form of jewelry and numismatic coins. To stimulate the economy, President Frank-

With the current inflation rate hovering around 3 percent, the recent strength in gold's price suggests that investors expect the inflation rate to rise. But will gold be their hedge of choice?

Perhaps gold's reputation as a viable inflation hedge is merely a popular misconception. According to studies reported in his book *The Golden Constant*, Roy W. Jastram maintains that gold has failed to keep pace with inflation throughout history. In fact, Jastram claims that gold did not hold its value as well during inflationary periods as it had during periods of deflation! Gold retains its purchasing power because of what Jastram calls the "Retrieval Phenomenon": "Gold prices do not chase after commodities; commodity prices return to the index level of gold again and again."

Furthermore, inflation is a double-edged sword: Rising inflation generally causes higher interest rates, which tend to tarnish gold's allure as an investment.

lin Roosevelt raised the official price of gold to $35 per ounce, effectively devaluing it an astonishing 69 percent!

Preparation for World War II restored the U.S. economy, but the global monetary chaos that followed the war prompted leaders of the allied nations to meet at Bretton Woods. They agreed to reestablish the international convertibility of their currencies into gold or the U.S. dollar, which was backed by gold and considered the strongest. As dollars continued to flow overseas to assist war-torn Europe's recovery, foreign banks and speculators traded them for gold stored in Fort Knox, significantly depleting the world's greatest cache.

Calamity Hedge

For decades, investors had turned to gold during periods of political unrest. Indeed, the price of gold often rose during times of world crisis, but declined as soon as peace was restored. But when the stock market crashed in 1987, gold did not attract investors—they fled to bonds. When Iraq invaded Kuwait in 1991, gold's price increased by only 5 percent, and then fell to even lower levels after U.S. troops returned home. Even the European currency crisis in September 1992 wasn't enough to spark the smallest blip in the price of gold, which later dropped to a seven-year low. So despite its reputation as a safeguard against calamity, as an investment, gold itself has been calamitous.

Demise of the Gold Standard

The persistent costs of the Vietnam War and the Great Society programs further exacerbated inflationary pressures on the already very weak dollar. Foreigners continued to swap dollars for gold, which they resold overseas for profit. In 1971, in an attempt to stem inflation and the further fall of the dollar, President Richard Nixon put an end to the government's selling of gold. Thus, the fixed-exchange rate system based on the gold standard succumbed to the present-day floating monetary system. (World currencies are no longer backed by metals but by confidence. Exchange rates are decided by currency traders who buy and sell globally around the clock.)

Supply/Demand

Some analysts suggest that the fundamental and technical aspects for gold investment may be improving. With gold trading at half its peak, there is little perceived downside risk relative to that of other investment options. Or perhaps the price of gold has dropped to a level that calls for a technical rebound.

Some analysts predict that supply/demand fundamentals will determine gold's price. Gold production added only 2 percent to the world's supply in 1993 versus the double-digit growth rates of the late 1980's. If mining costs increase, production may decrease or remain stable. Demand for gold, which comes from the world's jewelry trade, electronics indus-

President Gerald Ford eventually signed a bill legalizing the purchase and private ownership of gold in all forms. After four decades of artificial restraint during which it had become grossly undervalued, the price of gold began rising to more realistic levels. Loss of respect for the dollar, still the key currency of the world monetary system, wreaked havoc on currency markets as inflation continued to rage throughout the 1970s. Nervous investors paid escalating prices for gold in the hopes that it would hold its value better than paper currency. In early 1980, the price of gold peaked at $852 per ounce, an amazing 2,000 percent rise in less than a decade.

Almost immediately, the U.S. economy slipped into recession. As inflation slowed, the price of gold began its decline. Ten years later, gold was off more than 50 percent. During this decade, the U.S. stock market gained 300 percent.

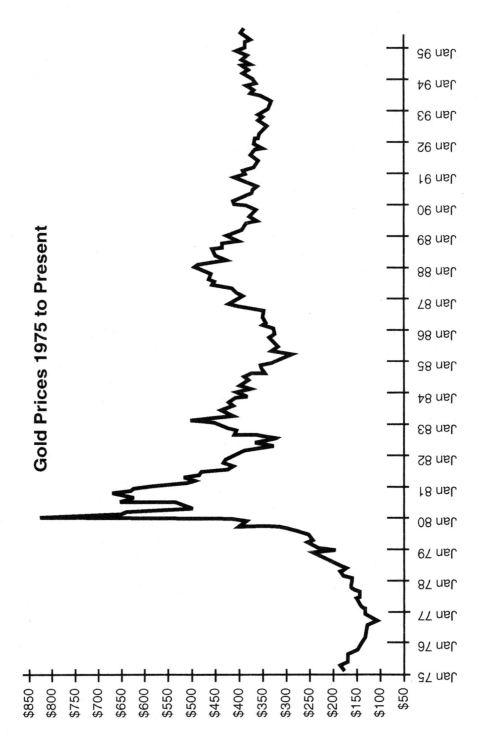

Gold Prices 1975 to Present

tries, and investors, has outpaced production since 1990; however, prices did not escalate because central banks were selling gold. Without such offsetting sales, demand could boost gold's price.

Ways to Invest in Gold

There are four ways to invest in gold:

Bullion Bars. Investment in gold bullion pays no interest or dividends and is quite impractical for small investors. Charges for storage, insurance, assay, and delivery represent a high percentage of funds invested, and some states impose sales taxes. Buying and selling in small quantities could be hindered by poor liquidity and stiff premiums.

Bullion Coins. Purchasing coins is the simplest and most liquid way to invest in gold bullion. The more popular bullion coins are the American Eagle, Canadian Maple Leaf, Australian Kangaroo Nugget, British Britannia, Chinese Panda, South African Krugerrand, and Mexican Peso. Dealers add a premium to gold's market price, based on the coin's weight.

Rare Coins. A limited supply of numismatic (rare) coins have produced profits for investors because their prices are based less on the price of gold than their value to collectors. Factors that determine value are a coin's age, metal content, condition, and type, as well as supply and demand. Numismatic Guaranty Corp. of America and Professional Coin Grading Service are the two leading grading services.

When you purchase coins, the dealer will declare them to be of a certain grade. Make sure you get a written guarantee stating that the dealer will honor his assessment of the grade should you want to sell the coins back to him.

Because the rare coin market is unregulated and often a target for scams, check out a dealer by calling the Federal Trade Commission, (202) 326-3303. Ask for the FTC's free brochure *Investing in Rare Coins*.

Common Stock. Shares in gold mining companies may be the preferred method for investing in the gold sector. Besides offering a speculation on the price of gold, common shares stand to participate in cash dividends as well as any improvement of company fundamentals such as decreased labor costs and rising profit margins.

The major U.S. producers of gold are Barrick Gold, Battle Mountain Gold, Echo Bay Mines, Helca Mining, Homestake Mining, Newmont Gold, Newmont Mining, Pegasus Gold, and Placer Dome. South African companies available as ADRs (American Depository Receipts, p. 206) are Driefontein, Hartebeestfontein, Vaal Reefs, Free State Consolidated Mines, Western Deep Levels, and St. Helena. A few sector mutual funds invest in these shares.

Summary

If you are considering an investment in gold, you must recognize that the gold market is subject to speculative booms, busts, and scams. To invest safely and pay decent prices, read more than one book on the subject. Also, it would be prudent to follow and study global economic and political indicators such as investor sentiment and inflation. Safe and profitable purchase of any hard asset including gold, real estate, art, or baseball cards requires considerable expertise, and you must not expect to receive unbiased advice from salespeople who market these assets.

*B*rokerage firms offer several types of investment accounts and the chances are good that at least one of them is appropriate for you, regardless of how much money you plan to invest.

Chapter **20**

Opening and Maintaining an Investment Account

*"Money makes money.
And the money that
money makes makes
more money."*

Benjamin Franklin

In most states, a brokerage account may be established by anyone 21 years of age or older (18 years of age in some states). Rarely do brokerage firms have investment minimums for opening a *cash account*, the simplest account that requires cash payment for securities purchased.

When opening an account, the broker asks you to provide information such as your address, phone number, Social Security number, birthdate, employment, marital status, dependents, net worth, annual income, and investing experience. Your broker must also ask about your investment goals so that he can make appropriate investment recommendations. He is not just being nosy—he is abiding by industry rules that require him to note your investment objectives on the new account form (*income, growth,* or *speculation*).

Account Ownership

The brokerage firm must be advised how you want to take title to your investments. The most common ways to own securities are

- ***Individual, or Sole Ownership.*** Only one person owns all the account assets.

- ***Joint Tenants with Rights of Survivorship.*** One or more owners have equal rights to the account assets. Any owner may enter orders, but all checks and securities distributed must designate everyone on the account. If an owner dies, the account's assets are transferred to the other party(s) on the title.

- ***Community Property.*** A married couple owns the assets equally.

- ***Tenants in Common.*** Two or more individuals hold fractional undivided interests in account assets that can be deeded, sold, or given away without the consent of the other owner(s).

- ***Trust accounts.*** The account assets are part of a trust arrangement, such as a living trust or charitable remainder trust.

Security Certificates

Certificates for securities purchased are either registered with the issuer in your name and sent to you or held in your account and registered in the name of the brokerage firm, *street name*. If the firm holds your securities, it is responsible for mailing you documents such as annual reports as well as collecting dividends and interest payments and crediting them to your account.

If you take possession of your security certificates, keep them in a safe or a safety-deposit box because fees are charged to replace certificates that are lost, damaged, or stolen. There is an industry movement to replace certificates with electronic book entry, and many issuers no longer print certificates. You must custody book entry securities at a financial firm. Dividends and interest payments are then credited directly to your account.

Account Statements

Account statements are sent to you monthly if you traded during that period, or quarterly, regardless of activity. Your statement lists securities held by the firm, cash and security deposits to and distributions from your account, money market fund interest credited, margin interest debited, money market fund and cash balances, and all transactions that occurred during the period covered.

Read your statement carefully as soon as you receive it, and verify that all deposited checks and interest and dividends earned by your securities were credited. Check for cash balances that are not earning interest, and ask the broker to purchase money market fund shares. If the account value has changed from the previous statement, check to see why. Did you withdraw money? Did security prices change? If you find a mistake or omission, advise your broker immediately. The sooner the broker is notified, the easier it is to correct. A transaction error not reported in a timely manner may be considered ratified.

One of the most common complaints brokers hear from customers is that statements are difficult to interpret. You must thoroughly understand this document, so if you have questions, be sure to have your broker explain it to you.

Open all mail sent by your broker. Do not assume any mail is promotional—some envelopes may contain important information, or even checks.

Note . . . Carefully read anything you are asked to sign, before you sign it. Never allow a firm to send your checks or mail to any address other than your own, and report any broker who makes this request of you.

Trade Confirmations

A transaction in which a security is bought or sold is referred to as a *trade*. For every transaction made in your account, the brokerage firm sends you a trade confirmation, or *confirm*, which is a record verifying a transaction. The confirm is not a bill, and payment is due regardless of whether or not you receive it. Check the confirm for accuracy as soon as you receive it and file it. You will eventually need the confirms for filing your taxes.

Payment Obligations

Payment for security purchases must be deposited to your account on or before the settlement date. *Regular way* settlement for most securities is three business days after the trade date; however, settlement for U.S. Treasury securities and options is one business day after the trade date, or *next day* settlement. If you sell securities when the certificates are in your possession, you are obligated to deposit them to your account on or before the settlement date.

If you do not make timely payment, the firm sends you a mailgram indicating what action the firm must take. If you fail to cover a transaction properly, the firm must cancel the trade, which could result in a financial loss for which you, not the firm, are responsible.

Payment by Check. Brokerage firms rarely accept cash deposits. Make your check payable to the brokerage firm, never to a broker.

Maintenance Fees. Most brokerage firms do not charge annual fees for simple cash accounts, although some charge for accounts that fail to generate minimum commission revenue.

Transferring Assets to Another Firm

To transfer an account's assets from one firm to another, sign the appropriate transfer document with the new custodian. Cash and securities are transferred between firms via computer. The transfer generally takes two to three weeks, depending on the type of assets in your account. Most firms will not hold another firm's proprietary investments (created exclusively by one brokerage firm). Certificates for securities that cannot be transferred may be sent to you. Some firms charge to deliver certificates and to transfer an account.

Securities Investor Protection Corporation

All brokerage firms that hold securities for clients are required to be members of the Securities Investors Protection Corporation. SIPC (pronounced *sip ick*) is a nonprofit corporation created by Congress in 1970 to protect customers against the loss of security certificates and cash if their brokerage firms become insolvent. SIPC is responsible for assisting with the liquidation of an insolvent brokerage firm and may arrange for a financially strong firm to acquire a failing firm, ensuring that all securities are properly transferred. To date, no SIPC funds have been required to cover losses of any sizable firm, only those of several smaller firms.

SIPC protects each customer's account up to $500,000 in securities and $100,000 in cash, excluding money market funds, although many firms have increased these limits with additional commercial insurance. *Insurance covers only the certificates and does not protect against losses incurred when prices of securities or money market funds decline or from losses that result from broker fraud or negligence.*

TYPES OF ACCOUNTS

The Central Asset Account

Most brokerage firms offer a type of investment account that provides more benefits and services than the simple cash account. *Central asset accounts* generally require a minimum deposit of cash and/or securities in addition to an annual fee. These accounts, which are known by a variety of names depending on the firm, generally offer

- special monthly statements,
- margin borrowing,
- various money market funds,
- credit card/debit card,
- check-writing privileges,
- canceled check return,
- ATM, and
- credit line.

Margin Accounts

All brokerage firms lend money to their customers when securities that qualify as collateral are deposited in their accounts. Just as you might borrow money using real estate as collateral, you may borrow against these marginable securities. The Federal Reserve Board regulates minimum margin requirements. Currently, investors may borrow up to 50 percent of the market value of their marginable stocks and mutual funds, and 70 to 90 percent on investment-grade bonds.

Margin loans may be a very efficient way to borrow because they are readily available regardless of your credit rating. Costs for borrowing may be less because no fees or points are charged, and you pay interest only for days you actually use the money.

To establish a margin account, you must sign the firm's *margin agreement* form. Although you may borrow for any purpose, investors typically use their loans to purchase securities. Sometimes brokers advise customers to *double up on margin*, to purchase more securities by borrowing against securities held in their accounts. In addition to increasing risk, this strategy results in more commissions.

Although many sophisticated investors exploit margin, such an aggressive strategy is rarely appropriate for novice investors. Before trading on margin, request a brochure, *Margin Trading Guide*, from your broker or write or call the New York Stock Exchange.

NYSE—Publications   (212) 623-3000
11 Wall St.
New York, N.Y. 10005

Margin Call. If you borrow against positions in your account, you carry a *debit* balance, which is money owed the firm. If the market value of your securities declines, you may receive a *margin call*, a notification to deposit additional funds or securities to your account to protect the firm against losses. If you fail to comply, the Securities and Exchange Commission requires the firm to sell, without your permission, sufficient securities in your account to reduce the debit balance. You, not the firm, are responsible for any loss this action may incur.

Margin Rates. Although they fluctuate and change without notice, rates for margin loans are competitive with rates charged by other lenders. The higher your account's debit balance, the lower your rate. If your debit balance is more than $100,000, you may be successful in negotiating a lower rate than the one offered. Just like banks, brokerage firms profit from margin accounts on the *spread*, the difference between what they charge customers and what they must pay to borrow.

Tax Implications. Margin interest is generally tax-deductible against investment income and gains when borrowed funds are used for investment, although there are exceptions. To be on the safe side, consult your tax adviser.

Discretionary Accounts

A *discretionary account* is one in which you grant limited power of attorney to a broker, empowering him to trade in your account as he sees fit without further permission. You give this authority to the broker by signing a *limited* power of attorney form. A *full* power of attorney, which is rarely conferred, grants the right to take funds from the account, but a limited power does not.

Although a broker's manager is required to regularly oversee trading in all accounts, there appears to be an increase in irregular activity when brokers have this discretion. Many firms discourage discretionary accounts because of the high frequency of client complaints for churning and unsuitable trades. It is far more prudent to require your broker to have your approval before executing any and all transactions in your account.

Custodial Accounts

A minor is not legally entitled to own securities, but a custodial account regulated by the Uniform Gift to Minors Act may be established on his behalf using his Social Security number.

The UGMA is probably the optimal way to invest children's money and can also serve as a terrific educational vehicle. The earlier a child learns about saving and investing, the easier it is for her to develop good financial habits. Many successful investors started learning about their craft at an early age.

Any adult may be the designated custodian for the minor, who is the account's *beneficial owner*, but it is usually a parent, grandparent, or guardian. Only one custodian and one minor are allowed on an account. The custodian has sole discretion over the account and may not delegate trading authority to another party. The custodian is obligated to transfer account assets to the minor upon reaching majority (age 18 in some states, 21 in others). Certain states allow the custodian to extend the age of transfer to 25 years of age.

Restrictions. The custodian, as a fiduciary of the account, may use the assets only for the benefit of the minor. The funds must not be spent on the minor's support or any legal obligation of the parent or guardian, but they may be used for certain items such as college expenses or piano lessons.

Any gift of securities or cash as well as money the minor earns may be deposited to a custodial account, but all deposits are irrevocable. Account assets may not be transferred to any other account if it results in a change of beneficial ownership. No margin or borrowing against assets is allowed, and the only allowable option transactions are covered calls.

Tax Implications. Custodial accounts provide tax savings on income and capital gains; however, because the law changes often and each situation is so different, consult your tax adviser about your particular situation.

As of 1995, the first $650 of annual income generated in a UGMA account is not federally taxed because it is offset by the minor's standard deduction. The next $650 is taxed at the minor's federal tax bracket. Income above $1,300 is taxed at (1) the minor's rate if 14 or older on the last day of the tax year or (2) the parent's rate if the minor is under 14 on the last day of the tax year.

Tax regulation requires that assets in a custodial account be taxed as part of the *custodian's* estate upon the custodian's death. So, if you make a gift to your child but do not ever want the gift to be considered part of your estate, neither you nor your spouse should be the custodian. Perhaps a close relative with fewer assets may agree to be the custodian.

Recordkeeping

Investing in securities generates quite a lot of paper. It is important to save certain documents, especially those that pertain to your taxes, but you do not need to save everything the firm sends you. It is safe to discard items such as annual and quarterly stock reports, statement stuffers from brokerage firms, and various marketing brochures for investment products.

You should maintain a separate file for each brokerage account, mutual fund account, and any investments not held with a custodian. Be sure to file prospectuses, statements, and confirms. For mutual funds, you may discard all but the year-end statement that recaps the entire year. When you sell securities, file copies of the confirms with your tax return.

RESOLVING DISPUTES WITH YOUR BROKER

Investment risk permeates the brokerage industry, so it's not surprising that misunderstandings occur between the broker and the client over who is responsible for a financial loss. Even operational and human errors may be expensive to correct. While most complaints are readily resolved to the client's satisfaction, some issues are sufficiently complicated and polarized to warrant formal airing.

Before doing business with any investment broker, you should be aware of some of the laws governing broker activities. In some states, brokers are considered *fiduciaries*, individuals held to a higher standard of conduct because they hold a position of trust such as a bank trustee or an investment adviser. Although industry standards do not require brokers to be infallible in their judgments, their recommendations must be suitable for their clients.

Suitability issues may be subjective, but industry guidelines and precedents exist. For example, if an elderly woman sued her broker for putting her in stocks that lost money, the broker might have a strong defense if the woman had been investing in stocks for several years. However, if she had never before bought stocks and had a history of investing only in high-grade bonds, the stock purchases might constitute "undue risk," and the broker might be found liable for her losses.

Attempting a Resolution

Brokers, like other professionals, may be held responsible for their negligence and misconduct. Recognizing that disputes will occur, the brokerage community has instituted a system for resolving them. If you believe your broker was responsible for your loss, first attempt to settle the matter directly with him. Date and file copies of all letters, and document phone calls and conversations by keeping a log. If this does not achieve a successful resolution, submit a written complaint to the broker's supervisor or the firm's compliance department.

Brokerage firms often make arrangements to accommodate customer claims if they determine that the losses resulted from broker misconduct. Brokers are legally precluded from personally reimbursing their clients for losses, but the brokerage firm may do so.

If discussions with the firm are unsatisfactory, you may pursue a resolution through the industry's arbitration process, mediation, or sometimes in a court of law. Technical aspects surrounding such disputes are complex, so you may need to consult an attorney specializing in securities law. Brokerage firms spend thousands of dollars defending most customer claims, and claimants with legal representation usually fare better than those without it.

Your local bar association should be able to assist you in locating an attorney who specializes in securities law. When a case has merit, the lawyer generally agrees to work on a contingency basis whereby he takes a percentage of the award or damages in lieu of an hourly fee. A lawyer may refuse to work on contingency if he believes your case is not very strong and charge an hourly fee regardless of the outcome.

Arbitration

Starting in the early 1800s, members of what is now the New York Stock Exchange settled disputes and resolved conflicts through arbitration. Over the years, the process evolved to include members' employees and their customers. In 1987, the U.S. Supreme Court handed down a landmark decision that generally binds investors to resolving their disputes in industry arbitration proceedings rather than taking their brokers to court. If you signed any firm documents, you probably forfeited your right to sue in a court of law.

The National Association of Securities Dealers and stock exchanges provide forums that handle nearly all cases arbitrated. For information regarding arbitration and to get the necessary forms for filing, call any industry self-regulatory organizations such as the NASD at (212) 480-4881 or the NYSE at (212) 656-2772. These organizations cannot advise you on the validity of your claim—for that you must consult an attorney. The time allowable to file a claim may be as short as one year or, if fraud is alleged, several years.

How It Works. The arbitration process begins when you file a *statement of claim* with one of the regulatory agencies. This document names the respondents, usually the broker and the brokerage firm, and states your position on why you deserve to be compensated. Once this document is filed, the broker and the firm must respond, and the arbitration is scheduled.

The opposing sides proceed with *discovery* as each side requests from the other pertinent information such as copies of documents regarding security transactions. If a settlement cannot be agreed on at this stage, a closed hearing commences.

The opposing parties present their cases before a panel of

three impartial arbitrators chosen by an industry organization. Arbitrators are individuals who are generally far more knowledgeable than judges or juries about the securities industry. Only one of the arbitrators may be associated with, or employed by, a brokerage firm or other securities industry organization. Each party may challenge the appointment of any arbitrator for good cause, and each party may challenge one arbitrator without cause. Before the hearing, both sides agree to abide by the arbitrators' decision, for which there is little possibility of appeal.

As in court, the claimant states his case first, and then the respondent presents their defense. Each side is entitled to cross-examine the other side's witnesses, who are sworn to testify under penalty of perjury. After final arguments are heard, the panel deliberates privately to decide if an award is to be made, the amount, and who must pay the costs of the hearings. Their decision is sent to the parties by certified mail.

Costs. Initial filing fees for an arbitration range from $400 to more than $1,000, depending on damages claimed. An average hearing runs about two or three days and costs about $1,500 per day, not including attorney fees. Your attorney may recommend that you hire, at your expense, one or more expert witnesses to support your testimony.

The arbitration process is a practical alternative to the court system for both the brokerage community and its customers. Arbitration is far less costly than trying a court lawsuit, and not nearly as time-consuming. While a court case might take two years or more, most arbitrated disputes are resolved in about one year.

Simplified Arbitration. A type of "small claims" procedure called *simplified arbitration* handles claims of $10,000 or less. Because lawyers rarely accept cases this small, this is a viable option for investors. Formal hearings are seldom required. The claimant submits his case in writing along with a check for minimal fees. The other side responds in writing. Only one arbitrator rules on the case. The decision, which is binding, is communicated to the opposing parties by mail.

How Cases Are Decided. Arbitrators examine the accountability of both claimant and broker, and assign responsibility for losses on the basis of several criteria. Although investors are not expected to know as much as their brokers, compensatory damages are not awarded simply because an investor lacks investment knowledge or his investments declined in value. Arbitrators are not inclined to rule favorably on frivolous claims. To prevail, you must convince the panel that the broker breached a duty that caused your loss.

Many securities are marketed by prospectus, which means that the broker must furnish the client with this document describing the investment. Regardless of what the broker may have actually told a customer, arbitrators might conclude that the prospectus properly informed him. Phone calls are generally not recorded, so cases often hinge on the customer's word against the word of the broker.

A substantial percentage of cases are settled before any arbitration. Between May 1989 and June 1992, the 10 most active brokerage firms paid out $165.7 million to investors on more than half the 4,962 claims brought against them. Punitive damages, awarded to punish a defendant who acted recklessly or to send a message to the brokerage community, have been awarded in only 2 percent of all cases, but they are becoming more frequent.

"When a person with money meets a person with experience, the person with the experience winds up with the money and the person with the money ends up with the experience."

Swim With the Sharks
Without Being Eaten Alive
Harvey Mackay

HOW TO MINIMIZE DISPUTES

Although most brokers are committed professionals with their clients' best interests at heart, all brokers are vulnerable to ethical breaches that could compromise your rightful yield and ultimate investing success. Prudent investing requires that you arm yourself with adequate investment knowledge as well as healthy paranoia.

Write your broker a short letter recapping your investment goals, and keep a copy.

Do not expect your broker to know everything or be able to read your mind. Be sure to communicate your investment goals and objectives.

Do not give discretionary power to any broker. Require that a broker have your permission to transact before every execution.

Ask your broker to explain in writing his rationale for recommending an investment you believe may be unsuitable for you.

Don't excuse unauthorized trades, even when they are profitable. Don't set a precedent that could result in problems later.

Report unauthorized transactions and any other problems with your account immediately to your broker or his manager or the firm might take the position that you ratified the trades.

Never allow a broker to pressure you into making an investment decision. "Deadlines" are generally sales tactics.

Never invest in any business that a broker is personally involved with or has an interest in.

Always check your statements to determine the market valuation of your account. Some brokers have advised clients they were making money when in fact they were losing it.

If a broker recommends an investment that yields a higher rate of return than the current market, make sure you know why before investing.

When investing your money, never make a check payable to an individual investment broker or adviser. Make checks payable to the financial institution, such as the brokerage firm, mutual fund, or insurance company. Write your account number legibly on the check.

Always ask your broker about the costs and underwriting fees for every transaction. Ask to see the prospectus and read the section on fees.

If you are told there is no commission, don't believe it. A commission is probably built into the price.

There could be underwriting fees, ongoing fees, or an exit fee charged upon liquidation.

Summary

Learn to take prudent advantage of the variety of investment accounts and brokerage services available. Ask plenty of questions to determine the best account/services package for your financial goals. Although a broker may facilitate your investment transactions, *the ultimate responsibility for investing your money is yours alone.* Consider yourself responsible for financial losses from trading securities about which you know very little. If you learn just one thing from this book, it should be to become as informed as possible BEFORE committing money to any investment.

W̶e all need to save money for retirement—a period that may arrive sooner than we think. The government promotes such savings by allowing them to grow on a tax-deferred basis when we establish qualified retirement accounts.

Retirement Accounts

"Save a part of your income and begin now, for the man with a surplus controls circumstances and the man without a surplus is controlled by circumstance."

Henry H. Buckley

Whenever possible, you should take advantage of the benefits of tax-deferred retirement accounts. The growth of savings accounts is taxed, but contributions to eligible retirement accounts grow tax-deferred, resulting in greater accumulation of wealth. You also save tax dollars because most contributions generate tax deductions.

Financial institutions such as banks, insurance companies, mutual fund companies, and brokerage firms offer *prototype* retirement plans for your convenience. A prototype is a plan that has been preapproved by the IRS, eliminating the expense of designing a plan. Individual Retirement Accounts and Simplified Employee Plans are the simplest, but Profit Sharing, Money Purchase, Defined Benefit, and 401k plans are also available. Your tax accountant should be able to determine which account(s) would be most beneficial to your individual situation.

To establish your tax-exempt retirement account, complete and sign the adoption form provided by the custodian. If your account is held at a brokerage firm, contributions are deposited immediately to a money market fund, where they earn interest until you decide how to invest them. As long as you qualify, there is no limit to the number of retirement accounts you may open, but the amount of your annual contributions is limited.

INDIVIDUAL RETIREMENT ACCOUNT

In 1982, the U.S. government enacted a law to encourage individuals to save for retirement by contributing to a special trust called an *Individual Retirement Account*. Anyone under the age of 70½ may contribute annually a maximum of $2,000 of earned income, which includes wages, tips, commissions, salaries, and alimony. Dividends, interest, capital gains, and child support do not qualify as earned income.

You must establish an IRA with a custodian such as a bank, brokerage firm, or mutual fund company, and complete and sign the adoption agreement the custodian provides. With a *self-directed* IRA, you select and manage the investments yourself, perhaps with the assistance of an investment adviser or broker. Many choices are viable including stocks, bonds, and mutual funds, but you may not invest in life insurance, commodities, artwork, precious gems, short sales, call options, or precious metals (except for certain U.S. minted gold and silver coins).

Allowable Contribution

You may deposit your annual IRA contribution all at once or over time, as long as it does not exceed $2,000. All contributions must be made in cash by April 15th following the calendar year to which it applies. (For a contribution made between January 1 and April 15, designate whether it is for the prior or current year.)

If you are married and either you or your spouse does not work, together you may contribute as much as $2,250 as long as you file a joint return, neither of you is older than 70½, and no more than $2,000 is contributed to either IRA.

Non-Deductible Contribution

Whether or not your IRA contribution is tax deductible depends on your adjusted gross income and whether you or your spouse are covered by an employer-sponsored plan. Because the rules change from time to time, consult your tax adviser. (Non-deductible contributions must be reported on Federal Income Tax Form 8606.)

Even if your IRA contributions are not tax deductible, you may still benefit from an IRA's tax-deferred compounding of income and gains. Table 21-1 depicts the accumulated growth of a $2,000 annual IRA contribution, compounding at 8 percent, compared with a fully taxable account subject to 28 percent tax. As the table shows, after 35 years, the assets in the IRA are worth 66 percent more than the non-IRA assets.

Table 21-1. Accumulation of a $2,000 Annual Contribution.		
Accumulation Period	Non-Deductible Savings Account	Tax-Deferred IRA
10 Years	$ 27,568	$ 31,291
15 Years	48,342	58,648
20 Years	75,831	98,845
25 Years	112,201	157,909
30 Years	160,325	244,692
35 Years	224,000	372,204

For more information on IRAs, obtain a copy of IRS Publication 590 by contacting any district office of the IRS.

SIMPLIFIED EMPLOYEE PENSION

Self-employed individuals who want to contribute more than $2,000 to a retirement plan should consider the *Simplified Employee Pension*, known as the SEP/IRA. This plan is the simplest retirement plan available to sole proprietors, partnerships, corporations, S-corporations, and self-employed individuals because it involves less administration, maintenance, and paperwork. No IRS or Department of Labor filings are required. (When a self-employed individual sets up a pension plan, he designates himself as both employer and employee.)

To obtain a tax deduction, you must establish and fund a SEP/IRA before the tax filing deadline, plus extensions. SEP custodial fees are usually the same as those for an IRA.

Annual SEP contributions may not exceed an adjusted 15 percent of the participant's compensation up to a maximum of $22,500. If you want to contribute a larger percentage of income, consider a Money Purchase Pension.

DEFINED CONTRIBUTION PLANS

Defined contribution plans include *Profit Sharing*, *Money Purchase*, and *401k*. These plans are so called because the contribution is "defined," or specified, as a percentage of earned income. Unlike a SEP/IRA, annual IRS and Department of Labor filings may be required.

Profit Sharing Plan

The *Profit Sharing* plan is recommended for business owners or self-employed individuals seeking contribution flexibility. Contributions, which are voluntary, may not exceed an adjusted 15 percent of the participant's earned income to a maximum of $22,500 in a calendar year. Contributions may be made through the due date of the tax return, including extensions.

Money Purchase Pension Plan

A *Money Purchase Pension* accommodates business owners and self-employed individuals who do not want their contributions to be limited to $22,500. Contributions are based on a fixed, predetermined percentage of compensation up to 25 percent of earned income, not to exceed $30,000 in a fiscal calendar year. Once the pension has been established, participants are expected to contribute annually. Contributions may be made through the due date of the tax return, including extensions, but not beyond 8½ months.

Note . . . By establishing both Profit Sharing and Money Purchase Pension plans, you may be able to contribute as much as 25 percent to a maximum of $30,000 annually; however, you are never obligated to fund more than 10 percent of your annual income in any year.

401k Plan

A *401k* is an employer-sponsored retirement plan that allows for employee contributions through a salary-reduction agreement. 401k plans also allow employers to make contributions to employee accounts. Amounts contributed by higher paid employees are limited by contributions made by lower paid employees. Contributions are optional, limited to a predetermined level, and indexed each year for inflation.

Most 401k plans offer a choice of stock and bond funds as well as a fixed account or *Guaranteed Interest Contract* (GIC). Changes in investment allocation are generally allowed on a specified schedule.

DEFINED BENEFIT PENSION PLAN

A *Defined Benefit Pension* promises to pay employees a fixed benefit at retirement. The plan is called "defined benefit" because contributions are based on a targeted retirement benefit rather than on annual compensation. An actuary computes the contribution on the basis of the participant's age, income, years of service, and projected retirement date. The actuary first identifies the targeted retirement objective and works backward to determine the annual funding required. Performance of a plan's investments may alter contribution levels. For individuals close to retirement, contributions to the Defined Benefit Pension could greatly surpass the limits of all other plans.

Note . . . Contributions to all retirement plans except IRAs depend on whether or not the business entity is a corporation. Contributions should be calculated, not by the investment professional, but by an accountant, tax adviser, or pension administrator.

IRA ROLLOVER

Assets of most terminated plans may be *rolled over* (transferred) to an IRA, deferring taxation. When you leave a job where you and/or your employer have funded your retirement plan, you may legally transfer the plan assets into an IRA rollover or other eligible retirement plan, thereby deferring any taxable event.

If your pension assets are not properly transferred, you may face a serious loss of funds to taxation. Recent legislation requires employers to withhold 20 percent of plan assets for payment of federal income tax unless all the assets are transferred to qualifying accounts. Assets that are not properly transferred are considered distributions of income, subjecting them to ordinary federal, state, and local income taxes, and potential penalties.

MAINTAINING RETIREMENT ACCOUNTS

Every type of retirement account has its own characteristics. However, Congress has ruled that all qualified retirement accounts abide by certain restrictions and tax consequences.

Withdrawals and Tax Implications

As long as assets remain in tax-deferred retirement accounts, no taxation is imposed. You may withdraw funds from your account at any time, although all distributions are taxed as ordinary income. If you have not reached the age of 59½, a 10 percent penalty is imposed in addition to the income tax (with certain exceptions).

The 10 percent penalty does not apply if the funds are properly transferred to an IRA, or if you are totally or permanently disabled. Also, you may avoid the penalty if you receive distributions in substantially equal periodic payments that are based on your life expectancy (a minimum of five years) up to age 59½. The closer you are to retirement, the larger these payments may be. Consult your tax adviser before taking a distribution.

Note . . . When cash is needed, it is generally best to withdraw funds from tax-deferred accounts last to postpone the tax liability and to continue benefiting from the tax-deferred status.

Transferring Accounts

You may transfer retirement-account assets from one custodian to another by completing transfer forms with the new custodian. If your account contains securities that are not transferable to the new custodian, you may sell them, continue to keep the account at the old firm, or take a distribution of the assets and pay taxes on their market value. Unless you intend to keep your account with a particular custodian for a long time, avoid investments that are nontransferable or not easily liquidated.

Minimum Required Distributions

When you reach the age of 70½, the IRS wants to start collecting some of the taxes you have deferred on your IRA and pension contributions. The initial distribution must be made no later than April 1 following the year in which you attain 70½, and continued annually until the account is depleted. (You attain 70½ in a particular calendar year if your 70th birthday occurs on or before June 30 of that year.) If you wait until April 1 to take your first required distribution, you must take your second distribution by the end of the same year.

The minimum required distribution is based on your life expectancy or your joint life expectancy with your beneficiary. Failure to comply might result in penalties as high as 50 percent of the required distribution. Most banks and brokerage firms are happy to calculate the required minimum distribution for you, or you may refer to IRS Publication 590.

The mandatory distribution may be taken from one or more of your tax-deferred accounts. Rather than liquidate assets, you may distribute assets *in kind* by transferring them to a taxable account or by taking possession of their certificates, making sure their market value is equal to the required minimum distribution.

Recordkeeping

Recordkeeping is extremely important. Keep a separate file for each retirement account and a log of all your contributions and distributions. For non-deductible IRA contributions, keep copies of form 8606 that you filed with your tax return as well as your annual IRA statements.

Summary

IRAs and prototype retirement plans are especially beneficial because they provide access to optimum investment options as well as tax-deferred investment growth. To secure your retirement, fund all qualified retirement accounts for which you are eligible to the maximum allowed.

Until recently, the only individuals who did more than write a simple will to transfer their money and possessions at death were the very rich. But with the increase in estate taxes and greater involvement of the probate courts, just about everyone can now benefit from estate planning.

Planning Your Estate

"It's a kind of spiritual snobbery that makes people think that they can be happy without money."

Notebooks
Albert Camus

Your estate is composed of all the earthly goods that you leave behind at death. Estate planning involves legal arrangements whereby your estate is smoothly transferred with the least expense and in the most efficient manner to selected beneficiaries such as a spouse, children, grandchildren, or charity. The goal is to complete this transfer with minimal tax assessment and complications.

Estate planning is about authority, power, and control over your assets. It is a lifetime project that requires you to make far-reaching, often irrevocable decisions. With adequate planning, the hassles and costs of probate are eliminated, tax dollars are saved, and assets are transferred efficiently to people or charities of your choice.

Although death and taxes are everyone's least favorite subjects, the ramifications of poor estate planning can be major. The following hypothetical scenario should give you a practical sense of the potential dilemmas.

Max and Sara Rentier have been happily married for many years during which they have accumulated stock and real estate valued at more than $1.5 million. The couple was always very fond of Sara's niece Nancy who has been very kind in looking after them. They were planning to leave most of their estate to Nancy and to their friend, Frank, who helps Max manage all his properties.

But the Rentiers could never bring themselves to consult an attorney specializing in estate planning. Like many people, they found the subject distasteful and a bit ghoulish. Unfortunately, when both were killed in an automobile accident, it became impossible to respect their wishes.

Because the couple had not written their wills, the state of California determines who will be their heirs. And because the Rentiers failed to plan properly, their entire estates are going to Sara's estranged brother whom Max and Sara had detested. Their devoted niece and their good friend Frank are receiving nothing—and the IRS is extracting more than $300,000 in estate taxes.

Adequate planning resolves many potential problems, as the following hypothetical story illustrates.

Mary Smith, a 65-year-old widow, instructs her attorney to arrange her affairs so that her son and grandchildren will inherit her $2 million estate. The estate consists of her home and some growth stocks that had greatly appreciated over the years. Smith has held off selling her stocks to avoid incurring the tax on the gains, but now she needs more income.

Because her health is poor, Smith wants to move from her large home to a small condo. The attorney counsels that Smith will be liable for significant capital gains taxes on profits from both the sale of her residence and her stock. To reduce this tax liability as well as estate taxes that would be due upon her death, the attorney advises Smith to establish a trust that will enable her to bequeath both her stock and her home to charities of her choice.

Because the trust, and not Smith herself, will sell these assets, no capital gains tax will be imposed. The trust will then have more of the sales proceeds to invest, increasing the income it pays Smith for the rest of her life. Upon her death, her son receives the income from the trust for the rest of his life.

Smith's attorney advises her to execute a Durable Power of Attorney for Finances to provide management for her assets should she become unable to do so. He further suggests a Durable Power of Attorney for Health so that Smith's wishes regarding termination of medical treatment and donation of organs will be respected.

Unable to secure life insurance because of her poor

health, Smith is able to qualify for a survivorship in-
surance policy paid for by the tax savings that result
from the charitable gift donation. The policy, which
also covers her son's life, provides for her grandchil-
dren to receive, after both their grandmother and
father are deceased, a benefit equal to the assets
Smith gifts to charity.

The result benefits everyone but the IRS, who loses
out on both the capital gains taxes and estate taxes.
The strategy generates a charitable deduction that
lowers Smith's income taxes to boot! Of course,
Smith's charity is very grateful.

If you fail to write a will that is properly signed and witnessed, and thus die *intestate*, the state effectively writes one
for you and becomes intimately involved in your affairs. Your
estate is transferred according to state laws, usually to your
next of kin who may not be your heirs of choice. If you leave
minor children, the state makes all decisions regarding their
welfare. If you become physically or mentally incapacitated,
the court appoints a conservator/guardian to oversee your
care and manage your finances.

Whether or not you have a will, the court takes control of
all assets in your name at the time of death. *Probate* means
"to prove"—the probate process proves that a will was validly
drawn, signed, and witnessed, and ensures that the government and heirs receive their proper share of the estate. The
executor files the will in probate court, and notices go out to
heirs, relatives, and newspapers so that creditors may make
their claims. The executor is responsible for locating and
valuing assets, paying legal fees and taxes, and paying off all
creditors. Only then do the heirs receive the remainder of the
estate's assets.

The probate process can be very lengthy, and probate fees can eat up 3 to 8 percent of the estate's value, or even more if the will is contested. The estate is no longer private because the documents are publicly recorded.

ESTATE TAXES

"Money talks, they say.
All it ever said to me
was 'goodbye.'"

None But the Lonely Heart
Clifford Odets

Without careful planning, a staggering percentage of the assets you intend to leave to your heirs may end up in the hands of the IRS. In fact, the IRS is counting on its share of the trillions of dollars in assets that make up the estates of U.S. taxpayers. Fortunately, there is tax relief for those who take appropriate and timely action.

Under present law, every individual is entitled to gift or leave to heirs a total of $600,000 without incurring estate taxes. This reflects the current *unified tax credit* of $192,800 granted every individual. Any amount over $600,000 will be taxed if inherited by anyone other than the surviving spouse (except when the spouse is not a U.S. citizen.)

You may also make individual gifts of $10,000 or less to as many people as you desire within the calendar year without reducing your exemption. A married couple, for example, may together gift $20,000 to each of their children and grandchildren annually. Gifts exceeding the limit reduce your unified tax credit by the amount of the tax due; however, gifting assets that are expected to appreciate significantly may be advantageous.

Upon your death, the tax due on your estate assets valued at less than $600,000 is offset by the unified tax credit, but your estate will be taxed starting at 37 percent on any amount over $600,000. An individual's estate is appraised as of the date of death. (Although an estate of $600,000 or less is not federally taxed, some states impose taxes on smaller estates.) When estimating your potential estate tax liability, be sure to include your pension plan, IRA, real estate, securities, investments, and businesses. Proceeds from life insurance are included unless the policy is owned by a party other than the deceased.

Because federal estate tax regulations are complex and subject to change, anyone with an estate greater than $600,000 should consult professional legal counsel. If your situation is complex, consult your tax adviser as well. You may discover that you are not holding title to property in the most beneficial way. For example, it may be unwise for a married couple to hold title in joint tenancy, especially in a community-property state.

Estate Tax Schedule*

Size of Estate	Rate	Tax
$600,001 to $750,000	37%	$ 55,500
$750,001 to $1,000,000	39%	153,000
$1,000,001 to $1,250,000	41%	255,500
$1,250,001 to $1,500,000	43%	363,000
$1,500,001 to $2,000,000	45%	588,000
$2,000,001 to $2,500,000	49%	833,000
$2,500,001 to $3,000,000	53%	1,098,000
$3,000,001 plus	55%	1,650,000 +

*Based on present tax law and subject to change.

After the attorney estimates your potential estate tax liability, anticipate how your heirs will pay the tax. Estate taxes are due in cash within nine months of the date of death. Without proper planning, your heirs may be required to sell a treasured asset. One way to avoid this is to buy a life insurance policy equal to the amount of the taxes on the asset in question.

TRUSTS

A trust is a legal ownership arrangement used to reduce taxes and smooth the transfer of assets from one owner to another. Trusts have existed for hundreds of years. They are not just for the wealthy—they are strategic tools for anyone's estate planning.

The trust document directs a *trustee* who holds title to an asset to undertake its management and/or disposal for the benefit of a designated person(s) or organization. A trust may hold any asset—real estate, securities, collectibles, art, businesses, cash, or combination thereof.

Parties to the Trust

There are three basic players in a trust arrangement:

- *Trustor or Grantor.* The person who establishes the trust and relinquishes the ownership of assets by transferring them to the trust.

- *Trustee.* The party who holds temporary title to the assets, manages the assets, and/or disposes of the assets.

- *Beneficiary.* The party who receives income or principal from the trust.

The Living Trust

Most estate planning starts with the *inter vivos* trust, commonly called a *living trust*. While you are alive, your assets are transferred into the trust, which stipulates how and to whom your assets will be transferred upon your death. The trust is *revocable* (any number of changes may be made) as long as the trustor lives; however, the trust becomes *irrevocable* (cannot be amended) upon the death or incompetence of the trustor.

In many ways, a living trust is similar to a will, but it offers additional benefits that may

- Increase from $600,000 to $1,200,000 the amount gifted or transferred by a married couple without being subject to federal estate tax liability.

- Allow an estate to bypass probate, saving attorney fees and probate costs that could be several times the cost of establishing the trust.

- Save time because the trustee gains access to assets immediately after the grantor's death, avoiding probate, which generally takes at least a year.

- Reduce the expense and complication of a conservatorship should the grantor become incapacitated.

- Reduce publicity because a trust, unlike probate, is not part of the public record.

A living trust might also accommodate extenuating circumstances such as a spendthrift child, handicapped beneficiary, or a child who is too young to handle her finances. The grantor may, for example, withhold a gift until a beneficiary is of a certain age to ensure that she has the maturity to manage it responsibly.

If you have a physically handicapped or emotionally disturbed beneficiary who is eligible for public assistance, it is important to provide a *discretionary trust* to supplement public assistance. If you do not, inherited gifts may render the beneficiary ineligible for public assistance.

Because it would be an easy way for the government to raise revenues without increasing taxes, the U.S. Congress may reduce the current federal estate tax exemption. However, an estate planning attorney can advise you on how to lock in the present exemption through gift trusts before any legislated decrease.

Selecting Trustees

To maintain complete control of their assets during their lifetime, most people elect to be designated the trustee of their trusts for as long as they live. The choice of a backup trustee is yours—it may be any adult or corporate trustee such as a bank or trust company. Be sure to select someone who is both honest and financially literate. If you become physically or mentally incapacitated, your backup trustee manages your trust affairs for as long as necessary. When you recover, you automatically resume complete control.

It is the trustee's job to collect, preserve, and distribute your assets after you die, according to the terms of the trust. Select a successor trustee in the event your first designee dies or becomes incapable of handling the assignment for any reason. Discuss your trust in detail with your chosen trustee because it is not an easy job. If the responsibilities are not made clear, your nominee might decline the appointment after your death.

If you do not have a suitable individual, consider a professional corporate trustee such as a bank's trust division. Corporate trustees are highly regulated by the government and are generally reliable and objective. Their fees are usually reasonable, negotiable, and typically about 1 percent of assets, depending on the estate's size. The fee may include investment management, tax filing, recordkeeping, and handling distributions. Be sure to meet with your proposed corporate trustees and make sure they address investment performance if that is important to you.

Charitable Remainder Trust

Many people confuse estate taxes with probate, and believe that by establishing a living trust they have done all they can to reduce their taxes. In reality, a living trust provides very limited tax savings, but the *charitable* remainder trust not only saves estate taxes but capital gains taxes as well.

By establishing a charitable remainder trust, you may avoid the current capital gains tax that you would have to pay when you sell any appreciated assets. The CRT also provides an immediate tax deduction for assets you give to a qualified charity at your death, but you may use the assets while you live.

Although the CRT is irrevocable, it can actually be a very flexible planning tool. Certain requirements must be met, some of which may be considered disadvantageous; however, when properly implemented, the CRT may provide significant benefits that include

- capital gains tax and estate tax savings,
- charitable tax deduction,
- higher current income,
- protection of assets from creditors, and
- significant charitable donations.

The CRT is particularly appropriate if you wish to sell appreciated assets subject to capital gains taxation. As donor, you would irrevocably transfer your appreciated assets to the CRT. The trustee then sells the assets and invests the proceeds in income-producing assets such as bonds that pay income to you.

With no tax due on the sale of the appreciated assets, more proceeds are available to invest, providing you with higher annual income for the remainder of your life, and perhaps for the lives of your spouse and children. Additionally, you may reduce your current income taxes with the charitable gift tax deduction.

If designated the beneficiary, some charities pay all or part of the legal fees for establishing a CRT. Consider discussing this possibility with your favorite charity.

The Grantor Retained Income Trust

With a *Grantor Retained Income Trust*, or GRIT, taxes are reduced when wealth is transferred to heirs. The most practical use of this trust is to fund it with your personal residence (or vacation home). You may continue to occupy the property for a specified period; however, at the end of the term, the trust terminates and the residence is distributed as a gift to your beneficiary.

Insurance Trusts

When you establish a charitable remainder trust, you are, in essence, choosing to leave some or all of your assets to charity rather than to your family or other individuals. You can provide for them, however, by purchasing a life insurance policy with the tax savings generated by your gift to charity via the CRT. At your death, the insurance benefits go to your heirs. Perhaps your estate contains a home or business you want your heirs to keep, but if they do not have the funds to pay the estate taxes, the IRS will force a sale. The purchase of life insurance is often the only way to avert a forced sale.

Make sure the insurance policy is owned by your heirs or an irrevocable trust so that benefits are not subject to estate taxes. It is generally best to set up the trust before purchasing the insurance policy. Consider transferring the ownership of policies you already own to a trust or another party to reduce potential estate taxes.

Note . . . All trusts and wills should be regularly examined and revised when necessary. Keep the original documents in your safety deposit box or with your attorney, but place copies in a home file marked "Estate Planning." (Some states limit access to safety-deposit boxes when the holder dies.) Keep a list of your financial and legal advisers along with a letter explaining your finances in the file. Destroy obsolete wills and drafts because they might lead to disputes among your heirs.

Summary

If you have children or assets, it is time to plan your estate. Consult an attorney who specializes in trusts and wills to determine if you hold title to your assets in the most beneficial manner. Discuss your estate matters with loved ones so that they may accommodate your wishes in the event you become incapable of caring for yourself.

Financial information is not that difficult to understand, but because there is a lot of it, it takes time to digest. You may feel overwhelmed and put off taking those first steps. This action plan will help you to apply what you have already learned.

Chapter **23**

Your Investment Action Plan

"Man must sit in chair with mouth open for very long time before roast duck fly in."

Chinese Proverb

The following basic plan identifies the more important tasks to address and points to the relevant chapters. The particular financial issues you should consider often depend on your age and, the more you can do, the better. Even though you may not have been able to accomplish certain tasks in your younger years, you may still reap the benefits of financial security by taking action now.

The Early Years: Your 20s and 30s

- Although it may be difficult, exercise discipline to cultivate the habit of saving money on a regular schedule. Set very specific financial goals, and construct a plan for reaching them.

- Learn about brokerage services and how to find a good broker. (Chapter 3)

- Set aside sufficient emergency funds and start saving for a down payment on a home. Consider a brokerage firm's money market account that allows you to write checks. (Chapters 10, 20)

- Learn to invest in the financial markets to maximize your savings growth potential. (Chapters 4, 5, 9)

- Check out all investment advice and learn the difference between prudent risk and gambling. Learn how to reduce risk through diversification and dollar-cost averaging. (Chapter 13)

- Learn how to invest internationally. (Chapter 11)

- When you start working full time, establish a tax-exempt (technically, "tax-deferred") retirement savings account that may be funded with tax-deductible contributions. If your company offers an employer-supplemented pension plan, fund it to the maximum allowed. After funding your pension, contribute to a self-directed IRA if you qualify to have one. Even if you cannot deduct your contribution, your savings grow tax-deferred. (Chapter 21)

- If you have funded all your qualified retirement accounts to the maximum, consider placing any additional savings in a tax-deferred variable annuity's equity fund. (Chapter 15)

- Organize your investments by creating files for the pertinent paperwork. Know where all your assets are located. If you transfer assets from one account to another, make sure everything gets transferred.

- Write your will. If you have dependents, purchase life and disability insurance. (Chapters 16, 22)

- To provide your children with college educations, establish custodial accounts and contribute regularly. Inform your children as to how their money is invested. This serves two purposes—funding educations and teaching your children the importance of saving and investing. (Chapter 20)

The Prime Earning Years: Your 40s and 50s

- These are the years when your income is likely to peak and you can save more. Make sure your savings are on track for funding your retirement by estimating your future retirement income on the basis of your current savings growth. Your broker can help you with this rather complicated calculation.

- To obtain an estimate of your future benefits, call the Social Security Administration, (800) 772-1213, and order a *Personal Earnings and Benefits Estimate Statement (PEBES)* request form SSA-7004. Check your annual earnings on the statement carefully every other year. If you find a discrepancy, call a Social Security representative at (800) 537-7005.

- Contact your company's personnel department to find out what benefits you can expect to receive upon retirement.

- If you discover that your savings may not be growing sufficiently to finance your retirement, address the short-fall as early as possible. It may be necessary to trim discretionary spending to make larger contributions to your savings accounts. (Chapters 13, 15, 21)

- Review your investment portfolio for asset allocation. Continue to invest in stocks—the ultimate risk is not a volatile stock market—it's outliving your money. (Chapters 4, 12)

- Educate yourself about estate planning and establish a living trust. Determine if you need professional legal advice. (Chapter 22)

- Review your insurance policies to make sure that your financial obligations are adequately covered should you become disabled or die. Reduce coverage when your dependents become self-supportive. (Chapter 16)

The Later Years: Your 60s and Beyond

- You are now better able to project your ability to retire with adequate financial support. Before you retire, make sure your savings are sufficient to support your lifestyle for the remainder of your life expectancy plus a few years.

- Review your need for life insurance. Perhaps you can reduce your premiums if you no longer need as much coverage. (Chapter 16)

- Scrutinize your investment portfolio. You should be investing conservatively, but it may be necessary to allocate part of your savings to common stocks to outpace inflation by any significant margin. (Chapters 4, 5, 6)

- Learn to invest safely in bonds because they may be your best vehicles to secure the regular income you may soon require. (Chapters 7, 8, 9)

Summary

It is my hope that you will continue to use this book as a guide for all your future investments. You may need to read some parts more than once. Remember, as your knowledge increases, your anxiety about investing decreases. You might even find yourself excited about the prospect of investing. At that point, you are well on your way to financial security. So relax and enjoy it.

Index